RESCUING REGINA

To My dear Friend You Bui
from S. Josephe Marie Flynn, SSND
What a blessing you are to all of us
Americans — here at Notre Dame of Elm Grove!
You have opened our minds and our hearts
to your own beautiful lives and country. —
Every blessing on your future!

RESCUING REGINA

The Battle to Save a Friend from
Deportation and Death

JOSEPHE MARIE FLYNN, SSND

Foreword by HELEN PREJEAN, CSJ

Sister Josephe Marie Flynn, S.S.N.D.
Regina Bakala

Lawrence Hill Books

Library of Congress Cataloging-in-Publication Data

Flynn, Josephe Marie.

Rescuing Regina : the battle to save a friend from deportation and death /
Josephe Marie Flynn ; foreword by Helen Prejean.

p. cm.

Includes bibliographical references and index.

ISBN 978-1-56976-624-8

1. Asylum, Right of—United States. 2. Deportation—United States.
3. Emigration and immigration—Government policy—United States. I. Title.
JV6601.F55 2011
323.6′31—dc22

2011011117

Interior design: Scott Rattray

© 2011 by Josephe Marie Flynn, SSND
All rights reserved
Published by Lawrence Hill Books
An imprint of Chicago Review Press, Incorporated
814 North Franklin Street
Chicago, Illinois 60610
ISBN: 978-1-56976-624-8
Printed in the United States of America
5 4 3 2 1

"Josephine's Children"

When I, Regina, was ten, my mother **Josephine** died. I cried every night, longing for her. I promised to someday honor her by helping Congo's orphaned children.

Today countless street children, victims of rape by foreigners, must beg or steal just to survive. At night these little ones hide in the forests or under bridges.

December 13, 2017, a court in the Democratic Republic of Congo gave life sentences to 11 militia men for raping 40-some children, 18-months to 12-years old. One soldier said a "spiritual advisor" claimed that raping infants would guarantee their militias supernatural protection.

In the past, orphans were adopted by other families, but decades of conflict and corruption led to insecurity and rampant poverty. Today in Kinshasa, the capital city of over 18,000,000 residents, there are only a few orphanages.

As an American citizen, I am now welcome to travel between countries. I own the property in Idiofa 400 miles east of Kinshasa where my mother **Josephine** gave birth to me. Years ago I hired a caretaker to guard the house and land for *"Josephine's Children"*. I also bought land in Kinshasa for an extension.

"Josephine's Children" needs financial support. For more info, books, speaking engagements, etc., contact:

Josephine's Children
P.O. Box 20743
Greenfield, WI 53220

To asylum seekers and refugees, arguably the most needy
and courageous of all the world's migrants

CONTENTS

FOREWORD

Some have called me a hero for my fight against the death penalty. If anything, I'd call myself a reluctant hero, someone who simply cannot turn away from cruelty and injustice. The same could be said of Sister Josephe Marie Flynn, who, after years of shying away from anything remotely resembling advocacy, found herself in the forefront of the struggle to save from deportation Regina Bakala, a Congolese torture survivor in the United States.

Rescuing Regina: The Battle to Save a Friend from Deportation and Death is a chilling look into the dysfunctional US asylum system and our byzantine detention and deportation system. Regina, a wife and mother of two young children living in Milwaukee, fled persecution in the Democratic Republic of Congo, where she had been sexually tortured, as had her husband, David. One early evening, as she walked out of the shower in her pajamas, she was picked up by Immigration and Customs Enforcement and whisked away—to a destination unknown. In a panic, David called their good friend and supporter Josephe.

Josephe—aided by the hastily assembled Save Regina group—quickly learns how difficult it is to work with a nameless, faceless, inhumane bureaucracy reachable only through lawyers or elected officials. Immigrants are presumed guilty, not innocent. The system is harsh, making no distinction between immigrants and convicted criminals. The lawyers tell Josephe this is a dead-end case.

Rescuing Regina describes how Josephe and the Save Regina troops create a media campaign to spotlight Regina's plight. The book portrays Regina's fierce determination to keep her children from being orphaned as she had been. The story of friendship between the reluctant advocate and the tenacious mother will both warm your heart and outrage you. It is a powerful book.

Helen Prejean, CSJ
Author of *Dead Man Walking*

PREFACE

Someone recently asked me, "So, how did you get involved in advocacy work?"

"Me?" I laughed. "Most of my life, I avoided the very thought!"

Marinated in fear from childhood on, I remember my mother, an avid John Birch Society member, warning me in my early twenties that a covert Communist plot was already poised to take over the United States by 1976. I quickly became squinty-eyed about everything politically controversial. In fact, it wasn't until my thirties that I finally mustered enough courage to take a graduate course in social justice. When the teacher required three major papers—"See," "Judge," "Act"—my stomach clenched. Ambushed by my own panic, I sheepishly took her aside, begging for an alternate assignment or at least an exemption from the paper on social action.

That I would one day lead a major advocacy effort was unthinkable.

Thirty years later, as adult and family minister in St. Mary's large parish in Hales Corners, Wisconsin, I found myself sitting across from a beautiful Congolese couple, Regina and David Bakala, each of them torture survivors seeking asylum in our country. They welcomed me into their journey, and years later, when their lives veered again into terror, they turned to me. While pulling out all the stops to help them, I found myself also being healed.

This is a story that needs to be told.

PART I
TRAGEDY UPON TRAGEDY

1

"THEY TOOK REGINA!"

"Sister, we have a problem."

"Hi, David. What's the problem?" David rarely calls. I cradle the phone between my cheek and shoulder and continue unpacking my groceries.

"They took Regina!"

"What?" I stop. "What do you mean 'took Regina'? Who took Regina?"

"Immigration!"

"No!" I grasp the phone with both hands.

"Yes! At six thirty tonight. Two policemen with guns."

I glance at my watch. An hour ago? But Regina's done everything right. This makes no sense. Pacing back and forth, I struggle to wrap my mind around what he's saying.

David and Regina Bakala's home country, the Democratic Republic of Congo (formerly Zaire) in sub-Saharan central Africa, is one of the most dangerous and unstable in the world. Each of them fled after being tortured for advocating democracy. Regina was beaten, raped, and imprisoned. If sent back to Congo, she faces grave danger, even death.

I freeze. *O God, what if they've already taken her to Milwaukee's Mitchell International?* What flashes to mind is another case, that of a local immigration lawyer awakened in the dead of night two years ago by a panicky client calling from an airport in Paris. She had been picked up by Immigration and Customs Enforcement (ICE) and promptly put on a plane back to Pakistan. They took her newborn to the father who had tipped them off—an abusive alcoholic against whom she had a restraining order. ICE did not know her asylum petition was pending with US Citizenship and Immigration Services (USCIS). Nor did it matter anymore. I know from working with other immigrant families that once deported, the person has no legal standing in our system, so all pending petitions are simply dropped—an all-too frequent occurrence.

"I'll be right over, David!" Their house is less than three miles from my upper flat, the unit I rent in a two-family house. I grab my winter jacket from the clothes tree, toss the carrots into the refrigerator, slip on boots and gloves, scoop up my purse, and fly down the stairs.

As I pull away from the curb, a wave of depression engulfs me. *O God, how can I deal with this now?* It's Tuesday of Holy Week, my busiest time of year, and these six weeks of Lent have been full of tears. Long-standing digestive problems are forcing me to retire. Probable cause—childhood abuse. I'm more than tired, I'm emotionally exhausted. Writing the autobiography required for next fall's sabbatical has dredged up years of unresolved psychological pain. I stop at the red light, feeling shaky and unsettled. Gone is the private retreat I had been banking on for Easter week.

My tires crunch over an ice-crusted patch. As I turn onto the parkway, my worry leaps to Regina: *Where* is she? *How* is she? I tighten my grip on the steering wheel.

———

David and Regina had come to St. Mary's five years before, in early 2000, to have baby Lydia baptized. Regina had asked Sister Martha at her workplace to recommend a parish they could join. "We tried a church called St. Jacobi's," she told Sister Martha, "but then we found out that it is Lutheran, not Catholic."

Sister had gestured across the street. "Just go there, Regina. It's close to work and to your apartment."

I was not there the day the Bakalas registered, but several women on staff delighted in the baby girl and at the prospect of a young African couple joining our suburban congregation. Regina and David never asked for help and, in fact, kept their circumstances quite private. No one knew what the new members had endured.

Regina said later about that day, "When we come outside, David and me, we say to each other, 'See how they love us? This is our church home God give to us.'"

I remember how happy she was when we first met a short time later. To her delight, David, baptized an Evangelical Christian, had decided to join the Catholic Church. It was late April 2000 when they arrived in St. Mary's front office for his initial interview for RCIA (Rite of Christian Initiation for Adults). Regina, a short, sturdy woman in a yellow turtleneck, cradled their baby in her arms like a spray of flowers. Lydia's tiny ponytails in multicolored clips bobbed about as she squirmed to see everybody and everything in our front office. Regina feigned annoyance, but I caught flashes of delight in her eyes. Her quick smile and silky complexion were clouded only by weariness. "Sorry we a little late," she said, bowing her head slightly. After her shift as a nurse's aide, she had to drive home to change clothes and pick up David and Lydia.

I ooh-ed and ahh-ed the baby while giving Regina a sideways hug.

Behind her stood David, broad-shouldered and handsome, with tight-cropped hair, the baby's diaper bag dangling from one hand. He looked older than his wife, his forehead marked by worry lines.

I extended my hand, using a bit of French remembered from college days. "*Bonjour, monsieur! Je m'apelle Soeur Josèphe Marie.*" David's wide face, staid and stoic, suddenly came to life. I had to confess, "*Mais non, monsieur. Je ne parle pas le français*"—I held my index finger and thumb a pinch apart—"*mais seulement un tout petit peu.*" I introduced

Bob Roesler, the gentle young man I had invited to be David's translator and RCIA sponsor.

Meeting weekly over the summer months, we quickly became friends.

———

In early June, as our fifth RCIA session closed, Regina handed the baby to David and asked to speak to me privately. With head bowed and smile slight and tentative, she said, "Sister, I am pregnant."

"How wonderful!" I gave her a spontaneous hug, but her return hug was flat. I pulled back a bit but did not let go. Her eloquent eyes would always tell me more, not only of hard-won courage but also of a persistent fear. This time I saw her fear.

"David is very worry, Sister. Lydia is just now eight months." She teared up. "What we gonna do? We cannot pay for a second baby."

I knew that David, preparing his asylum petition with immigration attorney Hal Block, would not be eligible for a work permit for many months. Regina was the sole breadwinner. Somehow she had managed through a difficult pregnancy back in North Carolina, but here she worked sixty-four-hour weeks juggling two nurse's aide jobs, first shift at one facility and second shift three times a week at another. In a role reversal unusual for Congolese, David cared for their infant daughter while Regina ached for time with her little one.

"Regina, you can welcome this new baby," I said. "The parish will help you."

"Sister, last night I had a dream. Everything is dark, dangerous. I see our little family—David, me, and Lydia—all close together like this." She curled her shoulders and arms into a huddle. "We are outdoors. Nothing around to protect us. The sky is black and"—she swirled her palms above her head—"is like a big storm coming. We are very scare, but God come. He say not to worry. He put a big blanket around our family."

"See?" I smiled. "God is reassuring you."

She looked straight at me, her eyes flashing from worry to faith to worry and back again. "God said the blanket is St. Mary's."

St. Mary's? Suddenly I realized the blanket was *me*—me and my big mouth. There was no way I could take on more responsibilities. I forced myself to keep smiling as I hugged her.

That night I told myself, *Just start. Do what you can. If you help one immigrant family, you help generations.*

The next morning, our pastor, Father Art Heinze, offered rent assistance and suggested I ask the St. Vincent de Paul Society for groceries. I began scouring ads for a desk job for Regina. Within weeks, the Development Office of the Sacred Heart Fathers hired her as a donations processor. After we introduced them at weekend Masses, more folks got involved. One idea spurred another—household goods, car repairs, baby shower—and for David, English classes and driver's lessons. When David got his work permit, Sacred Heart School of Theology hired him for maintenance, a half mile from Regina's workplace.

———

Over these first six months, I learned bits and pieces of their stories.

About six weeks after Regina and David's wedding on August 30, 1994, two of President Mobutu's soldiers had raped then imprisoned Regina for teaching democracy in the villages around Idiofa, her hometown. Nine months later, she was again beaten and raped by his soldiers on her way to Kinshasa, the capital city, to help organize a democracy rally. After the second incident, she fled Congo by night, forbidding her helpers to mention anything to David or other family members lest they, too, be endangered.

For two and a half years, neither she nor David knew what had happened to the other.

In June 1997, David was arrested by the regime of Laurent Kabila, the man credited with overthrowing Mobutu. I remember David's face contorting as he told of awaiting execution in a small, filthy underground cell. While Bob translated, David had pointed to his badly chipped front teeth, then demonstrated how a prison guard had used the butt of a Kalashnikov to smash them.

"They did unspeakable things to me—too terrible to tell."

Laurent Kabila had turned against the coalition of military/political parties responsible for his speedy victory, unleashing the far greater, more vicious 1997 war. With an estimated four million lives lost, the Democratic Republic of Congo is still locked in conflict.

The West acts as if the Congo war were an African implosion that has nothing to do with us, but four UN reports (1998–2003) held that it was endorsed, fueled, and funded by Western economic interests, its bloody spoils in our cell phones, laptops, and PlayStations.[1]

The problem is, the Democratic Republic of Congo (DRC), with a land mass the size of Western Europe, is richer in resources than almost any place on the planet, holding vast stores of gold, diamonds, copper, cobalt, cassiterite, and 80 percent of the world's coltan (vital to electronic circuit boards). Fighting to control this treasure trove, warlords and military leaders, both foreign and national, have created a self-sustaining war economy, lining their own pockets while destroying Congo. Proceeds do not reach the working people. In 2000, when I met David and Regina, the DRC's people ranked poorest in the world—annual GDP, $86.03 per capita.[2]

In January 2001, Laurent Kabila was assassinated in a failed coup. Regime power-brokers named his inexperienced twenty-nine-year-old son, Joseph Kabila, president. The younger Kabila won a UN-brokered peace agreement in 2003, but the slaughter shows no sign of ending. In the deadliest war since Hitler's massacres, 31,250 civilians are dying each month from violence or war-related causes.[3] Perhaps even worse are the ongoing atrocities—rape, torture, and genital mutilation of hundreds of thousands of women and little girls. In this war, rape is the weapon of choice.

How dare America return any woman to that fate?

2

"NEVER IN AMERICA"

Windows are dark, shades drawn, heavy drapes tightly closed. David once told me how frightened he was when he first saw windows in American homes so close to the ground. I park my car under the amber streetlight and pick my way over icy patches and up the concrete steps.

As he fumbles with the pesky lock on the storm door, through the foggy glass I see tonight's agony etched in his face. I wonder what specters lurched into consciousness when he faced armed men coming for his wife.

He offers a weak smile. "Ah, Sister Josephe." His jaw line and thick shoulders suggest strength, but he battles diabetes and a sharp ulcer.

"Oh, David, I'm so sorry." I glance around. "Where are the children?"

"They are sleeping." His face creases in pain. "All of us were crying. But I told them, 'We eat now, then go to sleep. Tomorrow we gonna get Mommy home.' But I could not eat." He gestures for me to sit on the couch and takes his place next to me. "What we gonna do now?"

"We're going to call an immigration attorney, but first I need more information. Who actually took her?"

"Immigration. Three policemen, two came in the house, one stays outside."

I'm confused. Policemen? This does not sound like Immigration.

"Were they wearing uniforms? Did they show you any I.D.?"

"No I.D. They say they gonna deport her. No uniforms, but they have big letters, P-O-L-I-C-E, on their"—he runs his big hand across his chest—"I don't know how you say in English."

"Vests? Bulletproof vests?"

"I don't know. They wear shirts, pants, like everyday clothes. But on top of their jackets . . . black with big white letters, POLICE." He gestures again.

"Did they have guns?"

His eyebrows lift. He nods, raises his pitch. "Yes! Yes!"

The story comes tumbling out. In the Bakala home, because work schedules have the whole family on the road by 5:20 A.M., bedtimes are early. Before dinner, everyone gets cleaned up and ready for bed. Regina was in the shower, their meal was in the oven, the kids were playing upstairs, and David was watching French cable news. Doorbell rang. Kids came running. David opened the front door. His eyes locked on the word "POLICE."

"The big one, he asks me"—David puffs out his chest and turns down the corners of his mouth—"'Does Andes Imwa live here?'"

Andes is Regina's official first name; Imwa is her paternal surname. Her middle name, Aboy, is her maternal surname. When she was eight, Mobutu had ordered Western-sounding baptismal names—hers is Regina Elizabeth—replaced with names of family ancestors. His campaign for authenticity tried to restore African pride after decades of colonialism, but it quickly deteriorated into a personality cult broadly derided as Mobutuism. Regina insists on using her "Christian" name.

"I say, 'Yes, she is here. She is in the shower.'" His voice turns gruff. "The big man—the main one—has a clipboard with many papers. He cannot find Regina's name. He go like this." David rifles through an imaginary stack. He shakes his head. "I think, how many people is this guy looking for? He does not know what he is doing—too many papers, nothing in order."

With typical African hospitality, David invited them inside to sit down, but neither did.

He demonstrates how the chief officer drew himself up to full height and muscled his way close to his face. "You got a gun?" David said no, backing into the children. "Knives? Weapons of any kind?"

David blurts, "No. No," showing me how he hiked his shoulders and opened his arms, palms up, fingers spread wide, his hands moving in tight circles. "Nothing. Knives for kitchen, that's all. No weapons."

Both agents moved quickly through the living room, examining shelves, and the kitchen, opening cupboards and drawers, then checking the back entryway. They searched the hallway linen closet, headed into the children's room and closet, and, last, the master bedroom—closet, drawers. When they returned to the living room, the hefty officer drew close to David's face. "You better not be lying!"

"The children—are they seeing all this?" I ask.

"Yes! Lydia, she push close to my leg, crying."

I imagine the kindergartner, her almond-shaped eyes staring at the big man's black gun inches from her face.

"Christopher was not shy. He say to the mean one, 'Stop talking to my daddy like that!'"

My eyes widen. "Little Christopher?"

David grins. "Yes, Christopher!" The grin disappears. "This man, he is not happy. When the kids start to cry, he says, 'Take them to their room and shut the door.'" He winces. "So I do."

Last spring, the Bakalas had been thrilled to put a down payment on their first home, a tiny bungalow with four small rooms and a bath that opens into a small hub—the hallway. With the children's bedroom kitty-corner from the living room, everything could be heard clearly on either side of the hollow door—the gruff questions, the fear in Daddy's answers, their wailing.

"Then this guy, he gets close and points at me. 'You!'" David jabs his index finger at me. "'*You* are not from this country. *You* are not a citizen, are you? Show me *your* papers.'"

David hurried into the master bedroom, the agents right on his heels. Taking his briefcase from the closet, he opened it and paged through the top papers, quickly finding the judge's decision. He pointed to the words "withholding of removal."

"That means I cannot be deported," David says. "But the agent, he say to me, 'Do not be so sure.'" He snaps his jaw up, imitating the officer. "'Next time we come, it will be for *you*!'"

I put my hand on his shoulder. "No, David. No one can force you to leave America."

He does not look convinced.

What David did not know, what I did not know, and what many others do not know is that all David needed to say was *I want to speak to my lawyer*. Nothing more.

The US Constitution applies to everyone in our country, including immigrants, no matter their status. Under the Fifth Amendment, both David and Regina had the right to due process, which includes the right against self-incrimination and the right to remain silent. In fact, if ICE had come to execute a warrant against a specific person, Andes Imwa, they were supposed to show David and Regina the seizure warrant for her arrest. Rifling through papers does not cut it. David was under no obligation to let them into his home without a warrant permitting them to search the home itself (Fourth Amendment against illegal seizures and searches). Furthermore, the agents' demand that he yield his identification amounted to an illegal search of his "person," also prohibited by the Fourth Amendment.

Later, I will also find out that withholding of removal is more tenuous than I thought. It stops David's removal to only one country, Congo. It also requires the government to periodically try placing him with a third country. If the third country says yes, he must leave the United States.

Arriving in late 1997, David was too terrified to leave their North Carolina apartment lest someone in the large Congolese community betray him to Kabila. He knew nothing about the new law requiring him to apply for asylum within the first year. They moved to Milwaukee two years later, where he felt safer. Chicago's Immigration Court postponed his hearing three times in three years. Finally, in September 2003, Judge O. John Brahos kept him on the stand for seven exhausting hours, then delayed his decision for another four and a half months. David had hoped Judge Brahos would find that his post-traumatic stress disorder (PTSD) constituted the "extraordinary circumstances" preventing him from filing on time. However, the judge wrote in his 2004 decision that, though he believed David's testimony of torture, he did not grant asylum because he found the closing sentence of the psychologist's PTSD diagnosis not strong enough to overcome the one-year bar. David's fate had hinged on two words near the end of the detailed report of Dr. Joseph L. Collins: "*it appears*" that he meets the criteria for PTSD.

Instead, Judge Brahos granted him withholding of removal under the Immigration and Nationality Act (INA), the basic body of immigration law in the United States. This allows David to live and work here temporarily but not to apply for permanent residency (a green card) nor for the prize, citizenship. Only asylum opens the way to those treasured benefits. If he leaves for any reason, he cannot come back. Under the INA, asylum depends upon a "well-founded fear" of persecution, but withholding of removal demands an even higher proof, "clear probability" that a person's life or freedom would be in danger.[1]

Since David had already met the higher burden of proof, why would the judge deny him asylum based on something as flimsy as a one-year filing rule? When David told me, he was furious. "So what does this mean? I risk my life for democracy, but now I have no country?"

Within a month, Hal Block had appealed the asylum portion to the Board of Immigration Appeals (BIA), attaching a clarifying document from Dr. Collins, who insisted that his standard phrasing did not equivocate the diagnosis. In fact, Collins had based his report, point by point, on the criteria listed in *The Diagnostic and Statistical Manual of Mental Disorders (DSM-IV)*, the bible of the American Psychiatric Association. The case is still in appeal.

David's face tenses as he tells of Regina opening the bathroom door to see the officers' stony faces, POLICE on their vests, guns on their hips. Her eyes flew to David. "What could I do?" His eyes brim.

Regina's case had been mismanaged by three lawyers. Lawyer #1 took all her money, did the paperwork, but later refused to appear in court, saying he was not an immigration attorney. Lawyer #2, a pro bono attorney, had no time to prepare Regina for court. Not ready for adversarial questioning, she fell apart on the stand—mixed up details, wept, couldn't remember dates. The judge denied all relief—asylum, withholding of removal, and voluntary departure. With one month to appeal, Regina trusted Lawyer #3, who met with her once, studied the previous mess, and submitted Regina's appeal on time. This was Attorney Anne Lybeau.

The decision of the BIA is sent to the lawyer who, in turn, is to notify her client. After eight years and numerous calls to Lybeau, Regina was still waiting.

David continues, "When they said, 'We are here to deport you,' Regina, she cry out, 'No! I did not do something wrong!' The chief officer, he shakes his clipboard, says today is March 22, 2005, but the order to report for deportation come from the BIA back in May 2002."

"Was he saying that the Board of Immigration Appeals had already ruled in her case?"

"Yes. We find this out four months ago, but her lawyer still did not get the official notice. I show you the letters."

He plucks his dollar-store reading glasses from a shelf on the entertainment center, goes to the bedroom, and returns with an envelope and a fax. The envelope, dated four months earlier, is not from the BIA in Virginia but from a United States Citizenship and Immigration Services center in Nebraska that processes forms. I scan the letter. They were refusing to renew Regina's work permit. Reason? Her asylum appeal had been denied on May 17, 2002.

David points to the date. "Look, November 24, 2004. This is the first time we hear this! We were both scared. Attorney Lybeau said she never got the notice. Then she remembers she forgot to tell the BIA that she moved her office. So she apologize. She says, don't worry, she gonna take care of it. But Regina was so afraid, she felt sick. Every time she calls, Anne Lybeau says not to worry, she's taking care of it." David shakes his head. "Regina went into our bedroom to get the proof, but when she gave it to the guy—the mean one, he just threw it on the dresser."

David hands me Lybeau's fax asking the BIA for their official decision. "See? March 4, 2005. This lawyer did nothing for three months! Look. Right here she explains this is her fault."

Again, the officer had tossed it aside.

David props his glasses above his forehead. His face contorts in anguish. "When the man threw the papers, Regina's eyes got big. She shouts, 'No! No! I did not do something wrong!'" He describes her sitting abruptly on the speckled carpet before her legs gave way, pleading in choking sobs to the mean one towering over her. "She was crying out, 'I must leave my husband and my two little kids? Why?' She shouts again, 'Please! You *know* I did not do something wrong. Just this lawyer make this mistake. *Not me.* Why you do this to *me*? *Why?*'"

I can see her head, shoulders, and open palms punctuating each plea.

"Then she cross her hands over her heart like this and rock forward and back, 'O God, please help me, please help me! Lord Jesus, please!' I look at the other officer—the short one. I think he is with Regina. He looks like he wants to cry." David hikes his shoulders and open palms. "But he's young, he says nothing."

By this time, the kids, hearing their mother, had come into their parents' room.

"Can you believe? Christopher again tells the mean one, 'Why you talk to my mommy like this? You gonna take my mommy to jail? Why? She did not do something wrong!'"

"He's only four years old!"

David smiles. His glasses slide down onto his nose, "I was surprised! Regina, too. We did not know he could do something like this."

When the officer demanded to know why she did not report for deportation in 2002, Regina found her fire. "I told you why! Why you not listen?" she shouted. "I did not get notify! Just my lawyer make this mess, not me. I gave you the letters. You did not look at them."

Typical Regina. I remember her telling me how she stood up to four of Mobutu's soldiers when they charged onto a soccer field in Elom, her mother's home village, shouting threats and swinging their clubs at the fifty or so folks gathered to hear about democracy. People scattered, screaming. The soldiers quickly tied Regina's hands. Her voice was strong, insistent. "I say, '*Why* you arrest me? *Why*? Did I do something wrong? Tell me!' They say, 'You try to change people's minds about Mobutu!' but I say, 'That's not true! Did you hear me say something wrong about Mobutu? No! I am here to help these people understand democracy! I don't talk about Mobutu.'"

"You dared to argue with them?"

"When it's your life, Sister, you have to speak."

David's shoulders sag. He sets his glasses on the glass coffee table, looks down, and blows out a stream of air. "Then I think Regina realized her situation. She said, 'God, I gonna be killed! I not gonna see my husband or my children again!' She crossed her arms over her body like this, 'Lord Jesus, please help me!' We were all crying."

When the pint-sized truth-speaker spoke up again, the lead officer demanded that David get the kids out. With them wailing through the flimsy door, he ordered Regina to find her passport, but the only passport she knew was the false one.

"When she say, 'I gave it to my lawyer,' the officer, he was very angry. He ask why. Then he wrote on his clipboard and said, 'We're going to deport you, but not right away.'"

"Oh, thank God." I sink against the couch. "I was so afraid it would be tonight."

"No. Not tonight. He say, 'Tonight we take you to Dodge County or to Kenosha County, whichever has room.'" David gets up to retrieve a small piece of paper from the entertainment center. "He gave me these numbers to call tomorrow morning for information. You call, OK?"

I recognize the Illinois area codes. Though I dutifully copy the numbers, I'm skeptical about whether either will connect me to an actual human being.

"Did you ask to phone a lawyer?"

"Regina ask to call her attorney, but they say they do not allow phone calls."

"He lied to you, David! You *always* have the right to call a lawyer!"

He leans forward, elbows on his legs, hands dangling between his knees. He turns his troubled face to me. "Then they took her . . . in her pajamas and slippers."

I jerk upright. "What?"

David nods, his voice echoing her horror: "She said, 'Like this! You take me like *this?*'"

She panicked, begging to at least put on her underwear.

The officer refused.

I remember Regina describing to me how two soldiers of Mobutu's elite presidential guard had dragged her by the arms, twisting and kicking, toward a stand of shrubs in the middle of a desolate savannah. Behind low-lying bushes, one clamped his hand over her mouth so that the third officer, manning the checkpoint, would not hear her screams. She shook as she told me.

When they got her pinned flat on her back, the second soldier yanked her jeans down past her knees and forced himself between her legs. She twisted and writhed as he gripped her underpants in both fists. Regina frowned as she told how he tore them off her body. Her mouth was taut. She held both her fists close together in front of her forehead, then yanked them with all her might down and out in opposite directions. Then her body sank, her hands fell limp at her sides. I saw her lower lip trembling.

She looked at me, eyes wide with tears, voice a mere whisper. "It was very hard, Sister."

––––––––––––

David's voice is angry. "I think, *What kind of men, these? They treat my wife like this!*"

The chief officer wanted no more delay. He told Regina that when they were ready to deport her, they would phone David to bring a suitcase with her clothes. She asked to hug her children good-bye, but he said no.

David's face comes alive. "But Regina, she look straight at the mean one. She said, 'No. I gonna hug my kids!'"

"Good for her!" I know Regina. I can picture her lifting her chin like African royalty, looking him straight in the eye. When she is adamant, she doesn't just say no. She purses her lips to signal the coming pronouncement. Her *no* is loud and firm with a period at the end. I can see her lips lingering in that perfect O while her eyes laser through every conceivable objection forming in his mind.

David returns my smile. "Lydia and Christopher come running to hug her. The mean one, he say, 'This is highly objectionable, highly objectionable!' But nothing could not stop her."

Regina hugged and kissed her children, assuring them, "I'll be gone just a little while."

"When Regina come to me, the officer said, 'You're not supposed to do that! Stop it! This is not acceptable! Stop!' But I hug my wife. I tell her, 'We will get you home soon, I promise. Somehow we will do it.' She says to me, 'Call Sister Josephe.'"

Me? My eyes widen. My stomach falls. I can try finding a lawyer, but then what?

The officer pushed open the storm door and waved Regina ahead. In the muted glow of the streetlights, David saw two dark, unmarked cars with Illinois license plates. Twice in recent weeks he had remarked about cars with Illinois plates idling on their block. Regina, too, had seen them.

After the men escorted her out, David quickly locked both doors and turned to shepherd his little ones into the kitchen. He did not want them to see her being driven away.

"Tomorrow, what should I tell Regina's boss?" David asks, then answers his own question. "I think I gonna tell him she is not feeling well. The same with my work." His eyes flash fear. "I don't want people to know about this. They will think she did something wrong."

"I'll stay home from the parish office tomorrow, too, so we can figure out what to do. Is it OK if I tell Father Art what happened? The principal should know and Lydia's teacher, too, just in case Lydia needs some special attention."

David nods.

I think of my coworkers. "May I also tell Father Todd Budde and the others in the parish office so they can pray for Regina? They love you. I know they will keep this confidential."

"Yes, but tell them she did not do something wrong."

"Of course." I glance at my watch. "I have the cell phone numbers of three immigration lawyers. If I reach one tonight, I'll call you right away. If not, we'll be in touch in the morning."

David looks drained.

I pause. "How are you feeling right now?"

His eyes soften. He smiles, gives me a half shrug. "OK, I guess. I just never . . . I never think something like this will happen in America. In Congo? Yes, they do things like this. But in America?" He shudders, turns down his mouth. "Never in America."

3

CARING FOR ONE ANOTHER

The moon is shrouded as I inch my way down the Bakalas' concrete stairs. *O God, is she OK? Where did they take her?*

I flip up the hood of my jacket against the bitter night and hold it bunched under my chin. She told David to call *me*. Hot tears flood my eyes. As I open my car door, I look up to see David's face boxed in by the small window high in the front door. My throat clenches. How will he make it without her? Regina is everything to him. I remember asking them years earlier how they met.

Regina had coaxed me to join her on the squishy old couch in their second-floor apartment. "One day when I go to Kinshasa to visit my uncle Jean and aunt Regina," she began, "David was at their house." She turned toward her husband, who had handed me a glass of orange juice before taking his place on the matching settee. "What year, David? 1992?"

"I think so. Your family was in Belgium, but you were teaching in Idiofa."

Idiofa is 417 miles from Kinshasa.

Orphaned at age nine, Regina and her seven brothers and sisters had moved to Kinshasa from Idiofa to be raised by their maternal uncle Colonel Basil Mondele, longtime friend and bodyguard of the dictator Mobutu. In the mid-1980s, Mobutu reassigned Basil to serve as military attaché on the diplomatic staff of the Congolese Embassy in Brussels, but when he returned in December 1989 for his mother's funeral, Congo was down-spiraling into turmoil. He urged the rest of his family, including his eight adopted children, to come with him to Belgium.

Twenty-six-year-old Regina was too heartsick to go. She had been caring for her maternal *grand-mère* Gabrielle, who had been "like another mother," while completing her history degree and student teaching. Nonetheless, after the funeral, Basil convinced her to take a break.

Four months later in Belgium, when Regina heard that Mobutu was promising multiparty elections, she joined Parti Lumumbiste Unifié (PALU), the political party named after Congo's first and only elected prime minister, Patrice Lumumba, who had been assassinated fewer than six months after his 1960 election. She returned to Idiofa the following year, moving into her father's house, where her cousins now lived. As history teacher at École Centrale des Filles, a Catholic secondary school for girls, she also volunteered with PALU to teach democracy in neighboring villages.

On one of her visits to relatives in far-off Kinshasa, she met David.

"Yeah, it was in the early nineties," he continued. "I was visiting my best friend, Regina's uncle, Jean Biletshi. Jean is close to my age, ten years older than Regina." He paused, then grinned. "When Regina is busy talking to her aunt, I say to Jean, 'I'm gonna marry your niece.'"

"Whoa! And this was the first time you saw her?"

David laughed. "Yes! But Jean, he don't believe me. He says, 'No, no. Don't play with me about my niece!' But I said, 'Jean, I am serious. I will marry her.'"

Regina smiled coyly. With eyes lowered, she shook her head.

David started to chuckle, *kee-kee-kee-kee-kee.* "But, Regina"—he glanced over to her bowed head—"Regina did not like me."

"He laughs all the time. I want someone . . . you know, a man can protect me, can provide for a family. Not this one." She harrumphed. "This one, he laugh like a woman with no worries."

David kept smiling, telling how Jean broke the news to his wife, who then told Regina.

She cut in, "When my aunt Regina, she tell me, 'David is interest in you,' I say, '*Nooo*, I don't like him.' She argue, 'But he's a nice guy. He is best friends with your uncle Jean.' I tell her, 'No. I am not interest.' On another day, I was with my best friend Faustina when Uncle Jean himself said, 'David is a good man, Regina, not rich, but good. He has a good job, too.' Faustina ask me what kind of man do I want. I say, 'I am not interest in a rich man. I am independent, a strong woman. I want one who can listen to me, one who likes me the way I am.'"

David leaned back, glowing. "I was happy to hear Jean say this because I am not rich like her father—a teacher and later a civic leader, who could afford two wives, maybe three, or her uncle who work for Mobutu. So, now I keep asking Jean, 'When is Regina coming to visit?'"

She wrinkled her nose. "I think, what about this guy? Every time I visit my aunt Regina, he comes at the same time?" She flashed him a tiny smile. "Then I begin to see what was going. So I think, *Well, he talks to me each time . . . and he's nice.*" She twisted her gold wedding band. "Then one time, he ask me himself, 'Will you marry me?'"

"But," David said, leaning forward, his mouth turned down, "Regina, she did *not* say yes."

Regina cocked her head a little to the side. "I just say, 'We give everything to God.'" She lifted her shoulders and raised her palms. "'And then we see.'"

David's laughter ended with another *kee-kee-kee-kee-kee.*

Congolese marriage customs take about a year. First, the prospective groom writes a letter to the woman's father or guardian—in Regina's case, her adoptive father (whom she still calls Uncle Basil). He introduces himself, "I am David, son of David Bakala and Lidia Bantani of Matadi. I would like to marry your daughter Regina." He asks the bride's father to choose the date and place for their families to meet.

On the big day, Uncle Basil and Aunt Julienne flew into Kinshasa from Belgium to join other family members and friends at Uncle Jean's house where the couple had first met.

Regina shook off her sandals and curled her feet under her. It was her turn to chuckle. "David's family came an hour late."

One corner of David's mouth turned up.

Regina's family hosted the dinner, and the Bakalas brought a bottle of vintage wine. As part of the ritual, the prospective bride stays hidden in a separate room while the groom's family barters for the opportunity to meet her in person. In explaining how the dialogue usually goes, David used US dollar equivalency, rather than the fluctuating Congolese Zaire.

"Where is the bride? We want to see her."

"She is far away. We need money to pay for her plane ticket."

"We will give three hundred dollars."

"Oh, but she is coming a long way."

"Five hundred dollars!"

"Hmmm, that is not quite enough."

"Fifteen hundred dollars."

"OK, but she will first need to take a cab to the airport."

"We will pay thirty dollars for the cab fare."

"Thank you, but she lives *far* from the airport."

"One hundred dollars!"

"And when she arrives, she will need to take another cab to our house."

"Ah, then we will give you another one hundred dollars!"

So it goes, until the inflated price impresses everyone with the bride's incalculable worth and, from what I surmise, sets a high bar for months of negotiations over the dowry.

Finally, the father of the bride presents her to the groom's family. Both families share a glass of fine wine and a wonderful meal. If all goes well, the bride's father invites the groom to begin negotiating the dowry by mailing him a list of what he is willing to pay for this beautiful bride. The dowry is to compensate the bride's parents for raising her. Once the dowry process is in full swing, the couple is considered married and may begin living together.

On July 2, 1994, last day of school nationwide, Regina resigned as school principal in Idiofa, a position she had held only a few months, and moved to Kinshasa to live with David.

"You should see how nice he made the apartment for me, lovely furniture, everything. I was surprised by how much he did for me."

David gave her a small smile.

In August, both families gathered again at Uncle Jean's, where they celebrated with a special dinner. The next day, August 30, 1994, the newlyweds and parents testified in civil court that the tribal marriage had taken place.

"But that's not our anniversary, because we did not have our big church wedding until we reunited in America," Regina said. "In Congo, it is like three marriages: the tribal marriage with our families, the civil marriage at the Bureau d'Etat Civil to get the legal proof, and, finally, the big church wedding."

David anticipated my question. "No, Sister. It is not possible to do the big church wedding right away. Only when the dowry is all paid can the couple celebrate the church wedding." With upturned palms, he added, "I agreed to a *big* dowry for Regina because her uncle Basil spent a lot of money to raise her, sending her to good schools and to Kinshasa University. I could not pay all the dowry at once." His palms flew up. "Then all these bad things happen to Regina, I get put in the jail—how am I gonna to pay this dowry? After I was baptized in a Protestant church in North Carolina, we don't want to wait anymore. We both want God's blessing, so we went to my church for our big church wedding."

"That's our anniversary, July 18, 1998," said Regina.

High on the living room wall across from us hung their gold-framed portrait—she, all in lacy white, eyes demurely looking down, he in a smart navy suit, smiling at the viewer.

"I still did not pay Uncle Basil the rest of the dowry," David admitted with a sheepish half smile. "But I will pay soon . . . as soon as I can."

I shook my head. "David, Regina's uncle is rich. Surely, he no longer expects you to pay."

"No, Sister. It's not the money. It is a man's honor. I will pay as soon as I can."

I tried over the years to press a tight budget, avoiding credit card debt, having a minimum three-month cushion for emergencies, but they still struggle from paycheck to paycheck. One day David said quietly, his eyes kind but resolute, "Sister, my mother in Africa never worked for pay. When I was a boy, she would get up before dawn to walk all day to her garden, a field with a little shed. She picks a big sack of vegetables, then sleeps in the field. In the morning, she carries that heavy sack on her back all day to feed our family—we was ten children. Now five are dead and my father, too. There's no social security. If my brother in Belgium and I do not send money, she eats maybe only one meal a day. My family—someone is sick, there is no medicine. Regina's orphan niece, my orphan niece—how can we put money in a bank when those in Africa need so much?"

A Ugandan friend later explained, "For Africans, Sister, life belongs to all, not just to the individual. To live is to give. Not even beggars are exempt. We care for one another."

So where did ICE take her? And where will we find money to pay an attorney? I park my car and hurry upstairs. In my small home office, I flip open the address section of my day planner and run my index finger down the "B" page for the number of my logical first contact, David's lawyer, Hal Block.

In May of 2000, when David told me about finding Block's name in the yellow pages, I called to inquire about his fees—no, truthfully, to grill him. I feared some hot-shot lawyer taking advantage of David. I need not have worried. I met Hal Block for the first time in Chicago's Immigration Court at David's asylum hearing. He wore a natty pin-striped suit, but his bulging, battle-scarred briefcase, as much as his worn face and thinning hair, marked him as perpetually overworked. For thirty years, Hal Block has been slugging away for the hopeful nobodies who take seriously the inscription inside the pedestal of our Statue of Liberty, "Give me your tired, your poor . . ." No local immigration lawyer has his breadth of experience. He's smart, conscientious, honest. Regina had hoped he would take over her case if the BIA ruled against her.

But my call tonight goes unanswered. I try Attorney Godfrey Muwonge—same story. Attorney Barbara Graham of Catholic Charities—zilch.

I go back to Block's listing, leave messages on his cell phone and at his downtown office, then boot up my computer to pour out tonight's fears in an e-mail to Muwonge, himself a refugee from violence. Godfrey has said Hal Block steered him into law after "delivering me from the brutal barrel of the deportation gun." Though the former seminarian is a sharp and avid advocate, his health is not good because his own African experience mirrors the experiences of his clients. Godfrey's heart—both literally and figuratively—bears the wear and tear of getting too enmeshed in the dramas of his clients.

As I write, the phone rings. I glance at my watch—10:44 P.M.

"This is Correctional Billing Services. You have a collect call from"— I hear my friend's voice, inserting her own name, "Regina," in the recorded message—"an inmate at the Kenosha County Jail. To accept charges, press . . ."

I can hardly breathe. I hit the button so fast, I cut off the message. The system jams, and I lose her. On her second try, we are connected, but I can't hear her.

O dear God, please!

4

A RAG IN THE WEEDS

"I'm in the jail tonight, Sister. I gonna be here just to sleep overnight." Her voice is weak, shaky. "Tomorrow morning they gonna take me back to Milwaukee because I go to court."

"Court? Regina, there are no immigration courts in Milwaukee."

"I don't know. They say I must go to a judge, give money or something." She begins to cry. "Sister Josephe, I'm so scare." Her voice is faint. "How are my kids? Are they all right?"

I blink back my tears, steady my voice. "They were asleep before I got there, Regina. David told them you'll be home soon. They're fine."

"There's something wrong with David's phone. You call him for me, please?"

"I'll call him tonight." I explain that I left two messages for Mr. Block. "He should know where this 'court' is, Regina. Tomorrow morning I will ask him to take over your case, OK?"

Her clipped *yes* blurts out on a short, shallow breath.

"Whatever happens tomorrow, don't answer any questions unless Mr. Block is present. If Immigration will let us in, David and I will come. If not, say nothing without a lawyer, OK?"

"OK, but I am so scare in this place, Sister." Her voice cracks.

"I'm so sorry, Regina. We're going to get you out as soon as we possibly can."

"These men who took me are not nice. They swore in front of my children when I cry for mercy. I want to wear my clothes because I am embarrass, but they say no. I was *very* scare."

She says that when they left, the younger officer got into a black car in front of their house, but the head agent—she also calls him the mean one—pointed her toward a car in front of the neighbor's bungalow. A third officer was already in the driver's seat.

"They talk *mean*. Their language—I think what kind of men, these? They have no morals."

They have no morals. Regina had used the same words to describe the men who raped her near Kinshasa—Mobutu's elite Division Spéciale Présidentielle (DSP). To protect his power, Mobutu had kept a number of armies and militias. When one got too powerful, he manipulated tribal rivalries to raise up another. Their rivalry is what held the system together. But for his private militia, the DSP, Mobutu brought in Ngbandi tribesmen from Équateur, his home province, surly young men nursing a hicktown grudge against urbanites. He housed the elite fifteen thousand in Camp Tshatshi's special hillside barracks next to his private villa in Kinshasa. In contrast to other Congolese armies, they were well equipped and paid royally. No soldiers were more fiercely loyal to Mobutu nor more cruel toward the Kinshasa populace than the DSP.

———

We had been sitting alone in Regina's kitchen the day she told me about the final rape that drove her far from Congo. They would set up arbitrary checkpoints, she said, "just a little string across the road," to stop any vehicle and demand whatever they wanted.

"It was because of the DSP that the rest of my family was no more in Congo. When Mobutu's wife died, he married his mistress, Bobi

Ladawa. He already had four children with her. Bobi was afraid my uncle Basil might introduce Mobutu to another mistress, so she got her DSP Ngbandi relatives to make trouble for him. That's why Mobutu gave my uncle the attaché job in Brussels." She chuckled. "But Mobutu got his own mistress—Bobi's identical twin Kossia!"

Basil's appointment as *l'attaché militaire* to the Congolese Embassy made him part of a group later known as Service National d'Intelligence et de Protection (SNIP), Congo's secret police, whose officers reported directly to Mobutu. In Congo, it was SNIP's dreaded presence that kept the DSP, among others, in check.

"Regina, when the DSP stopped the lorry, did they know your uncle was Colonel Basil Mondele?"

"No, because I have my father's name, 'Imwa,' not 'Mondele.' But I was *very* scare. I worry, did I make the right decision not to stay in Belgium?" She shivered. "When the DSP demand us off the lorry, everybody is afraid. These are terrible men, Sister. They do anything they want—torture, rape, kill. *They have no morals.*"

———

As the immigration agents drove Regina through Milwaukee, she says, tears ran down her face, nose, and chin, but in handcuffs with no Kleenex, she could do nothing about it. Over the men's crude language, she kept praying. They parked in an underground garage, then took her up into an office area where they pelted her with questions: "Why don't you use your husband's last name?" In Congo, a woman keeps her own name. "Why didn't you report for deportation? How long have you been working? How much do they pay you? When did you buy your house?" On and on.

This line of questioning rankles me. *By what right . . .* I feel a sudden chill. Of course. They were fishing for stuff to use against her. After barging into her life, terrifying her family, and not even letting her get dressed, they have Regina right where they want her—scared and compliant. Now that she's malleable, they'll haul her back to Milwaukee tomorrow, probably to get her to sign off on challenging her own deportation.

ICE is known to use an administrative procedure called *stipulated removal* to avoid court hearings. Without legal representation, Regina could easily be conned into waiving her rights to a hearing: "Want to get out of jail fast? Sign here." Regardless of her eligibility to stay in the United States, her signature would allow ICE to quickly close her case and deport her. The process is quick. Private. And wide open to abuse.[1]

"Regina, did they tell you, 'You have the right to remain silent. Anything you say, can and will be used against you. . . . You have the right to have an attorney present during questioning?'"

"No. Nothing like that."

No? I wonder how ICE "police" could neglect something this crucial.

Only later will I learn that Miranda warnings are not mandated for noncitizens accused of civil violations. Yet they face possible deportation, a consequence far greater than a jail sentence.

Each immigrant has the human right as well as the right under our Constitution not to be deprived of liberty without due process.

"I don't know where they took me. There was no sign. They told me to sit on the window, the stone part . . . in French, *saillie*, like a bench. It was *very* cold."

The men fretted with staff about requiring at least two immigrants for transport to the county jail in the city of Kenosha. After an hour, they locked her in an adjacent room where she watched from behind soundproof glass. At 9:30 P.M., they put her back in the car and swung onto the interstate. Kenosha was less than an hour away.

"I was so cold, but I think, pretty soon I will be in a warm bed. I begin to relax."

Suddenly, she jolted to attention. The driver was taking an off-ramp, but not into Kenosha. Beyond the glittering string of gas stations and fast-food places lay a vast dark area.

"I began shaking bad. I could hardly breathe. I am in handcuffs and my nightclothes. No underwear." Her voice trembles. "I think—I am all alone. Nobody knows where I am. Just me and these two men with their guns."

It all came hurtling back. The rape.

Thursday, July 10, 1995, Mobutu's DSP soldiers had chosen an isolated spot on a vast savannah southeast of Kinshasa to set up one of their notorious checkpoints. The sun was already bleeding into the western sky. Regina, coming home after her two months of pro-democracy work in the villages surrounding Idiofa, knew N'Djili Airport was close, though all she could see above the sea of dry, tawny grasses were a few bushes and acacia trees. By her calculation, the capital city was about seventeen miles away. She hoped she would be with David before dark.

"Suddenly there is shouting!" she told me, her eyes electric with fear.

As she described the scene, I could picture the lumbering lorry jerking to a stop, kicking up a cloud of red dust. In the cargo area, three women—two in traditional dress and Regina in jeans and a white T-shirt—plus eight to twelve men, muscular rural types in faded T-shirts and well-worn pants, sat wedged between and on top of tall stacks of gunnysacks bulging with corn and dried manioc roots for cassava. Several, like Regina, had been on the lorry for more than fifteen hours, bumbling along mud-rutted roads as hard as concrete. The canopy frame clattered forward and back as startled passengers bounced against the rails and one another.

"Then we see them—three DSP. Their guns point at us."

The soldiers shouted in Lingala, the hybrid tongue Mobutu had mandated to replace French as the national language. "*Bo kita! Bo kita!*— Get down! Get down off the lorry!"

"I know it's the DSP by their Équateur accents and their skin color, very black."

The soldiers shouted for them to bring their belongings.

Regina leaned forward. Even after all these years, her eyes flashed panic. "My PALU membership card and headband for the pro-democracy rally are in my little handbag! I also have a suitcase, not very big, with papers for the rally. I think, *O God! What I gonna do?*"

As the others began moving, Regina used her foot to shove her brown suitcase between the gunnysacks. "But I can't get my PALU card out of my handbag. The DSP are watching me."

She tucked the small black purse under her arm, then climbed down from the lorry.

"Everybody is scare, Sister. I look all around, but there is no place to go."

The soldier wearing the DSP's trademark sunglasses with flashy, feminine-looking gold rims approached the first woman and demanded her purse. Regina held her breath. "Maybe they just want money, I think. But if so, why her? She is poor."

When he returned the woman's wallet intact, Regina realized they were looking for someone—someone in particular. She wrapped both arms around her stomach to demonstrate how she held her purse against her body. "I say to myself, 'They will not kill me. Not in front of all these people. *O God, please don't let them kill me.*' But I could not stop shaking."

The soldier held out his hand for Regina's purse. As soon as he had the PALU card, he slapped her—hard—across the face. "You rebel! You are against Mobutu!"

Regina said she staggered, gasping for air. "'Stop!' I shout in Lingala. 'I am your sister! You should not treat me like this!' But he keeps hitting me. The other soldiers, they come, too. They decide to take me to jail." Regina trembled as she spoke. "Then the worse thing happen. The soldier tell everybody but me, 'Get back on the lorry.' I think now for sure they will kill me."

Watching the lorry rumble off in a fog of red dust, she felt suddenly weak, dizzy. Soldiers were coming toward her in a red haze. She sat abruptly on the hard ground, her arms falling limp at her sides. Head down, she closed her eyes, forcing herself to breathe as she heard their boots and felt the heat of their bodies closing in. "I cannot stop crying. I beg, '*Please!* Don't kill me!'"

When one angrily accused her of belonging to PALU, Regina insisted there was nothing illegal about PALU nor any of the two hundred political parties Mobutu had authorized years earlier.

The soldier shouted, "But you are trying to turn people against Mobutu!"

Her voice got stronger, "'No! I never talk against Mobutu. I tell people we can vote for the leader we want.' They say, 'But you want to get rid of Mobutu!'" She looked at me, gesturing up and down with her palms. "I tell them, 'Don't you see? Mobutu can run for office. People can vote for him.' But, Sister, their faces, they were like stone."

She laced her fingers together, then shook her joined hands to show how she begged, "'Please, please, do not hurt me!' But they do not want to listen. I am *very* scare."

"Stand up!" ordered the one with the gold-rimmed glasses. Regina struggled to her feet, but she could not stop crying. An approaching car distracted him. "Move her off the road!" he commanded, waving the others on while he stayed to enforce the checkpoint.

"The one, he slap me—hard—on the butt"—her eyes flashed old fears—"like the soldiers back in Idiofa nine months earlier. They slap my butt right before they rape me."

The youngest pushed her forward. Regina recoiled from his touch, then bolted toward the side of the road, shoving away their hands as she did. A sudden blow from behind sent her to the ground. She landed on hands and knees. As she struggled to get up, a well-placed kick sent her reeling forward again, down into the weeds. She tried pushing herself up on her hands, but they laughed, kicking, hitting, calling her foul names. She curled sideways and managed to kick back.

"I fought as hard as I could. But they were big men, you know— young, strong."

One sneering soldier seized her arm. His partner grabbed her other arm. They dragged her, twisting and kicking, behind a stand of shrubs where the younger one pinned her down and clamped her mouth closed while the other ripped off her underwear and raped her.

As she described their violence, I could not hold back my tears. "I'm so sorry, Regina." I had no other words. When she reached out her right hand, I pressed it between both of my own. After a while, I fumbled through my purse to get us both some Kleenex.

"It was very hard," she whispered. "It was . . . I can't explain."

"Some say that when a woman is being raped, she dissociates. That means she feels everything, but it's as if it were not happening to her. It's as if she were watching it from—"

"Yes," she interrupted. "That happen to me. Physical I was there, but not in my mind. This body was not like my body anymore. I was like another person. It was so strange . . . But I feel everything—everything so violent. I feel my ribs like crush under his body. I cannot breathe. I hear the noises in his throat . . . but I was not like in my own body. I was not there."

As the first man struggled with his pants, the second began maneuvering to take his place. Scrambling for his turn, he loosened his grip on her mouth. Regina screamed.

The third soldier came barreling through the weeds but stopped cold when he saw her on the ground. He yanked off his dark glasses and shouted at the one pulling up his pants, "You raped her, you pig! Why? Get away from her! NOW!"

I sat upright. "Whoa! The soldier with the sunglasses came to your rescue?"

"Yes. He was *very* upset. He shout at them, why they do this to me. He say, 'We agreed to take her to jail! Why did you rape her? Did you see her do something wrong? Did you? Because I did not see it! Why you do this? Answer me!' The two guys, they back away."

Her rescuer gestured for her to come away from the bushes.

Regina drew in her shoulders and hugged her body as she described pulling up her jeans and leaving behind the torn rag, remnant of her underwear. With the denim chafing her body, she slowly walked back to the checkpoint, keeping a wide berth between herself and all three soldiers. There, close to the road, she knelt in the dirt.

"I was not trust any of them."

"But the one with the glasses seemed to be on your side. . . ."

Her eyes were insistent. "No! Because he was dangerous!" She lowered her voice again. "Sister, I was not trust *any* man after what happen to me. For a long time, I always scare of men."

Regina begged her rescuer to let her go. "I tell him, 'Please, I work only for the good of our country. I do not talk about Mobutu.' Then the three argue for a long time what to do with me. I argue for myself, too."

Finally the rescuer turned to Regina. "We will let you go on the next lorry. You tell the driver where you want him to take you." He said nothing further but simply stood beside her for the next two hours. The other two hung back, talking between themselves.

It was after dark before the next lorry arrived. Regina gave the driver the address of her cousin, a PALU member. "I could not go back to David." She covered her eyes with one hand. Her lips quivered. "In Congo, Sister, it's the worse, the very worse thing for a woman to be rape. I sometimes feel why I cannot just kill myself and nobody gonna know this happen to me."

In Congolese society, the husband is responsible for protecting his wife. If she is violently assaulted, it's her fault. She put herself in danger, bringing shame upon him. She deserves to be ostracized. Victimized by soldiers, she is then revictimized by her own people. Ironically, by ostracizing the victim, society itself emboldens the rapists, becoming party to the very evil it decrys.

In the current war, foreign soldiers in eastern Congo are using rape to lay waste to the whole society—destroying its women, fouling their progeny, tearing apart both families and communities. Not surprisingly, massive sexual assaults—including vaginal, anal, and intestinal mutilation with guns and makeshift weapons—quickly became the cheapest, most effective weapon for fighters on all sides. Today, hundreds of thousands of Congolese women as old as seventy-five and little girls as young as three are among the most mutilated, displaced, and shunned in all the world.[2]

"When people gonna know that these soldiers do this to me, who's gonna see me like I was before, you know? There is no respect for you.

Your husband reject you. No man will touch you again. Besides, they are afraid of AIDS or malaria or some other disease. You lose all dignity. Everybody look down on you. You are *dirty*!"

Regina got out of her chair, pushed it aside. "I am like this." She knelt on the tan linoleum facing me, then sank back on her haunches, her face contorted. Her dark tear-filled eyes burned into mine. "Can you see? I am nothing. A rag in the weeds. Nothing . . . dirty . . . nasty . . . I am nothing." She lowered her head, holding her fists tight against her cheeks. "I feel so dirty . . . so nasty. David not gonna pay attention to me anymore. This rape ruin me. It ruin my life."

On the off-ramp riding into the dark unknown, Regina relived the horror. "Sister, my heart was pounding so hard. These two guys, the guns, their bad language." Handcuffed in the backseat, she prayed, *O God! O God, please help me.*

As they pulled into a gas station, "I start to relax, but then they drove past the gas pumps and park away from the lights. Again, I cannot stop shaking."

A short time later, a second unmarked car drove up. An officer got out, spoke briefly in Spanish to the agents, then opened the back door and introduced another handcuffed woman. "Leticia will be riding with you to Kenosha," he said.

"Finally I start to breathe again."

5

In the Eyes of the Law

"Forget about going downtown, Sister. I know the building—Department of Homeland Security. It's Fort Knox, so well guarded, you won't be able to get near her. They'll take her back to Kenosha when they're done." Hal Block sounds lawyerly, ponderous, careful. He reminds me there is no immigration court in Milwaukee, jail personnel don't understand immigration, and ICE is probably bringing her here for an intake interview.

I describe how the police confronted David, scared the kids, searched the house, then took Regina away in slippers and pajamas.

In his usual, measured tone, he responds, "A little over the top, don't you think?"

A smile cracks through my worry.

"Who did you say arrested her? Sister, ICE agents are not police officers."

I later learn that the word *police* also misrepresents the scope of their authority. ICE agents do not usually have the search and arrest powers of local police. In fact, mixing the two undermines the work of local police who, in their role of protecting residents, need immigrant communities to cooperate without fear of immigration consequences.

ICE is the largest investigative branch in the massive Department of Homeland Security (DHS) and the second largest investigative agency in the country after the FBI. It is also the most militarized branch of the federal government after the Pentagon, employing tens of thousands in four law enforcement divisions and several support divisions. Almost all of its annual budget of billions is focused on immigrants.[1]

In 2003, when the George W. Bush administration dismantled the troubled Immigration and Naturalization Services (INS), most immigration functions landed in one of three DHS bureaus: Citizenship and Immigration Services (USCIS), Customs and Border Protection (CBP), and Immigration and Customs Enforcement. With Homeland Security's mission focused on preventing terrorism, it was almost inevitable that immigrants, once valued as contributors, were increasingly viewed through a terrorist lens.

Other immigration functions stayed in their five cabinet-level departments: Department of Justice (adjudication of immigration law); State Department (visa policies and implementation); Departments of Labor, Education, and Health and Human Services (integration of immigrants into society).[2]

Each year an estimated forty thousand noncitizens, mostly failed asylum seekers who agreed to voluntary departure or were ordered deported by an immigration judge, fail to comply. Through its Office of Detention and Removal Operations (DRO), ICE is charged with apprehending, processing, and deporting them.

"David and I are very worried, Mr. Block. How soon will they deport her?"

"As soon as they have her travel documents. But they're dealing with the Democratic Republic of Congo, Sister. You know how speedy things are in the DRC. This may take a while."

"How fast can we get her out of jail?"

"That depends on whether the Board of Immigration Appeals agrees to reopen her case."

I grab a pen and a pad of paper. "So we can appeal this?"

"No. You get only one chance to appeal. As you learned last night, the decision was no."

"Wait. Didn't I read somewhere that you can appeal the appeal?"

"You never get to retry the first case. However, there is a thirty-day grace period after a negative decision that allows you to file a motion to reconsider, based on some legal or factual error, as we did with David's case, or to file a petition for federal review in a US Circuit Court of Appeals. There is also a ninety-day window to file a motion to reopen, but the case must be new, that is, based on all new evidence not available at the time of the first hearing. New evidence could be 'worsening country conditions'—Congo becoming just too dangerous to send her back—or in Regina's case the arrival of her husband after her hearing was over.

"If David's appeal were already granted, the judge could choose to grant her asylum on a derivative basis. Withholding of removal, however, lacks a clear provision for the spouse. But who knows? The fact that the judge in David's case believed his testimony of torture may work in her favor—if it's too dangerous for him, then it's too dangerous for her. Besides, we filed an appeal in David's case, so maybe they'll also take that into consideration." He paused. "Then again, all of this hinges on their marriage, and you know what a can of worms that is."

I remember asking Regina years earlier why she had filed for asylum as a single person when she and David had been married in Congo the year before she fled to America.

"Because I could not contact David. It's too dangerous for him to be connect with me. Besides, I was raped. He will not want me anymore." She lowered her voice. "Sister, I am very depress. I think, no, I will never see him, I will never be with him again."

"But Regina, once he got here two years later, why didn't you explain this to Attorney Lybeau so she could tell the Board of Immigration Appeals?"

She shook her head. "No. It was too late. My appeal was already file. I don't want to mess up for my appeal. It could be big confusion because we did not have the church wedding yet."

I frowned. Was she married or not?

Congo's repetition of three marriages started during colonialism as a way to accommodate Belgian traditions, both civic and religious, while retaining revered African customs. Regina explained that any of the three is OK in Congo. However, for Catholics (the majority of the population), the church wedding is the heart of the matter.

She lifted her open palms. "But for me, I come to America before we have the big church wedding. So I think maybe this is not a full marriage."

"But Regina, if you were *legally* married in Congo, why would you think you are not *legally* married in the United States?"

"In Europe, you must have the civil marriage certificate, so I think it's the same here. But I have no proof because David have the document, not me, and I cannot contact David or he will be in danger. The judge will not believe me without the paper. Worse, the marriage is over. I think I will never see David again. So they say to me, just apply, be like a single person."

"Who's 'they'? Who told you this?"

"My Congolese friends."

I groaned. Immigrants advising immigrants on matters of US law. "But once David got here, you *did* have a church wedding. You should have reported that to your lawyer."

She smiled. "No, it's not a legal marriage. We did not go to the court. It's just in church."

"Regina, in America, the church wedding *is* the legal wedding."

Her face registered alarm. She translated for David who jerked upright, his eyes as wide as hers. He too had applied for asylum as a single person. They had planned a court wedding after securing asylum. She looked back at me, resolute. "It's too late now."

Hal Block continues, "If I remember correctly, we added the marriage information and both certificates at David's hearing along with the kids' birth certificates, but I wonder how that will sit with her judge, since he didn't believe her testimony in the first place."

My throat tightens. "You mean she would have to go back to Judge Cassidy in Atlanta?"

"That's how it works. If by some miracle the BIA allows her case to be reopened, it goes back to the original judge."

In America, an asylum seeker gets only one hearing—one crucial chance—and Regina's September 4, 1997, hearing before Judge William A. Cassidy had been a disaster. The transcript, a half-inch thick, had drawn me in like a sinister novel I couldn't put down because, at some point, the tide was sure to turn. It never did.

Regina's political asylum claim was based on two major assaults by soldiers nine months apart, one in 1994, the second in 1995. In her original French affidavit, she had written about both; however, in the English version, someone—translator, secretary, or first attorney—had omitted the 1994 events. Unable to read English, Regina had signed the incomplete affidavit. The lawyer then used it to fill out her asylum application, rendering both documents incomplete.

Months later, a new friend, Professor François Lumbu, reviewing her written case, asked Regina why the first rapes and imprisonment were not included. She reacted with alarm, "What? I wrote a whole paragraph in French!" Also alarmed, Lumbu himself drove her the 307 miles to Atlanta, Georgia, for her short *master calendar hearing* (similar to an arraignment), to correct the affidavit. But Attorney Jeanne Wyuna told them it was too late to add the 1994 Idiofa events. The affidavit was already in the computer.

On the day of the asylum hearing itself, Ms. Wyuna's last-minute instructions were—in Regina's words—"I'm gonna ask you the questions. After that, the judge gonna ask and you have to say *exactly* what you wrote on your affidavit. You don't have to change it or something."

"It sounds like she was telling you to omit the Idiofa events. Just stick to the affidavit."

"Yeah. . . . But then, I don't know if it was a misunderstanding to me or what, she say, 'Now to the judge, you have to tell him *everything* about your story. You gonna tell him *all* your story and he gonna listen.' You know, that's the one I understand. And then, I say, 'OK.'"

The hearing proceeded in fits and starts. The judge was methodical, but his phrasing was often difficult for the translator. Page after page shows translator, judge, and attorneys repeatedly interrupting Regina and one another to correct or clarify or rephrase. The judge seemed annoyed, the translator unnerved, Regina more and more rattled.

As they moved to the heart of her claim, Wyuna's question seemed to open the wrong door. "During the time you were active in PALU in Idiofa, did you ever have difficulty with local authorities because of your political activities?"

"Yes, I had very serious problems."

With Judge Cassidy listening for congruence between her oral and written testimony, she then described what was *not* in her affidavit—being arrested and jailed in Idiofa.

I was perplexed. Why open this incident at all?

When he asked for a date, she gave March through October.

Impossible. How could she forget teaching until July or getting married in August?

As she testified to the second rape, in 1995 near Kinshasa, she seemed more and more confused.

JUDGE: How soon after this attack were you examined at the hospital or clinic?

Ms. IMWA: We . . . we . . . the time was . . . the time spent was just a bit long, because I had to leave that place, and then meet my cousin. Then the party leader and then to the clinic. So the time spent was a bit . . . just a bit long.

JUDGE: How long?

Ms. Imwa: Yes. I don't know if you understand the . . . the situation in which I was at that time. It was difficult for me to know exactly . . . it was difficult for me, a very difficult situation.

Judge: OK. We . . . I . . . my question still remains, how long after this attack did you visit the clinic?

Ms. Imwa: I understand your question.

Judge: Can you provide me with an answer?

Ms. Imwa: See . . . see what happened to me, for me to determine and with the emotional—my emotional state all the things that happened to me, for me to determine that—what happened exactly, it was difficult . . . it was difficult.

Judge: I'm not asking you why you waited a period of time before going to the clinic.

Interpreter: Excuse me, Your Honor. Why?

Judge: I'm not asking her why she waited before she went to the clinic. I'm just asking how long after the attack did she wait? The period of time, how long? If she doesn't know, she can say I do not know or I do not remember.

Ms. Imwa: Yes. I was under emotions. It was . . . and, that's why anybody who is like . . . somebody who is in that state is to determine that time. You see, I understand the question. But I was in . . . in emotions.

Judge: Are you in that state now?

Ms. Imwa: [Inaudible]

Judge: Yes or no?

Ms. Imwa: Yes. You see, when I'm . . . I'm rewriting this . . . the scene, I'm . . . it . . . it hurts me.

What had mystified me earlier—the inaccurate dates, stumbling answers—suddenly became clear: Regina was being retraumatized by the courtroom experience itself. I later researched the phenomenon. Discrepancies in recall are normal for torture victims. Well-documented clinical studies show that dissociation during trauma leads to a fragmentation of the experience, making it common to have amnesia coexisting with vivid recollections. Furthermore, trying to recall the traumatic event causes memory and verbal skills to falter while deeper parts of the brain—amygdala, hippocampus, hypothalamus, and brain stem where the imprint of the trauma resides—fire up in terror. The traumatized person has difficulties thinking and speaking.[3]

Judge Cassidy didn't get it. He kept hammering for a date, threatening that if she did not respond to the questions, "it may have a serious impact upon my finding of your credibility."

Later, the government lawyer pounced on the omitted incident, ending his first volley of questions with, "Ma'am, there was no mention of the 1994 imprisonment, beatings, or rape in your application."

Regina struggled to explain. "When they . . . when they . . . one day when I made an explanation, I made the original explanation in French. It was all there. It was all clear. But then, they were changing from the French to the English, the person who was . . . when they were talking about the rapes . . . the rapes just mentioned some of the items of the rapes. And by the time they . . . they . . . they finalized it, they sent it like that. They sent it as . . . as it was. But when I made the . . . the report, I put everything in."

After the government lawyer made the same point about her affidavit, Judge Cassidy said, "Yet you signed your application and the affidavit leaving out this important information."

"Because I didn't know . . . I didn't know the language. Whenever I just signed, I just signed. I didn't know the language."

The government lawyer quickly pressed into another morass, drilling her with questions about her position in PALU (representative for Idiofa), isn't it odd that in PALU documents no title is listed (titles were not used), but she had major responsibilities (yes), and in the asylum application she listed herself as a "chairwoman." After six pages of his grilling her about being a chairwoman, her confusing it with her school title as "Madame Director," and his questioning the odd absence of "chairwoman" in party documents, she finally asked, "Please, I don't . . .

I don't quite understand. Can you explain to me what a chair . . . actually what a real chairwoman is?"

On it went for hours, the whole sorry hearing plunging toward its ruinous end.

"I have found your application to be fraudulent," Judge Cassidy pronounced. "As a result, I have denied your applications for asylum and withholding of deportation. And I have further denied your right to depart the United States voluntarily and have ordered you deported to the Democratic Republic of Congo/Zaire." After informing her that she had thirty days to appeal, he added this kicker: "However, I would state that it is this court's position that any appeal would be as *frivolous* as the application upon which it is based."

Frivolous.

As denials go, the legal term *frivolous* is the worst possible ruling, the death knell.

"Sister Josephe, I was . . . *sick!*" Regina crumpled inside her shoulders and clasped both fists against her heart. "I was almost like die. And inside of my heart I was *cry*. And you know, that's the time, I just feel it's not my country, and it's not easy to go stay to somebody's country, special if you don't know the language. Nobody gonna trust you, you know? I think about my family and David when I was very important to them. Now I am like nothing. I say, 'God, you know I was here hours talking, talking, for what?'" She sank back in her chair, drained.

In his oral decision, Judge Cassidy identified inconsistencies between her written and oral testimony, focusing on the absence of the 1994 events from her written application and supportive documents. Finding her explanation of the translator's error unconvincing, he concluded that she fabricated everything. "In viewing the whole of the testimony, I equate it to someone pulling the string on a sweater. As the questions were being asked, the story began to unravel until it just lay as a ball at her feet."

Because her replacement membership card for PALU did not give much information (she testified that the original had been confiscated by the DSP) and the wording of a letter from the PALU representative in the United States too closely resembled her written testimony, he threw out all personal supportive documents, including Dr. Kulasalana's signed report bearing the clinic's seal ("Bruises all over her body: face, hips, legs. Vagina wounds and bledings [*sic*]. Probable sperm traces on the body and on clothes.") as well as Congo's secret service directive listing her as forbidden to leave the country. With no report, the rape did not happen. With no secret service directive, Congo had no interest in her. She had no "well-founded fear of persecution" and, therefore, no claim to asylum. There was no "clear probability" that her life or her freedom would be in danger in Congo, therefore no withholding of removal under US law.

To my dismay, throughout his five-page ruling, Judge Cassidy paid no attention to the central claim of Regina's case—that she had been raped for her political work.

Anyone setting out to deceive the court would have done a far better job than Regina.

Nevertheless, before stating his judgment in formal terms, Cassidy added, "It is clear based on her attempts to present this claim that she has no respect for this procedure or the asylum process. I will deny the voluntary departure as a matter of discretion because this is clear [*sic*] without doubt a fabricated application."

How can I tell Regina she'll have to face this man again if we get her case reopened?

Block continues, "Of course, the whole idea of reopening her case based on David's case may be moot because, remember, her ninety days for reopening ended three years ago."

"But that was her lawyer's fault. Regina never got the notice because Attorney Lybeau forgot to notify the Board of Immigration Appeals that she had moved her office."

"Sorry, Sister." He sighs. "In the eyes of the law, Regina had her day in court, she appealed, her appeal was denied in 2002. It's over."

"But that's unfair!"

"Well. That's how the law works. Unless someone in the BIA has enough humanity to accept Ms. Lybeau's apology and allow her to file a motion to reopen, there's nothing much anyone can do."

"Who is on this Board of Appeals anyway?"

"Only eleven judges. Used to be twenty-three working in three-member panels who would study each case before agreeing on a decision, but after 9/11, Attorney General John Ashcroft decided it was paramount to make the immigration process more efficient."[4]

"By cutting their number? Isn't that counterintuitive?"

"He said it was procedure, not personnel, causing the backlog. Those eleven BIA judges in Falls Church, Virginia, handle all the appeals from about 220 judges across the country. They're backlogged on about 32,000 cases right now." He clears his throat. "Yeah. To simplify the procedure, each one gets a stack of cases to decide. Ashcroft also encouraged them to issue 'affirmances without opinion,' meaning they can simply say they agree with the judge without explaining why. This gives us lawyers nothing to contest. Eighty percent of cases are decided this way—a single board member giving a one-sentence opinion."

My stomach plunges. "But they could wind up just rubber stamping the judge's ruling."

"That's the big concern. Before these changes, a fair number of appeals were granted, but now there are far fewer. In fact, many BIA denials end up being reversed by a US Court of Appeals." He clears his throat again. "Anyway, Anne Lybeau may or may not have the BIA's written decision from 2002. If she has it, she may have already filed to reopen. Have you called her?"

"She's next on my list." I hesitate. "Mr. Block, we hope to transfer Regina's case from Atlanta to the Midwest Immigration Court in Chicago. Would you be willing to take it?"

"I'm not sure I'd be able to do this, Sister. Right now it's in Anne Lybeau's hands. See what you can find out from her. Meanwhile, I will try to reach Regina's deportation officer."

A week or more after her 1997 hearing, Regina had shared her plight with a Congolese man named Émile who happened to be visiting in Greensboro. He offered to get her a lawyer in his state, New Jersey, 445 miles north. True to his word, Émile arranged an appointment with Attorney Anne Lybeau, paid Regina's bus fare, picked her up at the station, and accompanied her to the appointment. This had been Regina's one meeting with Lybeau. The attorney studied the judge's decision and filed Regina's appeal on September 30, 1997, within the thirty-day limit. Once a case is in appeal, it is adjudicated by the BIA behind closed doors. Regina knew it was not uncommon to wait years. As required, she sent every change of address to the government and regularly phoned Lybeau for news on her appeal.

"Hello? Attorney Lybeau?" I explain who I am and why I am calling.

After her initial shock and ample apologies, she explains her delay. "Sister, I've tried for months to get the BIA to send me the May 17, 2002, decision. I can't do anything without it. This morning I will file an emergency request to expedite it. As soon as it comes, I'll file a motion to reopen her case in light of David's withholding of removal. The fact that the judge believed his testimony may warrant reopening. If he had asylum, she could get asylum on a derivative basis."

"The asylum part of his decision is in appeal, Ms. Lybeau."

"Good. That may help. Keep in touch, OK? I'll fax all my motions to you." She pauses. "Sister, I feel just terrible. This is my fault. I never got the decision because I forgot to notify the Board of Immigration Appeals that I moved my office."

She explains that while in the stress of moving the office, her mother, several states away, grew desperately ill. In moving her sick mom to New Jersey, she remembered only to notify the post office of the new office address and to tell building tenants to forward all mail.

"This is tragic, Sister. I'll do everything I can."

"Anne, we hope to get David's attorney to take over her case."

"Oh, please do. That would be so much better. She hired me for the appeal, and we met only once back in 1997. I'll do all I can, but see if David's attorney can do it."

At 1:45 P.M., Regina calls from Kenosha, proud of having followed my instructions not to say anything without a lawyer present. The officer, the same "mean one" who had picked her up the night before, was visibly annoyed, shouted accusations at her for refusing to cooperate, then ordered her to stand against the wall while he questioned Leticia. Regina asked him, "Why are you angry with me? I am not a criminal. I just want my lawyer to be with me."

"You are lying. You *are* a criminal," he retorted. "You came with false papers!"

"No, I am *not* a criminal. I am asking for asylum."

After a while, he said, "OK, don't say anything. Just sign for your passport."

Passport? Forget stipulated removal. They just want her out. They must have realized her only passport had been a false one. I hold my breath.

"So I sign the paper. Now I am back here in Kenosha."

"She's her own worst enemy," groans Attorney Block. "All ICE needs to deport her are her passport and an airline ticket. As soon as they have both, she's gone."

"It's my fault." I wince. "I forgot to tell her not to *sign* anything."

"Well, what's done is done. I contacted her detention officer, but I could not get much information from him. I'll say this much—he is not a mild man."

Hmm. Maybe he's the "mean one" who arrested Regina.

"Mr. Block, Attorney Lybeau is eager to transfer the case to the Midwest. Will you take it?"

There's a long pause. "Sister, it makes sense because I am handling her husband's case, but I can't. Her case demands a lot of work, all of it urgent, and my docket is full. I leave soon with my wife for three weeks in Eastern Europe. I'm sorry, but there's no way I can do it."

My hopes free-fall. "I understand," I say, hardly able to breathe. "Thank you, Mr. Block. I know you would help if you could." I hang up, feeling starkly alone.

Godfrey Muwonge e-mails that he is disengaging from deportation defense. "I cannot handle the stress. I am heartbroken, but my doctors say I have to let go to stay alive."

I debate about calling Barb Graham of Catholic Charities who would be great, but her pro bono caseload is staggering. I decide to save us both the phone tag it will take for her to say no.

Outside, leafless, gray branches poke aimlessly, each at its own patch of air. I have no idea where to turn.

6

WHY AMERICA?

"Sister, you talk to Attorney Block? He's gonna take my case?" After I explain, her voice falters. "What we gonna do? My little kids need me." I hear her crying over the phone. "I must get out of here. Last night they put me in this small room with another woman, a big white woman on the bottom bed. When I come, she woke up. She was nice. She said not to trust everyone because some can do bad things to you, but she say not to be scare, she's gonna help me." Her voice drops. "There is no privacy here, Sister. Behind the bed is a wall, and walls on both sides, but in the front, it's like bars—you can see what each one is doing. They watch you go to the toilet, everything."

Later I will learn that hers is one of five double-occupancy cells lined up on one side of an open day room. Each cell has its own steel toilet and small sink, but inmates share a common shower at one end of the open area. Cells are locked at night. During the day, inmates can walk into the day room where picnic tables are anchored to the floor and a TV is mounted on the wall. No one is allowed to enter another's cell, nor is anyone to use a blanket during the day. A single guard in another room monitors four such units at a time on video screens.

Her voice gets quieter. "Today I am so scare I can hardly breathe. Maybe somebody gonna touch me in a bad way, you know? When you take a shower, you have to walk naked all the way and they just watch you. I keep my head down, try to be fast."

I wince, my own mind spinning into fear. I try changing the topic. "How was it coming to Milwaukee this morning?"

"Not good. First they put the handcuffs, then . . . I don't know how you say . . . things on the ankles, then a big chain to connect them. I must lift the heavy chain with my arms so I don't trip. Then they put chains around our stomachs—we was four women—to attach us to each other."

"What!" The image of Regina in belly chains slams me in the gut.

Later, online I will find in the Department of Homeland Security's *Detention Operations Manual*: "As a rule, transporting officers will not handcuff women or minors. If an exception arises, the officers will document the incident, recording the facts and reasoning behind the decision."[1] Does DHS know these officers are not following the manual?

I also learn that immigrant detainees are not referred to as "prisoners" because the government claims detention is not a punishment but simply a "means to effect deportation."

Clearly, the DHS's meticulous legal distinctions mean nothing. These women—taken from their families, stripped of their belongings, put into prison uniforms, locked in with convicted criminals, deprived of privacy, and transported in belly chains—*are* prisoners. Why the duplicitous language? Could this be an attempt to categorize a whole class of people as not needing further hearings so ICE can deport them at will?

My later research reveals that because immigration courts are not criminal courts, the United States Constitution does not guarantee an immigrant the right to legal counsel at government expense nor to a full trial by jury. However, the Supreme Court ruled long ago that if the government of its own accord gives an immigrant a hearing, it must be a fair hearing.[2] On that basis, the court stopped the old INS from acting as prosecutor, judge, and enforcer in 1950. However, by greatly expanding its use of administrative decisions to avoid court hearings, isn't that exactly what ICE is doing?[3]

The Supreme Court also ruled in 1966 that the burden is on the government to show by "clear, unequivocal, and convincing evidence" that an immigrant is actually deportable. Then in 1979 the court ruled, by referring to the standard in another case, that "unequivocal" equals proof beyond a reasonable doubt that the person being thrown out is actually deportable.[4]

"When we come to Milwaukee, Sister, there is another woman, Norma, *very* depress. She has three American kids. Years ago the judge deny her asylum, but she got voluntary departure. When it was time to return to El Salvador, she was seven months pregnant and too scare to go. Good thing, because her baby was born with a hole in his heart, he needs emergency open heart surgery. Now they take her? Why? She did not do a crime! He *still* needs her. He's only five."

Same age as Lydia.

"Most immigrants in jail are not criminals, Regina. If Norma signed a promise to leave by a certain date but didn't, her voluntary departure automatically became a deportation order."

"Is it too late for her to appeal now?"

"I don't know. If you see her, urge her to get a lawyer to review her case."

It's next to impossible for detainees in removal proceedings to effectively contest their deportation without a good lawyer, yet according to the Department of Justice, approximately 84 percent of immigrant detainees have no legal representation.

"It's terrible here, Sister. I am afraid all the time and I'm so cold I am shaking, but they won't let you use the blanket even when you tell them you don't feel well. They say they don't care. When they feed you, they put the food on a shelf like it's for a dog. If you don't save the little cup from the apple juice, you gonna be thirsty all day. Right now I am cold and thirsty, but my head is like burning. I just want to put cold water on my head."

It's been less than twenty-four hours since ICE took her into custody.

I lower my pitch, hoping to sound confident. "Try to be calm, Regina. I know it's terribly hard for you in jail, but . . . well, at least you're still in the United States." I bite my lip, realizing how hollow, almost cruel, that must sound.

"I could not sleep last night, Sister. I struggle in my mind why God let this happen to me? My family did not want me to do the democracy work. If I just listened to them . . . or maybe it's because I use the false passport."

"Wait a minute. How else could you get to safety, Regina? Your own government was threatening your life. No. You turned the false passport over to your lawyer right away. You did exactly the right thing."

"For myself, Sister, I'm OK." She steadies her voice. "But now it's not just myself. I make this pain for my good husband and for my two beautiful little children."

Alarm bells go off in me. "Regina, this is *not* your fault."

"Then why is this happening?"

"Because your lawyer neglected to tell the BIA that she moved her office—that's why." I'm overtired. I feel my throat tightening. "Regina, you did *nothing* wrong."

"Yes, but why did God send me to America? Just to deport? That does not make sense."

I think of the many desperate people who flee violence or unlivable conditions believing that God is leading them to safety and new life—hundreds of thousands of them—whom the United States and other countries summarily deport every year. Surely their faith and prayers have been just as fervent. I glance at the small "P.S. from God" message taped to my desk lamp. Created by my friend Sister Caroline, it reads: *Remember, I need you . . . more than you can imagine.*[5]

If I can help just one . . .

"Sometimes, Regina, we just have to trust that God is with us."

"Yes, I know," she says. "But I think of all the troubles to get me here, how God help me through each one. Why now to deport me? I don't think so." She pauses. Her voice is resolute. "No. I am still *sure* God wants me in America."

I had been full of questions after Regina first told me of the Kinshasa rape: When did you decide to flee? Why America? How did you get here? She picked up the story one summer afternoon a few years before her recent arrest. I cleared a clutter of books from my kitchen table and poured us each a glass of juice.

"After the rape, remember I told you I could not go back to David. That night I told the lorry driver to drop me off not far from my cousin's house in Kinshasa."

Her cousin Chrétien and his wife Claire lived in a middle-class neighborhood, an irregular grid of brick wall enclosures higher than the houses they guarded, the only light a lamp or two near a front gate or at the door of the occasional unwalled home. Regina got off the lorry and crossed the boulevard to enter a dark maze. Head down, she hurried along the dirt walk flanking the blacktop, then turned onto an unpaved street, eager to reach Chrétien's redbrick wall and well-lit gate. "I argue with myself, why I didn't just renounce my party or say no?" she said.

Pounding repeatedly on Chrétien's red metal gate, she finally heard footsteps.

"Who's there?" he called.

"It's me . . . Regina."

"When my cousin open the gate, he go like this." She jerked back. Her jaw fell open.

"He wants to know what happen to me, but I just look down. 'No, no, I'm just tired, that's all.' He took me around the back to the kitchen door where Claire was. When she hug me, she *knew* something was wrong, but I don't say. I just ask to take a shower, that's all."

After the shower—"a hot, *hot* shower"—Regina dressed, then returned to the guestroom to sit quietly on the bed. Claire emerged from the hallway, closed the door, and sat next to her. "Something happened to you, Regina. You are not the same."

"My face is swollen and bruise. I cannot hold back my tears. When I tell her what happen, she cry, too, Sister. She told me she was worry about me for a long time. Then she say, 'This political work is too dangerous, especially for a woman. The family told you this many times. I hope you will stop now.' She put her arm around me. She wants me to see a doctor right away, but I think to myself, *What if I have the HIV?* I could not face that. Not tonight."

Nor did Regina want Chrétien to know she had been raped, but Claire insisted.

The two went back to the kitchen where Claire did the talking.

"My cousin Chrétien was shock. First thing, he was angry—*very* angry—against the DSP and the Mobutu regime. He shout, 'What? How come they can do this to a Congolese woman?'"

Then looking at her swollen face, his voice quieted. "I'm sorry for how you suffered."

"He say to me, 'You are a brave woman, Regina. You have done a lot for PALU and for our country.' I was grateful, but Claire, she did not like to hear that, *nooo*. She shout, 'No, Chrétien! She needs to *stop*! She has been raped—*raped*! She must stop this political work!' Then she shout at me, 'What kind of woman are you anyway, Regina? You should be home with your husband, starting a family!' Chrétien put up his hands like this. He say, 'Stop, Claire! You cannot tell Regina what to do! It's her life, not yours!'"

I interrupted, "Claire *shouted* at you?"

Regina shrugged. "It's how we argue in Congo. Claire is traditional like most Africans. I am the *only* one in my own family who volunteer for a political job. My sisters? My brothers? No. They are afraid. Many times they are upset like Claire—why I am not home with my husband, this work is too dangerous for a woman, things like that. Chrétien—

he is a member of PALU—he understands. I tell Claire there are other women in PALU, too, not only me. I teach the village women. But she shout again, 'Why you do like this, keep acting like a man? You will end up killed!' Then Chrétien says, 'Stop, Claire! Yes, it's dangerous, but Regina knows the risks.'"

While they argued, Regina worried. "Yes, I must think about my safety, but the people in Idiofa are my own people. I must think about them, too. But is it too dangerous for me now?"

After a while, Chrétien and Claire wanted to take her to David, but Regina refused, finally admitting that this was not the first time she was raped. They stared at her, stunned, as she told what had happened nine months earlier. After the first rape, David had accepted her back, but when he wanted her to stay with him in Kinshasa, she convinced him to let her return to Idiofa to recruit a replacement. She had no problems for two months. Ironically, she was coming home when she was raped for the second time.

Both still wanted David to know.

"No! He will not trust me anymore." Her next words opened a more immediate worry. "Besides, maybe I am sick now—HIV, malaria, or some other disease."

Chrétien quickly persuaded her to see a doctor he knew at a small clinic in N'Djili Zone.

On their way, he directed the taxi driver to stop at the home of PALU's president Antoine Gizenga, the man who had summoned Regina from Idiofa to help plan the Saturday, July 29, pro-democracy rally, nineteen days later. Gizenga and his wife had invited her to stay in their home with the other rally planners, but seeing her battered face, Gizenga worried aloud for her life. Cautioning her to stay away from the rally, he gave Chrétien money for her treatment.

At Clinique Munga, Dr. Kulasalana was horrified. "*Why*? Why would they do something like this to a Congolese woman? What is happening to this country?"

After the physical exam, he gave her medication for possible venereal disease and malaria. It was too soon to test for HIV. Though he prescribed five days of psychotherapy, the clinic was too far and too costly to return. The doctor told her to rest a while before going back.

"When he ask if I am married, I say I do not want to tell my husband. He knew why I felt this way. He said, 'I understand. Just take your time.' I was very grateful."

It was well after midnight when they got home.

"Claire ask me what I gonna do now, but I did not know what to say."

Regina's worn face and troubled eyes tugged at my heart. As a Catholic sister, I understood her drive to help people of the villages near Idiofa understand democracy, but I also remembered the wisdom of a friend: God created us in such a way that the deepest needs of one person will never conflict with those of another; conversely, if we ignore the deeper call within, we will end up hurting both ourselves and those we are trying to help.

"I ask Chrétien if he thinks the DSP knows about the rally. He says, since they were watching for PALU organizers, they probably do. He agreed with Gizenga I should stay away." She sat up, her jaw tight. "But the *big* thing Chrétien said was, 'Regina, Kinshasa is *dangerous*, not like Idiofa. Now that the DSP knows you are here, they will be watching for you.'"

She looked from one to the other. "What should I do?"

"Maybe you should think about leaving the country," Claire said.

Five days after the rape, Chrétien came home wide-eyed with news from PALU. "Kinshasa is *very* dangerous, Regina. We need to get you out of the country quickly."

Regina leaned in toward me. "I look at his face and"—her voice dropped to a near whisper—"suddenly I feel very, *very* scare. This time I say OK."

Again Chrétien urged her to contact David.

Again she refused. "To keep him safe, it is best." She made them both promise not to tell David or anyone else. "If someone asks, tell them you heard rumors of trouble in Idiofa. That's all. It is best for their safety and mine that nobody knows what happen to me."

When Chrétien suggested consulting her uncle Basil, Regina agreed, but she did not want to live with her family in Belgium nor with her brother Lucién's family in France.

"Sister, I was too scare Mobutu will find me! Europe has many Congolese. I want a safe place far from Congo where nobody knows me. When Chrétien ask what country I have in mind, I say I need a little time to think. Claire, she knows I used to go to a college prayer group, so she invited me to her weekly prayer meeting the next night."

Wednesday, July 16, Regina and Claire took their places in the second row on one of the backless wooden benches facing the pulpit. Fifteen to twenty others also attended.

Afterward, the pastor took Regina aside. "When you prayed aloud for the Rwandans suffering from the genocide, God told me you have something to tell me."

"I say, 'No,' but he say again, 'God says there is something heavy on your heart.' I shake my head. 'No. I have nothing to tell you.' But he did not go away. He say, 'I think God wants me to help you. You know I am a pastor, don't you?' Finally I talk quietly, say, 'OK. I must make some big decisions. It's too dangerous for me now in Congo. If God wants me to leave the country, where I gonna go? What does God want me to do?'"

She was grateful when he suggested that for the next three nights, he and his wife come to pray with her at Claire and Chrétien's house. The five prayed together.

The prerequisites for authentic discernment are inner freedom and a healthy humility. Both are essential, but neither is easily achieved. It all comes down to how honest one dares to be. A wise, impartial outsider asking the right questions can help a person let go of any personal agenda to come to a "holy indifference" about the outcome. When peace comes, the answer is usually clear. This process is generally trustworthy.

At the end of the third night, Saturday, July 19, the pastor noted that they had experienced God's peace every time they prayed—nothing disturbing, nothing to give them pause—only peace. He believed that God was confirming what was in her heart. The others nodded.

"So, Regina, what country keeps coming to your mind?" he asked.

"America."

He smiled. "Go to America, Regina."

"But he can see I am worry, so he ask if it's because I must use false papers. I say, 'Yes. I do not want to do something wrong.' But he say, 'It's OK. You are not going to kill or steal but to save your life. In the Bible, Abraham saved his life by telling his wife to say she was his sister. God's gonna use the false papers to save your life, Regina. Go with God's blessing.'"[6]

Regina's shoulders relaxed. "From that time on, I was at peace."

Chrétien and members of PALU immediately set about getting Regina a bogus French passport with a US visitor's visa.

Every year, tens of thousands of foreign nationals seek protection in the United States because they fear persecution in their home countries.

Those who apply while living in a third country *outside* the United States, usually in a refugee camp, are called *refugees*. The president in consultation with Congress sets that year's combined cap for how many refugees will be admitted. Those who apply while living here are called *asylum seekers*. There is no limit on individuals seeking asylum.

In either case, the person seeking protection must meet the international definition of a refugee.

A person who is outside his/her country of nationality and who is unable or unwilling to return because of persecution or a well-founded fear of persecution on account of race, religion, nationality, membership in a particular social group, or political opinion.[7]

Different programs serve each group.[8] Asylum seekers enter the United States any way they can: presenting a legal temporary visa (student, visitor, or worker); asking for asylum at a port of entry (airport, seaport, or border); sneaking over a border; using fraudulent documents. Falsifying a passport or a visa can be a federal felony, but under international law, which the United States has incorporated into its own law and is obliged to observe, anyone alleging persecution is entitled to ask for asylum in any country and is not to be penalized for having to use a fraudulent document to save her life.

To get asylum in the United States, Regina would need to prove a "well-founded fear" of returning to Congo based on one of the five categories in the definition of "refugee," in her case, political opinion.

───────

Nine nights after her decision to flee to America, Regina quietly stepped out of a taxi into a moonlit fishing village on the banks of the Congo River. She was wearing the same jeans and T-shirt as on the day of the rape, with new, white tennis shoes from Claire and Chrétien.

"The village is small," she told me. "Six or seven round huts with roofs like cones covered with grass."

Chrétien took her black duffle bag and paid the driver. They waited while the taxi rumbled off, then with moon and stars lighting their way, Regina walked with her cousin through the weeds and beyond a few short trees, toward the riverbank. It was around 3 A.M., Thursday, July 27, 1995, two and a half days before the PALU rally.

"It was not easy for me, Sister. I am going someplace—I don't know anybody, I don't speak the language, I just go. I have to go because I want to save my life. But, most important to me, I know God is with me."

7

MOONLIT FOG

Regina held Chrétien's hand as they descended the stony embankment leading down to the Congo River. She described the night as "cold, damp, smell like fish," its only sounds the rhythmic lapping of water against the shore, a steady hum of insects, and the occasional *whoot-whoot-whoot* of a distant African wood owl. A skinny fisherman in long pants and flip-flops waited on the fog-draped shoreline, his pirogue rocking in the shallows. His eyes were wary, his face tense. He didn't talk much, didn't have to. Chrétien handed him her duffle bag.

"I didn't take much—just clothes for my flight, black shoes, a purse with some money, personal items, and my new Bible—all gifts from Chrétien and Claire. When I hug my cousin good-bye, I cry. He was so good to me." She looked down, then brushed away tears. "I don't know how he did it, Sister. After he talk with Uncle Basil, he work with PALU people in five countries. In less than two weeks my cousin made it all happen. My brother Lucién in Paris gave money for the plane, but Chrétien save my life." She was quiet for a moment. "It was a miracle."

The fisherman, holding her bag in one hand, helped Regina to her place in the bow of his flat-bottomed boat. Then, standing behind her in the stern, he pushed his oar against the riverbed to propel the long, narrow canoe forward between tall bulrushes and dense mats of bulbous water hyacinths. By the time Regina turned back to wave, Chrétien was already lost in the bright fog.

Most people, even from the world's poorest countries, do not leave their homelands unless forced out by untenable circumstances. Home is home. Whenever Regina talks about Congo, she glows. Moving permanently to America uprooted her from all she cherished—her husband, relatives, friends, colleagues, the graves of her parents in their ancestral villages, her profession, language, culture, the singing and dancing, the laughter of village children, Congo's lush forests, bright rivers, circus-colored birds, and flowers everywhere.

As the fisherman threaded his pirogue between the weeds, she said, the fog was so thick she could see only the bow of the boat parting the water and on either side thick leaves ballooning from tall hyacinth stalks. I pictured the slender boat gliding in a bubble of clarity, as if light itself were cradling them through the Congo's mercurial waters.

"I am crying, Sister. I am thinking of David, our short life together."

It had been three months since she had seen him. Married less than a year, most of their time had been spent apart, first due to David's day job plus political work evenings and weekends, then because of her pro-democracy work and imprisonment in far-off Idiofa.

"It's too hard to think of him, Sister. So I think of Claire—how she took me to the prayer meeting, how we both cry when we kiss good-bye, and Chrétien—all he did for me, then the pastor, my PALU friends. I think of my father's house in Idiofa, the white fence around our yard, our three lemon trees, my beautiful country that David and I work so hard to save." She paused. "David again. I always come back to David. I cannot stop my tears. I say in my heart, *There is no one now but God. God, you are my Father. You gonna give me a new life. I depend on you.*"

Suddenly the weeds ended, propelling their boat into the wild current. Careening forward in moonlit fog, Regina could do nothing but hang on and trust. "I don't know how this fisherman did it. After the water hyacinths, he has to work very hard, and the fog was too thick."

I unfolded a map of the Democratic Republic of Congo on my kitchen table. On it, the Congo River looks like a giant hand draped over the top of the nation, its many long fingers spanning the country. The river begins quietly in the "fingers" of the southeast savannahs, then widens and breaks loose, looping over the equator in the north, swirling west between hundreds of islands through some of the thickest jungle on earth, then surging south-southwest, intensifying in volume and velocity on its way to Kinshasa. As it expands into the fifteen-mile-wide Malebo Pool between the capital cities of the two Congos—Kinshasa, DRC, and Brazzaville, Republic of Congo, it slows, but after the pool, it careens west over cataracts and rapids for two hundred miles, becoming navigable only for the last hundred miles to the Atlantic.

"Where were you, Regina?"

"Somewhere around here," she said, sliding her finger along the stretch before the capital cities. "But I'm not sure, because where we cross the river, the water was *very* fast. I was thinking, *God, what's gonna happen to me?*"

In approximately forty-five minutes, Regina caught the faint outline of the riverbank, the "other Congo," Republic of Congo, one-seventh the size of the massive DRC, its population twenty times smaller. Gradually, the silhouette of a tall man materialized out of the fog. After the fisherman helped her from his boat, she walked across the sand toward the well-dressed stranger.

"His complexion was very dark. He did not smile. 'I am Mr. Nkoufi, the person who will help you,' he said to me. 'Tonight we leave. You will pose as my wife.' I had many questions: Will I use the name of your real wife? Her passport? What if they suspect me?"

He frowned. "Don't ask questions. My wife and I will teach you what you need to know."

By the time they left Nkoufi's house by taxi late that night, Regina knew how to present herself as the wife of a wealthy businessman, poised and confident, standing back a bit, trusting Nkoufi to do the talking. They arrived at Maya Maya Aéroport in Brazzaville in plenty of time for their 11 P.M. flight. She looked the part in the outfit Claire and Chrétien had paid a seamstress to create—a midcalf black skirt, side slit to the knee, topped with a silky blouse, navy with white polka dots, gathered at the waist in a V-shaped ruffle. She wore gold earrings and a gold watch. Her hair was drawn to one side in a ponytail of loose curls.

I pursed my lips. "Ooh, *très chic!*"

"I am taking my wife on vacation," said Nkoufi, also looking smart in black suit, gold chains, and well-polished shoes. He handed both tickets over the Air Afrique counter.

After landing at 8 A.M. in Aéroport International Brussels, Belgium, they took a train to Amsterdam Airport Schiphol, the Netherlands, arriving about two hours early for Regina's flight to New York. She had been too nervous to eat on the train. All had gone well, but this was as far as Nkoufi could travel. When he presented Regina's ticket and passport at the check-in counter explaining that his wife was going on vacation, the no-nonsense blond looked over the top of her glasses and gestured for Regina to come forward.

"I was scare in my heart, Sister, but I have to act brave. '*Parlez-vous français?*' I ask. So the agent switch languages. '*Bagages?*' I answer, '*Un sac.*' Mr. Nkoufi lifts it on the scale. When the ticket agent open my passport, I hold my breath. The woman, she look at the photo, then look over her glasses at me. She frown, then look at the passport again, then at me again, the passport, then me. She straighten up, then she squint her eyes at me, say, 'This is not your picture.'"

Regina felt suddenly cold, knowing she would have to tell an outright lie. She frowned, then snapped, "Of course it's my picture! Whose else picture would be in *my* passport?"

The agent stared into her dark eyes for a few long moments.

"Oh, Sister, I was so scare!" Regina scrunched her shoulders. "I just pray, *Dear God, you told me to do this. Please, God. Please, do something.*"

"OK," said the agent, handing back the passport. She tagged the luggage, then handed Regina her boarding pass and an American I-94 customs declaration. "*Ne vous inquiétez pas*. Don't worry. They will explain how to fill out this paper on the plane."

When they had walked a safe distance, Regina finally dropped her shoulders and exhaled. Nkoufi, looking straight ahead, put his arm around her. "You're doing fine," he said. When they reached the concourse, he turned toward her. "This is as far as I can go. Shall we pray?" After joining hands in silent prayer, he looked at his watch. "It's time." Ahead were five gates labeled *Paspoortcontrole*. Mr. Nkoufi studied them for a moment, then directed her to the last line.

The inspector took her passport. "*O, je bent Europeaan*," he said, handing it back unopened. "OK. Gate 22." Nkoufi smiled and waved good-bye.

In the gate area, Regina spotted a black man with an empty seat beside him. When he answered her greeting in French, she sat down, happy to have someone to talk to on the plane. Also fluent in English, he helped her fill out the customs form. Just as he finished, a flight for Canada was announced. Regina was surprised when the stranger stood up.

"What? You are not going to the United States?"

"No," he said, equally surprised. "The US flight is over at that gate. Good luck."

Regina thanked him. At Gate 22, she boarded her flight, a bit disappointed to be alone yet grateful to be on the right plane with her I-94 customs declaration already filled out.

"There was no other black people on the plane. My seat was next to a pretty woman with red hair, name Judith, from New York. She was very nice. We try to talk, me with my very little English, and she does not know French." Regina smiled, then grew suddenly somber. She leaned forward. "But, Sister, just before the plane begin to move, the worse thing happen!"

A short airlines official bustled into the cabin and headed toward their row. "*Jij*," he said, looking at Regina.

She froze.

He nodded. "*Ja, je.*"

Her voice dropped to a whisper. "Sister Josephe, when he say that, I think, *Now here I am by myself! Dear God, what I gonna do?*"

The Dutch official said, "*Geef me je paspoort, alsjeblieft. We moeten het inspecteren.*" He ushered her off the plane into a small room between the Jetway and gate area, where airline officials sat at a desk accepting each passenger's boarding pass. The round-faced man gestured for Regina to sit down. Holding her passport open, he peered down at her. "*Wat is je naam?*"

She answered, "Hélène Nkoufi."

He looked again at the passport. "*Wat is je adres?*"

"Thank God I was prepare. I say to him, '*Pourquoi vous posez cette question?*' Then I ask for someone who speaks French. He left and got another man. I told him in French the address on the passport. He tell me to sign, so I sign my name, same way as on the passport."

"You had practiced the signature?"

"Yes, the day before. Many times." Regina leaned closer. Her voice was solemn. "Then he take my passport to another room. I am *soo* scare. I pray, *O God! You are the one told me to go to America. Three days we pray. I told you to stop me if it was not right. God, if I ever needed you, I need you now! Show me that I am your daughter! . . . Now, God, NOW!*"

The door opened. The original official emerged, an apologetic smile on his ruddy face. "*Sorry. We moeten nogiets.* We needed to check something," he said, handing back the passport.

Regina settled back on my kitchen chair. Her eyes brightened. "Sister Josephe, God love me. God really love me." But the sun splashing across the table quickly faded.

On Friday, July 28, 5:30 P.M. Daylight Savings Time, Regina's plane landed in New York at John F. Kennedy International Airport. As passengers came off the Jetway, airline agents routed Americans in one direction, foreign nationals in another. Judith, the New Yorker, wished her luck and gave her a hug before disappearing into the crowd. Regina, feeling suddenly alone again, followed the flow of foreigners. Three Customs and

Immigration stations had scores of people waiting to turn in their I-94 customs forms and have their passports stamped with US visas. When another inspector opened a fourth line, Regina stepped up to be first.

"Again, I was scare, Sister, and very tired, but what can I do? I just trust God."

Without looking up, the man opened her passport, stamped the visa page, then cut a section from the I-94 to staple inside. "Welcome to America," he said, handing it back to her.

"At that moment, I feel like I am free," she said.

Thanking him, she slipped her passport back into her purse and joined the sea of strangers surging toward baggage claim. It did not take long for her black duffle bag to circle into view. But as she scooped it from the carousel and turned to leave the international area, a tall female police officer appeared from out of nowhere. "I need to see your passport, please."

"I am thinking, No! Not again. I act confident, but in my heart, now I am *very* scare."

While the officer paged through her passport, Regina glanced around. "Nobody else from my plane was stop. Nobody."

The woman looked up, her eyes studying Regina. "Why did you come to America?"

"Vacation."

"Do you know anyone here?"

Demonstrating how she answered, Regina raised her chin and arched her eyebrows. Her voice sounded indignant. "Yes! They outside."

"Do you have any money?"

"I answer in my broke English, what I can remember from school, 'Yes, in my purse.' Then more questions." Regina's shoulders sank. Her voice fell. "I was so scare! What they gonna do to me now? In my heart, I am praying, just praying."

The officer clamped her right hand around Regina's upper arm. "Come with me." She steered her into a nearby restroom—small, maybe three places with toilets. Nobody else was there.

"She say to put out my arms and spread my legs. Next, she check my body, my ponytail, everything. It was terrible. She even feel in my bra and make me show inside my underwear."

"Not after all you had been through!" I put my hands on my knees, leaned forward, and mumbled in a low growl, "Welcome to America."

"*Why?*" she barked. "Why they do this to me?"

"They were probably looking for drug smugglers."

"But I am the *only* one they search, Sister Josephe, the *only* one!" Her voice was insistent.

"Nigeria and South Africa are known for drug trafficking."

Her eyes blazed. "My passport was from France."

My bright excuses crumple. My heart sinks. I put my hands on her knees. "Regina, I am very, very sorry."

After searching her body, the officer emptied the duffel bag, dumped out her purse, and to Regina's dismay, even fanned the pages of her new Bible. At that point, another female officer came in—a well-built black woman, middle-aged. She stood near the door with folded arms, then turned down her mouth. "Let her go. She has nothing. Look how tired she is."

"Sister, I *was* tired. This long time, I have to act like a strong woman, confident to do all these hard things. I was *very* tired." Her shoulders fell. She drew a deep breath and blew it out. "I don't know how I did that, Sister." She stared down at my kitchen rug, then looked directly at me. "I know I am a strong woman, Sister, but I could never do something like that again. Never."

Regina stuffed her things back into her bag. Hurrying from the restroom, she joined the flow of people heading into the main airport, scanning faces as she walked. Suddenly, there they were—two African men, holding up a sign with her name, Regina Imwa. The trim, more sober man in khaki pants and white polo shirt introduced himself. His companion in a raucous African shirt grinned as he thrust out his hand. "Welcome to America!"

"You know the first thing these men did, Sister?" Her eyes shone. "They give me a phone card! Uncle Basil in Belgium, he was surprise. He say, 'What? Already? Oh, thank God!' When I call my older brother Lucién, the one in Paris who pay for my trip, he began to cry."

Regina asked Lucién to phone Chrétien and Claire with the news and then to call the family of her best friend, Faustina, also in Congo, to learn where Faustina had settled in America. After promising to phone Lucién again soon, she came away beaming.

Walking through the airport between the two New Yorkers, she told them how grateful she was, but, as much as she appreciated their kindness, she was afraid to live in such a big city.

The men looked at each other. "Greensboro?" suggested one.

"Maybe," said the other.

"Then this guy say, 'North Carolina has a big Congolese community,' and the other say, 'I know a guy down there name Maurice. I can call him before we eat.' That's how they did, Sister. At McDonald's, they phone people. By the time we was finish eating, it was done."

"You mean they had a place ready for you in New York, but when you said you were afraid, they were able to find someone in another state willing to take you in? Just like that?"

She grinned. "This is how Congolese people are, Sister. It does not matter if they know you. You need a place, they open to you."

By nine o'clock Regina was on a Greyhound bus rumbling out of New York, traveling solo on her way to Greensboro with a bunch of strangers whose language she could not speak.

"I was too scare to sleep. The bus stop at every little town. When it stop in Washington, D.C., in the middle of the night, we have to change buses." She flashed her panicked-little-girl look. "It's a *big* place, Sister. I don't go inside to get something to eat or go to the bathroom. No, I was too scare the bus might go, so I wait outside and watch. I pray not to get on the wrong bus."

She repeated the routine in Richmond, Virginia.

The Greyhound pulled into Greensboro, North Carolina, Saturday at 9 A.M. By now, the PALU rally would be over, thank God. She hoped everyone was OK.

"*Pardonez-moi*, are you Regina?" asked a tall, very dark man with a shaved head. Seeing her face brighten, he extended his hand. "*Bonjour!* I am Maurice from PALU. You will stay with my girlfriend and me. Felicia, too, is from Africa, but she does not speak French."

Their apartment was a unit in a former motel. When Maurice pulled up, Felicia swung open the door. "Welcome to America, Regina!"

"She was nice, really good to me, but we could not talk. I was just happy to take a shower, eat a meal, and fall into bed. But I was so lonesome, Sister, so sad. I keep thinking about David, how I won't see him anymore. I worry if he will be safe. I worry he will miss me, too."

Later that day, when she phoned Lucién to tell him where she was, he surprised her with news that her college roommate, Faustina, lived right there in Greensboro.

"It was like a miracle, Sister! Faustina was my best friend in college, the one took me to the student prayer meeting in Kinshasa dorms where I learn to love the Bible and the singing. We are very close when we pray. She always say, 'Regina, you are my sister, God connect us.'"

Faustina immediately invited Regina to live with her family.

The next day, from Faustina's house, Regina phoned Chrétien.

The democracy rally in Kinshasa had erupted in violence, he said. As PALU protestors marched toward Parliament, the Civil Guard opened fire. Officials said four were killed and fifty-four seriously injured, but Reuters had reported nine dead, forty-seven wounded. No one knew for sure. The radio added that one soldier had also died. In the aftermath, soldiers also stormed the home of PALU's leader, Antoine Gizenga, in Limete Zone. They arrested Gizenga and his wife and, according to some eyewitnesses, raped his two daughters—Passy, twelve years old, and Wamba, fourteen. At least two other PALU women were severely wounded. The radio was also reporting that they raped and killed Pil-cherie, Gizenga's twenty-two-year-old niece.

"Regina! That's where you were supposed to be—in Gizenga's house, right?"

"Yes. Gizenga's house was our headquarters." She shuddered, then said in a sure voice, "God save my life, Sister."

Chrétien had something else to tell her.

On July 21, just seven days before they had sneaked Regina out of Congo, a PALU leader had given him a document intercepted from SNIP, Congo's secret police, ordering the president of the Civil Guard to prevent Regina and three others from leaving the country. When Chrétien told Uncle Basil, also a member of SNIP, Basil was alarmed, worried both for Regina's safety and—should their relationship be discovered—for himself and the rest of the family. With Congo in financial ruin, salaries had been suspended, so Basil was not even able to contribute toward her escape.

Regina was third on SNIP's list, under her surname and middle name: "Imwa-Aboy, Principal of Idiofa Girls Central School in Bandundu Province." Though she was no longer a school principal, the notice was current on her recent residence.

"Regina! How did SNIP know you were with Chrétien?"

She shook her head. "These people!' she spouted. "They have spies everywhere."

"Maybe the driver of the lorry? Maybe the DSP paid him to tell them the address?"

"In Congo, Sister, soldiers don't pay! *Nooo.* They steal, rape, kill! They do whatever they want." She turned down her mouth. "It does not matter how they knew. When Chrétien tell me what happen the day of the rally, I am more worry about my cousin and his wife *now.*"

Chrétien had known the Civil Guard could come for Regina at any moment, but rather than frighten either woman, he had kept the document secret while working against the clock on her escape. Now that the violence was drawing international attention, he assured her that he and Claire were no longer in any danger. Mobutu would order his troops to lie low while making a show of calling for an investigation, which they all knew, of course, would never happen. Besides, the soldiers had made their point by attacking Gizenga's family. The Civil Guard knew that no one in PALU would dare risk annoying them again for quite a while.

I leaned forward. "Regina, I don't get it. If the government knew that Antoine Gizenga was the leader of PALU, why didn't they just kill *him*? Why would they go after you . . . and the women staying in his house?"

"It's like Chrétien say, Mobutu is clever. He does not want the international community to pay attention that he is against the political parties. So he not touch Gizenga. No, he send his soldiers after the grassroots organizers. If the soldiers kill us, world leaders do not notice, but Congolese people, they know us. They get very afraid."

"But if Mobutu's men wanted to avoid international publicity, why would they break into Antoine Gizenga's house?"

"That surprise me, too. I think, is PALU this dangerous to them that they risk this? But the government knows Gizenga's house is also party headquarters and the women staying there are grassroots organizers like me."

Chrétien later sent his copy of the SNIP document for Regina's asylum application. The English translation read: "These people are wanted for inciting the populace to participate in the illegal and forbidden PALU march of July 29, 1995. We expect you and your border services to prevent these people from escaping from the country." It was signed by the "Repression Service Manager." I noticed that Regina's photocopy of the original showed handwritten scribbles plus notes in the margins and partly on the printed text itself. In immigration court, the scribbles should have added credibility to her story. No forged document would have such imperfections.

Safe in America, Regina's first order of business had been to petition for asylum.

I later googled "Congo, July 29, 1995." The US State Department's "Country Reports on Human Rights Practices for 1995" spelled out the facts:

In July, in the most egregious example of extrajudicial killing, Civil Guards used lethal force to put down an unauthorized demonstration by the Unified Lumumbast [*sic*] Party (PALU) in Kinshasa. Human rights monitors, press reports and the Kengo [prime minister under Mobutu] Government state that 4 protestors and 1 soldier died and that 54 others were seriously wounded. There were clear political objectives involved in the aftermath of the demonstration, when the military attacked the home of PALU leader Antoine Gizenga and raped and killed a member of his family. The military and the Government launched official inquiries into these incidents but failed to report any results by year's end.

8

SEARCHING FOR
A LAWYER

I should be preparing for Holy Thursday's RCIA session, but I can't concentrate. Less than twenty-four hours ago ICE upended Regina's life. Block and Muwonge have said no to her case, legal action is impossible until Lybeau gets the BIA decision, ICE needs only her passport and ticket to send her to her death, and the corker—Regina herself signed for her Democratic Republic of Congo passport. I can't sit still. On my way to the kitchen, I rub my arms to warm myself then grab a sweatshirt from the hall closet.

There's something else needling me, something about Regina's call. . . . I fill the teakettle, suddenly aware that the chill I feel is not from the air but from something in Regina's voice . . . not what she said, but . . . Dear God! It was *fear*! The fear in her voice! Panic races through me as a scene from my childhood comes hurtling back—the fury in Mama's eyes, the sting of the leather belt, the gut sense that I could never please her. My throat tightens. Tears start. "No!" I shout. I clear my throat, roll my shoulders, tell myself it's over, long past. Get a grip.

I turn on the gas burner to heat the kettle, then, walking to the window, I take a long, deep breath. Outside, day slides toward evening and shadows stretch across the melting snow. Staring into the darkening cold, I wrestle with my own neediness. *Dear God, how can I be strong for Regina?*

Bubbling water tugs my attention. I drop a tea bag into an empty mug. As I pour in the hot water, ginger-peach steam wreaths my face. I'm OK, I tell myself. I close my eyes to relish the fragrance, to breathe in the present moment, the now. God is here. God is right *here.* Regina knows God is with her, too. After all she's been through, I can bank on it.

———————————

I remember the winter night several years ago when I had stopped at their apartment to return the transcript of her hearing. With David at night class and the kids in bed, we were sitting at her kitchen table when I asked how she—new to this country and speaking no English—went about getting asylum.

"In Greensboro in 1995, Sister, it was not easy to find a lawyer."

Someone at nearby Lutheran Family Services had heard of a suburban attorney, Bradley Puzzola, who took immigration cases, but no one knew anything about him. When Faustina phoned his office to make an appointment for Regina, he had no openings until October.

"I did not want to wait two whole months, but what can I do?"

She needed someone to drive her who could also translate. One man said yes, but as the date approached, he cancelled. Another agreed but backed out the night before.

Regina's brow tightened. "This was *so* important to me, Sister. In the end, Faustina took off work. She don't know much about immigration, but she knows English. I was *scare*! He's gonna need the proof, you know? So I go with all my papers, everything they told me to bring— birth certificate, rape report, SNIP's document that Chrétien sent—all that. And I give the lawyer my résumé. Everything in French. He says it must be in English. Faustina cannot do that."

"When you say your résumé . . ."

"My story in French—what Mobutu's soldiers do to me. We have to find someone can do the translation. Later I ask a student from North Carolina A&T University. He promises to keep my story secret. He just came from Congo, but I think he speaks English very well. . . . Now I know better—speaking and writing are not the same thing.

"But this is the big problem. Attorney Puzzola did not do like David's lawyer, ask me about my story. I came with somebody to speak English, but he never ask me questions so I could be ready to tell to the government my story. *Nooo!*" Her lips linger in the long, disappointed *nooo*. "The one question he asks is how did I get into America. I explain to him and show the paper, the one they gave, so he can see the name I use. I give him my false passport and the I-94 customs form. Then he just says how much I have to pay and gives me another appointment. I don't see him much, Sister. He is very busy."

"So, all you did at your first appointment with Mr. Puzzola was hand over papers?"

"Then I pay him the four thousand dollars, and we make another appointment."

"Four thousand dollars?"

"Yes, all the money my family in Europe sent." She shook her head. "Sister Josephe, it was not easy to see this lawyer. For the next appointment, we wait and wait, but he is too busy. So I keep calling, calling. Each appointment I have to find someone to take me who can translate. It's almost like five or six months, maybe longer, I don't know, because sometimes they give you the appointment, you go there, but he is in court. You sit there, wait and wait, then the woman finally says, 'I'm sorry. You must make another appointment.' This happen maybe three, four times—getting people to drive and translate, then nothing." Regina slumped back in her chair, the kitchen window's dark sky framing the world behind her. "Finally it was a whole year later. He still did not send my application! I was very upset . . . and *very* worried."

"Wait a minute. Your first visit was in October of 1995 and this was the fall of 1996?"

"Yes. More than a year."

The provision in immigration law that mandates an asylum seeker apply within the first year of arrival did not go into effect until April 1, 1997. Of course, neither she nor David knew about this law until 2000 when they first met with Attorney Block.

Regina's tone darkened. She jerked her palms up and down. "I say, *why* this lawyer take so long! He's got my money, he's got everything, but he is not helping me. He does *nothing*! Finally, I leave a message in my broke English. It was a very sad message because I was crying."

Puzzola himself responded, setting an appointment for November. When she arrived, he filled out the I-589 Application for Asylum and Withholding of Removal, but again—even with the student translator himself sitting there—he failed to review her story.

The asylum seeker's story is pivotal. Written as an affidavit, it is signed in the presence of a notary public. Form I-589, Application for Asylum and Withholding of Removal, incorporates the affidavit by reference and must be signed in the presence of her lawyer and later, under oath, in front of the asylum officer at her interview or in front of the immigration judge in court.

I later examined the four-page affidavit. Besides the major omission, there were numerical errors—nine years as principal (should have been six years as teacher, and three months as principal, over a nine-year period), fifty people on the lorry (should have been fifteen), as well as the mistranslation "chairwoman" for her role in PALU.

"Did Bradley Puzzola keep a copy of the original affidavit in French?"

"No, the only one we give to him was in English."

"Did you keep a copy of either one?"

"No."

"Big mistake, Regina." I leaned toward her. "Never, never sign anything until you check every detail. Keep copies of everything. And be sure each document has the date on it."

"I know *now!* But at the time, I don't know anything, so I just trust someone." She bristled. "I blame Mr. Puzzola. He's the one should sit down and go over my story with me."

———————

After her I-589 application was filed, fingerprints taken, and FBI security checks completed, within a month or so, Regina received a notice addressing her by name and alien registration number (eight digits preceded by an "A") stating the date, time, and location for her *asylum interview*—an opportunity to tell her story to an asylum officer in a simple office setting. It was scheduled at the nearest Asylum Office, 250 miles away in Arlington, Virginia, just across the Potomac River from Washington, D.C.

"Again I have to find someone to translate. You know, Sister, if the interview was in Greensboro, it would be easier, but you have to go to D.C." She shook her head. "*Who's* gonna take two days off work to go with you? *Where* you gonna get money to pay the ticket? I have to call someone: 'You know someone in D.C. can translate?' And then, 'Yeah, OK, we know someone' or 'I remember a guy, I don't know if he was . . .' It was like that, you know. You just have to trust. They say, 'We know this one guy, and you can go there and sleep at their apartment.' These are people you're gonna meet for the first time and . . . it was *too* hard. When I got there, the guy says, 'OK. I'm not working but my wife is, so we gotta find someone to take care of my baby.' The little money I have, I have to pay a babysitter."

She dropped her hands into her lap. "Then I have to go with this guy who doesn't know me, and I have to let him read my private story. You know, if it was the same student, well maybe I could do it . . . but now it was this guy." Her shoulders caved.

The asylum process is extremely difficult for a rape survivor, especially one from a culture that shames the victim.[1] The asylum officer charged with determining whether she meets the definition of a refugee must ask the hard questions, but to answer freely, Regina needed to feel safe. How could she?

"You *have* to talk about it—the rapes. You have no choice. Or they can send you back to be raped again and maybe . . . killed."

I rested my hand briefly on her arm.

"And your lawyer is there, but the lawyer doesn't talk. He just sits there."

Apparently Mr. Puzzola had not bothered explaining that he was not allowed to speak until the end when the applicant and lawyer may each make additional statements.

"Then they say, 'OK. Come back next week to find out if you . . . if they accept you.'"

In the interim, usually two weeks, the supervisory officer checks to see if the decision is consistent with the law and, if need be, can refer it to Asylum Division Headquarters for further review. If all background checks prove negative for criminal activity, the officer can recommend approval. However, if anything in her case makes her deportable, the officer will refer her to the Executive Office for Immigration Review (EOIR) for a hearing before an immigration judge.

I frowned. "Another 250-mile bus ride just to get their decision?"

"You gotta do what they say, Sister. But I don't go to that man's house. I take a late night bus, get to D.C. about 5 A.M., then wait until it's time to take a bus to the Asylum Office."

Having used a false passport and visa, Regina was not surprised that her case was referred to the EOIR. She was then in *removal proceedings*, also know as the *defensive process*, preparing to request asylum in an adversarial (courtlike) hearing as a defense against removal from the United States.

Although the terms *court* and *judge* are used, the immigration court system is not part of the judicial branch of government but under the Department of Justice (DOJ) in the executive branch. Immigration judges are administrative, charged only with *applying* immigration law. As DOJ employees, they ultimately answer to the attorney general.

"When I come back, I call Mr. Puzzola for another appointment. I think now is the time we was gonna work because I have to go before the judge. But he says, 'OK, I'm looking for a lawyer. This lawyer Riley, maybe he can help you.' I was surprise. I say, '*You* are my lawyer!' He says, 'I'm sorry. I cannot go before the judge. I'm a criminal lawyer, not an immigration lawyer.'" She jerked her palms up and down. "I didn't know! He never told me! *Never!*"

My gut tightened. What business did a criminal lawyer have taking on an asylum case? Most American Bar Association–accredited law schools don't teach so much as a single course in immigration law. Perhaps he could handle a visa application—mostly paperwork—but an *asylum* petition? The life-and-death struggle of a tortured woman fleeing the government that wants to kill her? I tried to excuse him—perhaps he didn't know what he was getting into, was just trying to help—but no. He didn't even listen to her story. He took all her money to do paperwork, none of which he bothered checking with her; sat in on the interview; then abandoned her when she most needed him. Worse, her flawed application was now the only official record the government had of Regina's own account of the reasons for her claim, and she had literally sworn to that flawed account with her lawyer sitting there to second its purported accuracy. Kafka couldn't have devised a better plot. Without the intervention of an astute, tenacious attorney, her case was bound to get worse before it could get better. Before the government had even scheduled her asylum hearing, Puzzola had set Regina on a sure track to failure.

"I . . . I don't know how I'm gonna get a new lawyer . . . what's gonna happen to me."

Asylum seekers are on their own in our system. While the government pays lawyers to serve an indigent person accused of petty theft in criminal court, it provides no representation for an indigent asylum seeker who risks being tortured or killed if sent back to her home country.[2]

What could she do? Going it alone (pro se) invites disaster. How could she follow laws she knew nothing about or navigate a complex system she did not understand in a language she didn't know? Yet every year, this is what tens of thousands are forced to do. Having legal representation does not ensure success—64 percent are denied—but for those without a lawyer, more than 93 percent lose their cases.[3]

Regina's *notice to appear*, the official charging document, ordered her to appear for her master calendar hearing Tuesday, March 18, 1997, before Judge William A. Cassidy at the nearest Immigration Court, 307 miles from Greensboro in the Martin Luther King Jr. Federal Building, downtown Atlanta.

At the master calendar hearing, the judge asks whether the asylum seeker admits or denies the allegations of fact (nationality/citizenship; date of entry; manner of entry, as a visitor, student, etc.; visa violations) and the charge of removability—all listed in the notice to appear. This is the threshold required by law. The applicant can then deny the charges, asking the government to prove its case. After determining if she is eligible for any relief (asylum, withholding of removal, or voluntary departure), the judge sets a date for the *individual merits hearing*. At that hearing, really a trial, the judge listens to her as well as to the government attorney before issuing a final ruling on whether she should be removed from the United States.

If Regina failed to appear for either the master calendar hearing or the individual merits hearing, Judge Cassidy would rule in absentia on her removability from the country.

She was frantic. "One day Lucién call me and I explain everything. He was almost sick. He said, 'What we gonna do?' He had no more money to send."

Lucién gave her the phone numbers of two cousins he had recently learned were living in the United States. The nearest was Father Godé Iwele, OMI, in Washington, D.C.

Father Godé was delighted to hear her voice. He contacted a generous friend, Buck Goodman in Atlanta, who asked Attorney Jeanne Wyuna at Catholic Social Services to take her case. Buck also invited Regina to stay with his family when she was in Atlanta.

"Before the master calendar hearing, I gave my affidavit to a good friend, name François Lumbu—a professor. He and his wife call me their daughter. He's the one discover the omission. He said, 'OK, when you gonna see this lawyer, I'm going with you. We don't take a bus. I will rent a car.' Mr. Lumbu took two days off so he could tell Ms. Wyuna himself."

The day before the master calendar hearing, they drove to the Goodman home in Atlanta.

"Mr. Goodman is a *very* kind man. His daughter, too, was rape, so he really wants to help. He quit his job to help poor people, the homeless, and others. I was surprise he visited Congo and knew Mobutu very well. His best friend was Newt Gingrich. I think he even look like Gingrich."

By this point, Ms. Wyuna had told Buck she was too busy to take the case. Regina remembered, "He was very upset. 'After everything I do for the Church and she will not do this one thing?' The day before we went to the judge, he calls Attorney Wyuna again. He says, 'I want to call someone in Washington to talk to the judge to help this girl get asylum.' But she said, 'No. Don't do that.' He said, 'Why not? I'm a Republican, and if I say so, they're gonna help her.' Sister, this man would do *everything* to help me. He even came to the hearing with us."

Regina was quiet for a bit, then she slid forward on the maple chair. "I remember the way the judge was talking to me." She tossed her head about, barking out the words, "'You need a lawyer! Next time you come with the lawyer! If you don't come with a lawyer, if you don't come here, if I don't see you here, you're gonna go back to your country! They're gonna deport you!' That's the way he was talking—to scare me! He was not talking quiet! *Nooo!*"

Though his manner frightened her, the transcript shows Judge Cassidy issuing only the standard warning: "If you do not appear at that hearing, you may be ordered deported in your absence, and your application for asylum will be denied. You will also be ineligible for other forms of relief under the Immigration and Nationality Act for a period of five years." He also—surprisingly—offered a list of low-cost and pro bono attorneys and, coincidentally, suggested Jeanne Wyuna. He postponed the master calendar hearing for a month, adding that if Regina got an attorney, the attorney could request that Regina's presence be waived since she lived so far away.

Afterward, Regina, Buck Goodman, and François Lumbu stopped at Jeanne Wyuna's office. She told them it was too late to add the missing paragraph and again refused the case.

The following week, Mr. Goodman phoned Regina to say Wyuna had changed her mind.

Regina, arms crossed, raised a hand in caution. "But did she invite me to Georgia so we can work on this? No. She just ask the date for my new master calendar hearing. The one time I saw her again was the day before my asylum hearing. That's all. She ask me, 'You want to sign for voluntary departure or not?' Why she ask that?"

"Maybe, knowing how tough Judge Cassidy was, she thought your case was weak."

"I said, 'No! I want to stay here.'" Regina's mouth turned down. "She really didn't like to help me, Sister. She did not ask about my story or prepare me for court. No, just, 'OK, see you tomorrow.' She took my case to satisfy the guy. I saw that myself. Because when I got there, a lot of people was waiting. They said, 'She is the *best* lawyer! We don't know how you got her.'"

I hope Wyuna saw the cruelty of her passive-aggressive behavior—not giving her client time, not fighting to restore a critical part of her affidavit, not preparing her for court, not coming to her aid when she fell apart on the stand, offering no redirect. By withholding her best, Wyuna betrayed and abandoned her client. Regina left the courtroom feeling orphaned all over again.

"I was like sweating everywhere," Regina said. "I was *so scare*, I was shaking inside. My mouth was so dry. They drink water, but you don't drink anything, just keep talking, talking . . . . Then my own lawyer says no, she don't want to appeal. Inside I feel like my heart broke."

By the time New Jersey attorney Anne Lybeau agreed to craft the appeal, the case was almost hopeless. She was stuck with the record of proceedings that Regina and her previous attorneys had created before the judge.[4] Worse, the Board of Immigration Appeals would never see or hear from Regina herself. They would get only the printed record. How would this third attorney get them to reconsider Regina's case?

"No, Sister, I didn't tell Attorney Lybeau my story and she didn't ask me."

Outside, the wind moaned against the windows.

"Sister, all three of my lawyers, they was my lawyers, but they did not pay attention to me. They was not interest in me."

9

DAVID'S TRAGIC PAST

A far-off, pesky ringing burrows down through my toasty old quilt. I snap open my eyes. *Ohmygod! Regina!* I bound from bed to grab my phone before it switches to voice mail. I try to sound chipper. "Good morning, Regina! How are you this Holy Thursday?"

"Scared. I can't sleep—no pillow, only the thin blanket. I want to be home."

"David and I are doing everything we can think to do. Were you able to talk to him yet?"

Her voice is colorless. "I try many times, but the line is still block."

I look at my watch—7:30. "Regina, I have an idea. Call me again at 9:00. I'll get David here so you can talk to each other, OK?"

Unlike me, David had been up before dawn. "Good," he says when I tell him my plan. "I'll be there, Sister, but I have to bring Christopher. I found out this morning that his babysitter went on early Easter break."

As I eat breakfast, I quickly slide into worry. David knows too well what awaits Regina in Congo. I remember when he first shared in depth his own tragic past.

I plopped two paperbacks onto their mahogany coffee table. "These authors were in Kinshasa before you were arrested, David. Now I see what it was like." I leaned over to flip open Jeffrey Tayler's travelogue. "His ferry docks at Kinshasa's Ngobila Beach where he's greeted by amputees and disabled beggars. Next, it's fat men in silk suits and gold necklaces, soldiers demanding free service, and everywhere the poor trying to sell him stuff. I felt like I was there."[1]

They both nodded, smiling.

I pointed to the other book. "Michela Wrong stayed in Hotel Intercontinental where you once worked. She watched Mobutu's DSP forces hide their families in the guest suites as Kabila's troops threatened Kinshasa. And guess what? Just before they fled, the DSP families took their T-shirts and other things imprinted with Mobutu's face and flushed them down the toilets, clogging the whole plumbing system."

David's eyebrows flew up. Both he and Regina broke into laughter.

In 1965, after five years of turmoil following the assassination of Congo's first elected leader, Patrice Lumumba, Colonel Joseph Mobutu had seized power in a coup and declared himself president.[2]

In 1971, he renamed the country "Zaire" (Kikongo for "river") and himself Mobutu Sese Seko Kuku Ngbendu Wa Za Banga ("the All-Powerful Warrior Who, Because of His Endurance and Inflexible Will to Win, Goes from Conquest to Conquest, Leaving Fire in His Wake").

Mobutu presided over what came to be called a kleptocracy, literally, "rule by thieves." By expropriating European properties, he amassed a fortune estimated in the 1980s at $5 billion. The tall, imposing ruler with the leopard skin hat and Buddy Holly glasses accumulated fleets of Mercedes-Benzes, jets, and villas all over the world, including at least eleven in Zaire/Congo. Daily newscasts began with his face materializing from the clouds while folks sang and danced as if he were the Messiah. Meanwhile, he weaseled his way out of every reform, hanging on to power through bribery, sham elections, and brutality. Nonetheless, the United States bolstered his anti-Communist regime with millions of dollars' worth of weapons and military training. In 1989, President George H. W. Bush welcomed him to Washington, calling him "one of our most valued friends." While Mobutu and his entourage were flying his private jumbo jet on lavish state visits to curry foreign support, Congo's financial infrastructure and social order plunged into chaos. Six months after his US visit, Zaire was bankrupt, mired in foreign debt, its currency worthless. Most banks closed. Families lived on one meal a day. Major cities lost electricity and running water. The state-owned river transportation system collapsed, the national airline rarely flew, and most roads were impassable.

Under pressure at home and abroad, on April 24, 1990, Mobutu ended the one-party system, promising multiparty elections the following year. However—as always—he reserved the real power for himself. Ten days later, when students at the University of Lubumbashi (David's alma mater) protested, Mobutu unleashed his DSP forces. Witnesses called it a massacre with thirty to one hundred students killed, but his soldiers whisked away bodies, claiming only one death. When Mobutu forbade international inquiry, many Western countries cut off all but humanitarian aid.

David shook his head. "Like every young Congolese, I was sick in my heart."

Less than a year later, Mobutu's unpaid paratroopers went on a rampage in Kinshasa, provoking the worst violence since Congo's 1960 struggle for independence. France and Belgium sent hundreds of troops to restore order while America provided air transport for ten thousand foreign nationals who abandoned their businesses, leaving Kinshasa's economy in shambles.

David sat forward. "I had to do something! I see now that political action is not enough to get Mobutu out, so I join a military party, Conseil National de Résistance pour la Démocratie [CNRD], National Council of Resistance for Democracy. I was not a soldier, but I long admired General André Kisase Ngandu, president of this party, a good man, intelligent, too. People respect him. He had twenty years' experience fighting Mobutuism in eastern Congo."

Early in 1994, a CNRD leader asked to meet David at a bar in a Kinshasa suburb. Sitting at an outdoor table with blaring Congolese pop music preventing eavesdropping, he told David that party leaders had seen how intelligently and effectively he spoke about democracy. They also noticed how well he got along with people of all kinds.

David told me, "Therefore, they decide to appoint me an *agent de liaison*—a spy."

"A spy? You?"

He broke into a grin.

Espionage was usually full-time, but David was to dedicate weekends and free time. He would be briefed before each assignment and was to report weekly to CNRD's local leader.

"That's when I got active. In Kinshasa, we was maybe fifty spies, but I work all over Congo, talking to people door-to-door and on the streets to survey opinions about sanitation, education, infrastructure, and development. I study other parties' platforms. I also talk at CNRD conferences. Even in dangerous provinces, I am developing contacts and following leads."

Meanwhile, David was also preparing for Regina's arrival. On July 2, national end date for the school year, Regina moved from Idiofa, and by the end of August, they were married.

Regina said, "But I was not happy alone in the apartment, Sister. I was use to be a teacher and working for PALU. What can I do in a dangerous city like Kinshasa where no woman goes out alone? David is always at work, and on weekends he was travel for CNRD, so I told him, 'PALU needs me. Let me go back, work awhile in Idiofa. It's a lot safer for me.'"

Shortly after she left in October, violence erupted again in Kinshasa. David would see her once more for about three months in 1995 before she left again in April, then disappeared.

"For two years, I ask everyone everywhere if they know what happen to her, but nobody knows. No one in her family. No one in PALU. I travel near Idiofa, but nobody can say if she is even alive."

Meanwhile, Congo was roiling. As David and his compatriots shared reports with CNRD leaders, they were convinced that the populace was with them. The hour for change had come.

"This meant war?" I asked.

"Yes," said David. "At the end of September 1996, CNRD and three other political parties form a new coalition to overthrow Mobutu—AFDL, Alliance des Forces Démocratiques pour la Libération du Congo-Zaire.[3] They chose General Ngandu to be the military leader." He raised his eyebrows. "It was very, *very* political!"

Later I would learn what David meant from a firsthand source, Congolese refugee, now US citizen, Christophe Opanga. Colonel Opanga had been Ngandu's close friend and confidant, second in command of CNRD and later of AFDL. He explained that AFDL was actually a front for a larger plot hatched in Rwanda by defense minister and soon-to-be president Paul Kagame and his friend President Yoweri Museveni of Uganda. After quelling the genocide, Kagame needed to secure the future of his regime against retaliatory raids.

Hiding among the two million Hutus who fled into UN refugee camps in eastern Congo were the *génocidaires*—tens of thousands of extremist militias and Hutu soldiers of the former regime. To stop cross-border raids, Paul Kagame, in a move denounced by Mobutu, began arming the Banyamulenge, exiled Tutsis who had been living for years in eastern Congo's South Kivu Province. The Banyamulenge's claim to centuries-old roots in the region was rejected by most Congolese who charged them with coveting Congo's diamonds and minerals.

Kagame wanted to use his own Rwandan army, but since international law forbade preemptive war, he and Museveni conspired to use the Congolese rebellion to stage a two-pronged war—ending the Hutu threat while also liberating Congo from Mobutu. Spoils of victory would include Congo's mineral-rich eastern provinces. AFDL was to be their Congolese cover.

Museveni sought out General Ngandu, convincing him that CNRD needed their help to overthrow Mobutu. Ngandu brought his troops (estimated in the thousands) to train with the Rwandan army, but he grew leery when Paul Kagame wanted him to combine his CNRD militia with a multinational force to fight two wars at once. Ngandu wanted only Congolese liberating Congo.

Paul Kagame secretly began seeking another Congolese leader.

Opanga continued describing the situation to me. "So the President of Tanzania flies Laurent Kabila to meet Kagame, saying, 'Here's the leader you need. Kabila is Congolese but not tied to just one country.'"

Indeed. Best known for having built a business empire by smuggling gold and diamonds out of Congo, Laurent-Désiré Kabila had operated from Uganda for years. When Museveni frowned on his drinking and womanizing, Kabila moved to Tanzania to continue living the high life while lavishing gold on Tanzania's president. As for military skills, Laurent Kabila was a small-time Marxist revolutionary who once held Westerners for ransom. His avoidance of the front line had prompted his own soldiers to call him a "tourist."

"United States President Bill Clinton was tired with Mobutu," David explained, "so when the Tanzanian president brings Kabila to Paul Kagame, Kagame phones America. He says, 'We have this man Kabila who can get rid of Mobutu.' Clinton says he will support this cause."

I found through research that America provided "marksmanship training," arms funneled through other nations (Rwanda was under an arms embargo), spy satellite maps, and, according to some, advisors on the ground as well as mercenaries linked to American mining companies.[4]

Of the four Congolese groups Paul Kagame assembled to form AFDL, only CNRD was a viable party with an active army of thousands. Laurent Kabila's party had two members, himself and his son Joseph. A third group drew from the Bashi tribe. The fourth—key to Kagame's plan—was from the ethnically Tutsi Banyamulenge exiles whom he had been arming.

David said, "When Paul Kagame brings Kabila to General Ngandu, he tells Ngandu to give him a title, like he wants Kabila to help lead the army. But General Ngandu does not trust either of them. He named Kabila just 'party spokesman.'" David shook his head. "But Kabila right away starts talking to the media like he is the leader and acting like he is in charge."

I began to connect the dots. "So Kabila took over?"

"Yes. And after Kabila was president, he told all foreign troops to leave, but it did not work."

The foreign fighters claimed that Uganda, Burundi, and Rwanda relied on them for protection against armed groups in eastern Congo. Critics countered that Rwanda hoped to exploit Congo's mineral wealth, a claim later supported by a 2003 UN investigation.[5]

To purge Congo of his former allies, President Kabila called in the armies of Angola, Zimbabwe, Namibia, and Chad, promising them a stake in Congo's minerals to fight for him. This second war quickly expanded to include eight African nations and roughly twenty-five loosely organized militias in ever-shifting alliances.

"That's why they call it Africa's World War," said Regina. "Five times more people die than in the Rwanda genocide—*five* times, Sister! Mostly women and children, because soldiers and militias rape them, then they destroy the roads so no food or medicine can get through."

David shook his head. "Everything got worse under Kabila."

"But what happened to you, David? Why did Kabila turn against you?"

He leaned forward, his face animated. "In late 1996, when AFDL was still new, a party member reports to me. He says there is a large cache of weapons in the home of a Maï Maï chief. First, I verify the information. Then I report this to General Ngandu. But"—David threw up his hands—"this put me in big trouble with Kabila. When Kabila heard about my report, he sent his people to tell me he was angry, *very* angry. He said I was to come to him first." David shrugged, "But I think, *Why?* Ngandu is AFDL's military leader. He needs to know! Kabila is just the spokesman." He furrowed his brow. "But now I get afraid."

Weeks later, on January 10, 1997, General André Kisase Ngandu was murdered near Goma in North Kivu Province. Locals said he was killed by Rwandan soldiers loyal to Laurent Kabila.

David began to watch his back.

Later, Colonel Opanga, citing firsthand sources, told me that Ngandu's death was part of a written contract between Kagame and Kabila: Rwandan troops would secure Kabila's takeover, but he must first kill Ngandu; then when he became president, Kabila was to give a large part of Congo's eastern provinces to Rwanda. He later reneged on this contract as well as on others he had signed with US and Canadian mining companies as his troops were marching across Congo.

AFDL rebels had advanced quickly, because Mobutu's underpaid soldiers often changed sides or even fled. Meanwhile, America urged Mobutu, weakened by cancer treatment, to resign. He declined, but on May 16, 1997, with AFDL advancing on the capital, he fled, first to Togo and then to Morocco, where he died four months later in exile. His regime collapsed May 17 as thousands of rebels walked single file into Kinshasa, virtually unopposed, many just boys in flip-flops or bare feet, laden with munitions. People lined the streets cheering and offering them food.

Twelve days later, Laurent-Désiré Kabila had himself sworn in as president by Congo's Supreme Court. He immediately outlawed all political parties, especially those in AFDL.

Less than a month later, on Tuesday, June 25, 1997, Kabila's men had come for David.

10

BEHIND THE MASK

Four-year-old Christopher plops down on the red carpet in front of my glass coffee table. "I draw the policeman," he announces.

David and I exchange glances.

I had given him crayons and scrap paper to keep him busy while David and I talked in my adjacent office, but Christopher wanted Daddy with him in the same room. While David pulls up a side chair and I sit on the gray settee, he draws a brown circle above a large squared body.

"This is his hat," he adds in a bright voice as he positions a blue lump on top of the head then straightens up to admire his work.

He draws two small brown eyes next, then curls his body over the picture, tightens his hand around a bright red crayon, and presses down hard. "His mouth is ANGRY!"

David and I both frown.

After two long strokes for legs, Christopher grabs a black crayon. Again he bends over his work and pushes the crayon with all his might. "He has BIG boots!"

David's mouth turns down. He shakes his head.

Gradually, I realize that the low ring tone we hear is from my phone. I get there just before it goes to voice mail, then signal David that it's not Regina.

After the call, I return to the living room and squat down next to Christopher. "Honey, Daddy and I need to be closer to the telephone in case Mommy calls. Is it OK if you stay here and continue drawing?"

He nods as he grabs another sheet of paper.

In my office, I gesture for David to take the padded swivel chair. I pull up my desk chair.

He looks worn, exhausted. "I could not sleep again last night."

"Did you eat anything?" I ask.

"A little . . . this morning."

I lean forward. "Diabetes is a serious illness, David. You cannot go without eating."

He gives me a lopsided grin. "You, too, Sister Josephe. You are too thin." The grin slips away as quickly as it came. "You talk to Attorney Lybeau? To Mr. Block? What he say?"

I share what I remember of both calls, watching each piece of information stir a new ripple over his weary face. David's bony knees leave precise contours in his navy slacks, and his once muscular thighs no longer fill the pant legs. The sweatshirt drapes loosely. I watch his long, elegant fingers lacing and unlacing between his knees as I talk, fingers that produce such precise handwriting that Regina insists he fill out all Lydia's kindergarten forms and sign the family greeting cards. As I finish talking, it's the whole of him that touches me—this troubled transplant whose clothes don't fit; the financial manager at Kinshasa's five-star, five-hundred-room Hotel Intercontinental, now working in maintenance; the eloquent public speaker on democracy, fishing for English words; the long-time, happy-go-lucky bachelor whom his friends teased would never get married and whom Regina initially avoided because he laughed too much. His troubled face lays out all the hard-won credits and frightening debits of immigrant life in America.

"David, this must be terribly hard for you." I reach over to put my hand on his knee.

To my surprise, he immediately covers his face with both hands and plunges forward, collapsing into wrenching sobs.

I reach for my Kleenex box.

Then, just as suddenly, he jerks himself upright. Quickly passing the palm of his right hand over his face from forehead to chin, he transforms himself before my eyes. When he looks at me, he is calm and resolute. "I must be strong," he says.

I straighten up, taken aback by the sudden change.

"I have a wife. I have two children."

"It's OK to cry, David."

"I must be strong."

"You *are* strong, *very* strong."

I've often admired David. As potential witnesses at his asylum hearing, Regina and I were excluded for most of his seven grueling hours on the stand, but I watched him stay focused during the preliminaries when Judge Brahos sneered, "What kind of man are you anyway?" Hours later, the same judge commended him for his testimony. Few people would guess that he still struggles with nightmares from his own hellish torture.

David and Regina are among the 0.7 percent of Congolese with college degrees, but like most first-generation immigrants, despite their intelligence and education, they are not able to get jobs commensurate with their talents. In his fifties, David has had to learn English then start all over studying nights in hopes of resuming his white-collar career. Regina is doing the same. Yet they've bought their first house and are raising two beautiful children in a totally new culture.

I look into his bottomless eyes. "David, you have done things I could never do." I lower my voice. "But you also need to cry. Maybe not here, maybe not now." I gesture toward Christopher in the next room. "But sometime, David."

Regina once confided that after his arrival in America, David seemed extremely anxious—"paranoid" was her word. Understandable, since he had landed in America less than forty-eight hours after being snatched from a subterranean torture chamber. Two years later and still too afraid to leave their apartment lest some other Congolese betray him to Kabila, he insisted they move as soon as their baby was born. Greensboro transplants phoned to recommend Milwaukee. The timing could not have been worse for the new mother, but for David's sake, Regina quit her job, helped pack, then asked a friend to drive them and their two-month-old 645 miles in a rental truck, pulling their old car behind.

The telephone rings.

It's Regina. I hand the phone to David and slip into the living room where Christopher is absorbed in *Sesame Street*. Over the bouncy TV music, I can hear David talking in melodious Lingala. Though he has seemed generally better in recent years, I can't push aside the startling moment I just witnessed twenty minutes ago—his face, contorted in pain, flash-changing to complete serenity with a mere slide of his hand. He did it so quickly that it seemed automatic. How often does he do this? More to the point, how much trauma can he hold in check? And what is this doing to him? I often wonder if David can ever break out of his nightmare past. I remember him describing what Kabila's henchmen did to him.

He and Regina had been visiting with me in their living room one sunny Saturday when I asked, "What happened when you were arrested, David?"

"It was Tuesday afternoon, June 25, 1997. I came from my job to my friend's house. Dominique was a journalist, a member of AFDL like me. His wife and children were inside. He just finish locking the gate to his yard when suddenly"—he jerked his head back, his eyes wide—"I see a soldier coming over the wall."

The brick wall enclosing Dominique's house was fifteen to twenty feet high.

David told how Dominique whirled in the direction of his gaze. In a flash, the soldier was on the ground pointing an AK-47 at them with one hand, flipping open the gate with the other. In rushed ten or twelve soldiers, guns at the ready, followed by two plainclothesmen.

"The main soldier, he screams, 'Show us your identification cards! Now!'" David swirled his hands in tight circles. "It all happen so fast, we cannot think what to do."

As both men yanked their wallets from back pockets and fumbled for their party IDs, the soldiers scrambled to close in behind them. In front, the railing commander and two plainclothesmen stood with spread legs.

"I say to them, 'We are members of AFDL like you! Why are you . . .' but the leader, he shouts, 'Shut up! You betrayed Kabila! You are double agents, traitors!'"

David was kicked, jabbed with guns, and beaten. As he struggled, he saw Dominique being forced toward a nearby car.

"I never saw my friend again." I looked into David's open face, his deeply perplexed eyes. He ignored the box of Kleenex and used his thumbs to swipe at the tears. He looked down, drew a deep breath, then raised his face to me again. "Suddenly, other soldiers grab my arms, tie my hands behind. They force me through the gate, into a car . . . black car, black windows."

They sped through the city to some building, "not very big, like an office. The security officer wrote down some information. He took my watch, my wallet and business folder, my belt, shoes, and socks. Then he lock me in a tiny, dark room." David grimaced. "Very bad smell. Urine. And only one window"—he held his palms about six inches apart—"a very small window." He framed the top and bottom—same distance. No food. No water.

Late the next morning, a commander appeared at his door. He did not enter but fidgeted with his rifle while his eyes darted around the tiny cell. "I am ordering you to Camp Tshatshi."

Once the main barracks of Mobutu's elite DSP, the vast Camp Tshatshi was then under an ex–police officer from Katanga Province who kept up its notoriety as a military death camp. In Tshatshi, inmates were routinely tortured in small underground rooms before being executed.

David protested. "No, this is a mistake! I am a civilian, a member of AFDL!"

The commander batted the air as if chasing away a pesky insect. "At Camp Tshatshi you will be tried in a military court."

That afternoon he returned with two soldiers. They forced David, hands tied behind him, to lie facedown between them on the floor of a Toyota 4x4, then sped off under the blazing sun to Camp Militaire Colonel Tshatshi on the northwest side of the city.

When they arrived, they shoved him into a tiny one-room building. As David tried to describe the roof, I handed him a notepad. He drew a squiggly line—corrugated metal. Then he sketched the floor plan, a rectangle with a black circle near the upper-right-hand corner and a short line jutting in from the right wall—a privacy panel shielding a sewer hole, the toilet.

"The place is small, same size as the kids' room," David said. Nine-by-ten feet. "Only two tiny windows high up." With his hands, he framed another six-inch square. "One above the toilet hole, the other on the opposite wall." An empty socket dangled from electrical wires that looped across the wooden trusses of the tin roof. The floor was black with filth.

"When they open the door, I think I am gonna be sick from the smell. The soldier push me into the dark . . . too dark to see. He quick untied my hands, then leaves and locks the door."

Weak from dehydration and the sudden stench, David sensed thick body heat around him. As his eyes adjusted to the dark, he counted some twenty emaciated men jammed into the room.

"They were all thin like skeletons just staring at me. Maybe an hour, no one talks. Nothing at all. I can see from their clothes these are not military men. And they are not poor people or criminals but businessmen like myself. Some are old with gray hair. They have good clothes like mine but dirty like rags, and their hair and beards—very bad. I think they have lice. I look around. On the walls . . . I don't know the English word . . ."

"Graffiti?" I suggested.

Regina interrupted. "Sister, you don't understand. It's not like in the United States. There is nothing to use to write. A person poop, then he use the poop to write."

I winced, then hiked my shoulders, shuddering.

David nodded. "Is very bad. Very, *very* bad."

The filth, the stink, the . . . what? Anger? Defiance? *So this is what people do when they are stripped of their humanity,* I thought. Having seen vile words scrawled on American fences, buildings, restroom walls, I could only imagine the fury of these men against Kabila, who had ridden into power promising them democracy. "What did they write on the walls, David?"

His voice was gentle, even reverent. "Their names," he said. "Mostly their names."

I drew in a sharp breath. "Their names?" Dear God. These men felt abandoned. They were pleading, *I exist, I'm real, I'm here.* To whom? Themselves? God? Anybody? The realization sucked the air out of me. My eyes brimmed.

"Also, some write 'Jesus' or 'God.'"

My throat jammed. I broke into tears.

"Yes," he said, "prayers to God."

As I tried to regain my composure, David straightened up. "Sister Josephe, Americans cannot think something like this can happen, not in the whole world. But it is true."

For days afterward, I was not able to put these forlorn men out of my mind. Having often signed the small Amnesty International cards for political prisoners around the world—"You are not forgotten"—I now walked the length of my flat, back and forth, weeping, telling them over and over, "You are not forgotten. We grieve for how you suffered. You are not forgotten."

David described them, a few sitting, arms looped around their boney knees, dozing or numbed in their own thoughts, but most standing or shuffling about, their bare feet as dirty as the floor itself. Even if they wanted to, he said, there was no room to lie down. The silence was eerie. Two finally moved closer to ask David why he was there. After he explained, they said they, too, were civilians, insisting, "We are innocent! We don't know why we are here."

"Nighttime comes. One of those men, he push close to warn me, 'This place is dangerous. Do not sleep when it is dark. During the night, the guards come. Last night, very late, they took four people.'" David's eyes pulled me deeper into the horror. "He tells me when the guards take them, those men never come back. *Never*." He shifted in his chair. "At about maybe seven o'clock, two guards come for me. I think, *Now I will not come back.*

"They took me to military court. The judge says my situation is very, very bad. The government says many things against me—that I was not loyal to Kabila, that I reported to General Ngandu instead of Kabila. They accuse me of treason, say this crime deserves death."

After cross-examination, David was given the death penalty. Soldiers marched him outside and into another small building, where, by the light of an oil lamp, they took him through a short hall and down cement stairs to a single basement room. When they opened the heavy door, again he had to brace himself.

"I was almost vomit from the smell. They push me into this cement room, maybe the size like our bathroom"—five feet by six feet—"with a hole for the toilet in one corner."

Everything went dark as they slammed the steel door behind him.

David was not able to sleep. It had been two days since he'd had any food or water. He knew it was morning when a small haze of light filtered through the iron grate of a single, five-inch air shaft carved through the thick cement wall high above his reach, just enough light to make out the outline of his hand when he held it up. This was as bright as it would ever get.

Another night passed. Most of another day. Still no water, no food.

"Then I hear heavy boots coming down the stairs. A big soldier come in, push me against the wall. In Congo, they send very bad people to do something like this, soldiers who are very, very . . . *en français, méchant.*" Vicious.

David described trying to fight off his attacker, squirming to avoid his kicks and blows. Without warning, he felt the butt of a gun jab into his gut. David yelped. Then his shins, next his face. He screamed.

"My eyes are *enflés* . . . I don't know how you say in English . . . like they get bigger."

"Swollen. Your eyes were swollen."

Another crack broke both front teeth. He could taste the blood.

"Then he ties my hands and ties my feet. He pushes me against the wall. I see him reach into his bag. He takes out something small with a long electric cord. I don't know what it is."

Within seconds, the hulking stranger had yanked down David's pants. Suddenly, David felt his body explode in pain. He screamed until he blacked out.

David bent forward, his hands gripping both knees. His voice was quiet. "That torture is the worst." He let out a quiet moan. "It's too terrible. *Too* terrible."

After a few moments, he straightened up. "Then, can you believe?" he grimaced. "As I regain my conscious mind, I see the soldier standing over me. He is yelling, 'Give me money! Promise me money and I will set you free!'" David let out a wry laugh, shook his head. "Crazy. That's how these men are. Vicious and crazy." He grew silent again, then looked me in the eye. "Many times they did this torture to me."

It had been eight years, but the muscles in his neck still tightened.

"I was isolated, cut off from the world, Sister. No information. No contact. Sometimes I hear someone screaming. That's all. Sometimes they bring a cup of water, sometimes a little rice. Then two or three days, nothing. One time they give me a piece of moldy bread. I was waiting. Just waiting and praying and thinking. I was praying for Regina, that she be safe. Long time I heard nothing but rumors—maybe she was out of the country, maybe some trouble in Idiofa. Before I was in the jail, somebody said maybe America. Nobody knew. I pray for her all the time. I pray for my family. I worry about everything that can happen to them . . . and to me, because this time they was killing people. I was in jail, but my mind was outside. I was worried how it would be if I get free, because then Kabila's soldiers could come again and get me."

Almost two months passed.

"One day, I hear people coming down the stairs. The guards open the door, and they push in twelve men, maybe more. All of them was sick—malaria, typhoid, other diseases, too. Some have trouble, they cannot walk. They have open sores, and some have bullet wounds and bad scars all over their bodies. All of them are near to dying. That night, the guard came, took three of the sickest men. We hear the gunshots from up in the courtyard."

I found myself withdrawing emotionally, wanting this tale of torment to end.

"Yes, when prisoners get too sick, they shoot them. Then the next morning they bring more sick men. Everybody nervous, afraid. One time maybe fifteen men in that small room, some blind or wounded by bullets. I got sick, too, with malaria, then typhoid, and the ulcers I still have today. Little by little, I realize I was getting blind with so many days no light. At night we try to stay awake. We talk. We pray. We sing hymns." He paused, staring out the window, his face contorted in pain. "Until now I still wonder what happen to those good men." He looked back at me. "Because of them, I grew in my faith."

He was quiet for a while, his mouth pursing. Then he leaned toward me. "Sister Josephe, we was thinking . . ." His palms were upturned, his fingers beckoning for words. Finally he said, "We all know we are dying, we was living the last days for our life. There is nothing to do in our minds but to give everything to God. To everybody, it was . . . they say in French *spontané*."

"Spontaneous? You suddenly all thought of the same idea?"

He nodded vigorously. "Yes. We all think this at the same time. We was very, very sure we was gonna die now—all of us. Because when these people tell me where they are from, for me, I was thinking I am in Camp

Tshatshi. This is the finish for me. So we pray. We sing songs to God together. We give our lives over to God."

Their prayer of surrender also emboldened them. After an endless stretch of thirst, they pounded on the door, shouting for water—"*Mai! Mai! Mai!*"—until the guards came. But when the soldiers arrived, they simply grabbed three prisoners and removed them from the cell. They heard the gunshots.

"What to do? We decide it is better to be shot than to die of thirst. So we make a loud noise again. 'Shoot us if you want, but we must have water!' Finally, the head of the prison come. He agrees to give us water and a little rice. After one hour maybe, he come back, make us sit down against the walls like children before he gave to us."

One day, David and three others again clamored for attention. This time they demanded answers: "What happen to our friends you took by night? Why are we here? When will we be judged in civil court? Why you deprive us of food and water?"

The guard quickly left but returned later with another guard to transfer them to a different prison. The four stood their ground. Shots rang out. The soldiers dragged out two bodies.

Tshatshi's routine hell continued: nighttimes brought the gunshot executions of two or three at a time; daytimes, the sad arrival of their barely alive replacements.

Watching David's troubled face, I wondered if the men who died weren't the lucky ones.

His voice dropped. He looked intently at me. "Then in November 1997, during the night, the head guard came. He says nothing. He just grab my shoulder from behind, like this." David's right hand clamped down hard on his opposite shoulder and yanked it forward. He moved forward in his chair, nodding vigorously, eyebrows high. "*Moi seul! Moi seul!* Me alone! No one else!" He talked faster. "I was never so afraid in all my life. *Never!*"

The guard jerked him up the stairs and outside toward a waiting car, wrestled him into the trunk, slammed it closed. The car sped away.

David panicked. "I think, what torture they gonna do to me now?"

A short time later, the car stopped. David was pulled from the trunk at a small security post. Here two men in civilian clothes forced him into a Toyota 4x4 that then took off into the dark. On a remote road not far from the post, the driver suddenly pulled over.

The man on the passenger side turned around. "We received orders to make it look like you escaped. You cannot stay in Congo. Your life is in danger. Tonight you will be on your way out." With a quick glance over his shoulder, the driver pulled back onto the road. "We are taking you to a village southwest of Kinshasa where others will help you with what you need."

"They lie to me. I was sure of it."

For the next forty-five minutes, no one spoke. "In my mind, I keep worrying, what will they do to me? My morale is very, *very* low. I cannot give my attention to anything. I am exhausted. All I think is where they go with me? What they gonna do to me now?"

After skirting the south end of the darkened capital, they drove through a bleak savannah into a sleeping village. When the Toyota stopped, David could hear nothing but singing insects and the distinctive *prrrp* of an African Scops owl. The driver took him into a one-room hut where two solemn strangers waited. In the glow of an oil lamp, he saw a table with six chairs and a battery-powered radio.

"The driver says, 'Wait here. Someone will bring you papers and give you instructions,' but I did not trust any of them. After he left, one guy locks the door. I hear the jeep drive away."

The men offered him fish, rice, vegetables—his first meal. David said nothing. He ate. He drank. He took his first shower. Back in his filthy clothes, he sat on a chair and stared at the door. No one spoke. All morning and afternoon, they waited. As the radio crackled through news and Congolese pop tunes, they waited. All day, they waited. Finally, after dark, the knock came.

"I was so scared, I could not breathe."

One of the men unlocked the door. There stood a friend, Grégoire, originally a higher-up in David's party but now serving in the Kabila government. He flashed David a big grin.

"I smile back, but not a big smile," said David, his voice small, quiet. "I stood up, but I was feeling so scared. I could not understand what I was seeing. I could not think that this was my friend that I was seeing. My mind was not ready."

Grégoire, a big man, quickly set down his bag, walked over, and took the frail David into his arms. He spoke softly. "*Calme. Calme.* Be calm, David. Don't worry." His voice was almost a whisper. "You're going to be OK. Everything is going to be OK."

"Sister, I am not ashamed to say, I finally cry."

My own eyes filled with tears.

Grégoire apologized for the delay, telling David it was an extremely difficult challenge. From the moment they had learned he was imprisoned in Camp Tshatshi, his friends, both in Congo and abroad, had been working on a plan to save his life. "You leave Kinshasa tonight at eleven on Scibe Airlines," he said.

David's face softened. "At last, I have hope. Maybe I will be OK."

After David had changed into the fresh clothes Grégoire had brought for him, his friend drove him to Kinshasa's Aéroport N'Djili.

"Everything is secret," Grégoire told him. "When you arrive in Brussels, watch for a man who will give you the victory sign. I don't know his name. He is the only one who knows your final destination. He will give you an airline ticket and further instructions. Do not ask questions. Just do what he says."

Before walking David to his seat on the plane, Grégoire quietly added, "We know now that Kabila's rule is nothing more than Mobutuism without Mobutu." Grégoire's face was grim, his eyes piercing. David said he will never forget his final warning. "Remember, David, Kabila wants to kill you. You must *never* come back to this country!"

"Were you able to contact Grégoire once you got to the United States?"

"Yes. About a month after I was in Greensboro, I call a friend in Kinshasa to tell Grégoire I am safe. We reconnect for a while, but when Kabila was assassinated in 2001 and Kabila's son took over, I don't know what happen to my friend. Joseph Kabila is cruel like his father. Now I have no information about Grégoire."

In Aéroport International Brussels, a tall African man signaled David. Without a smile, he handed over a packet containing a French passport, a ticket to Newark Liberty International Airport on CityBird Airlines, $300 in US money, and a motel phone number to call for a car should he miss his contact. The contact would then meet him at the motel. The man left quickly, but David remembered him saying, "We are sending you to America to save your life."

He sank back into the couch. His arms fell to his sides. "I was so relieve, Sister. The first thing I think, *Kabila cannot get me!* The United States is far, far from Congo, far from Europe. Here I will be safe from Kabila."

Gradually his face lightened. "While flying over the ocean, I think— *America!* Everybody in high school, on TV, the news—everybody talks about the United States, the land of freedom."

Remembering David's experience only deepens my certainty that if his wife is deported, she will be seized, tortured, and killed. Current ruler Joseph Kabila is still beholden to his father's vengeful regime. Besides, Regina "defamed" Congo in a failed attempt to get asylum in America.

I glance at my watch. Regina's fifteen-minute call is nearly over. As I help Christopher put away the crayons, David signals him to come talk to Mommy.

The child scrambles to the phone, his eyes enormous. "Mommy, you come home now?"

David cringes.

The talking is mostly on Mommy's end with an occasional "yes" from her little boy. "I love you, too," he says, then hands the phone back to his Daddy but stays close, quietly staring up at his father, whose face stays calm as he says his own good-byes in Lingala.

As David reaches for their jackets on the hall clothes tree, I ask if he remembered to bring the contact information for their phone company so we can get his line unblocked.

"I cannot find the bill, Sister. Regina pays that one. Maybe today the phone will work."

I watch from my upstairs window as he buckles his four-year-old in the car seat, slides the door of their Honda Odyssey closed, then opens the driver's door. I wave, but he doesn't look up.

A different fear suddenly grips me.

Dear God, this current trauma could undo him.

PART II
WOUNDED WARRIORS

11

BEFRIEND THE FEARS
AND ANGERS

While this evening's Holy Thursday Mass continues, I lead my eight RCIA candidates from church into the soft-lit conference room where we gather around a table. The Bible, resting on a purple cloth, is opened to John 13, "Jesus Washes His Disciples' Feet."

"So, Scott, what was it like to have Father Todd wash your feet tonight?" I begin.

"You mean besides being up in front of hundreds of folks with the priest kneeling before me?" The group laughs. Scott gets serious. "Well, once I got into it, I guess I felt honored."

After discussing Jesus' example of service, I ask the group, "Is there anyone in your life whose feet you would like to wash? And anyone whose feet you would *not* want to wash?"

One wants to wash the feet of his terminally ill father; another, her beloved grandma. It's a loving gesture she says, so she admits she would tend to avoid a gossipy co-worker. One guy wonders how to wash the feet of an angry brother who rebuffs family help. Their honesty touches me. When my turn comes, I open my heart about what happened to Regina and David. Once I start, I notice I don't want to stop. I confess there are people whose feet I would find it very difficult to wash—the guys who barged into the Bakalas' home two nights ago, for starters.

"I guess I need some quiet time," I confess, "to see how I can use this anger for something good."

For five years now, I've been negotiating the immigration labyrinth with new parishioners. It started with Regina and David. They urged me to help reunite another family from Congo and, a year later, to assist a pregnant Indonesian now out of student status. As those cases dragged on, a Nigerian couple needed help bringing their young children here. I researched the system. I accompanied them to lawyers. I managed to help. But ICE swooping in out of nowhere to deport my friend? *God, I am paralyzed with worry.*

After Mass, the group disperses and a Eucharistic minister brings me a small, white cloth packet with a consecrated wafer. We pray a moment together, but I ask to receive the Eucharist by myself tonight. I feel as fragile as the little packet I tuck into my pocket.

The March air is crisp as I head into the parking lot, empty except for the cars of a few folks lingering to pray. The vast night sky, star-studded and silent, invites me beyond the urgencies of these days. Now I can be me, just me, with my God. When I get home, I clear off my kitchen table and light the gardenia candle I save for special occasions. I turn off the light.

"Lord, I am not worthy. . . . Say but the word and my soul shall be healed." As I put the Sacred Host on my tongue, I feel a new calm radiating from within. I let myself enter the quiet. Thoughts of Buddhist monk Thich Nhat Hanh linger in my heart: do not run from the suffering, befriend the fears and angers in your own heart, have great compassion on yourself. Gradually I let my shoulders relax and begin breathing deeply. As I let my troubled self feel the comfort of my own kindness, I begin to feel safe.

Suddenly, the thought comes unbidden—Jesus wants to wash *my* feet! Tears rise from some tangled knot deep in my gut, gentle at first, then surprisingly fierce.

Anger grips my throat. In words that are half prayer, half rant, I sputter, "God, how can this miserable immigration system get away with treating people like this? Have they no decency? No humanity? For years, I've wrestled this convoluted, backlogged system, but this? This is cruel. Demeaning and deliberately cruel. These good people, brutalized beyond anything I've known, and the United States violates them again. Disrupts their family. Throws their papers aside. Terrifies them in front of their little children."

I shove my chair back, grab a wad of Kleenex, and begin pacing. "And they turn to *me*! What can *I* do?" My pace quickens. "I am sick to death of this irresponsible bureaucracy! They bury people in paperwork, fees, restrictions, minutiae, regulations, endless waiting—'Just put your life on hold, folks'—then barge into their homes like secret police." I stomp through my house, each step drilling my anger into the floor. "'Who cares about their trauma? So what if we crush their spirits?'" Tears course down my cheeks as I head full-tilt through the dark. I picture Regina in a jail cell, weeping. And David crumbling into sobs this morning. I pray their names as I walk the length of my upper flat, "Jesus, David . . . Jesus, Regina." Again and again.

A wave of panic rushes through me.

I stop.

"What if they deport her before we . . . *I* . . . can get help?" I try to breathe, but the fear does not diminish. *O God, please.*

Back in the fragrant glow of the kitchen, I sit down, a jumble of emotions. Pulling the candle closer, I open my favorite prayer book, Nan C. Merrill's *Psalms for Praying*, at random, and read from her adaptation of Psalm 77: "In the day of trouble I seek the Beloved; in the night my hand is stretched out in prayer; my soul yearns to be comforted."[1] The single verse grips me with longing . . . longing to be comforted, gathered in, held. I close my eyes, trying to remember being held by my mother—

surely she held me—but no memories come. Instead, my fear shifts to a deeper place. I feel myself as an angry, frightened little girl still yearning to be mothered. Turning fully to God, I lean into my yearning.

An old poster once said that healing is like peeling an onion, you cry with each new layer. Recognizing the moment as grace, I curl my shoulders, wrap my arms around my waist, and begin peeling off memory after memory, sobbing out old angers, grieving the loss of Mama.

I was the firstborn of three, all girls. My mother, terrified she would do something wrong, had based her parenting on the writings of early behaviorist John B. Watson, who taught that through rigid training, an infant can be shaped into whatever the parents want her to be. A good mother keeps her baby on a strict four-hour schedule for changing diapers and feeding; she does not let her emotions interfere lest she spoil the child; she avoids cuddling and nurturing. "Never hug and kiss them, never let them sit on your lap. If you must, kiss them once on the forehead when they say good night. Shake hands with them in the morning."[2] Not surprisingly, Watson's only daughter attempted suicide multiple times. His third son succeeded on his second attempt. And— intriguing for me having battled digestive problems for years—both middle sons developed severe, chronic stomach problems.[3]

"You were a beautiful baby," my mother told me, "and I so wanted to hold you, but the book said I should not pick you up until it was time, no matter how hard you cried." Daddy worked nights manufacturing war machinery during those bleak World War II "black-outs." Meanwhile, night after night, she sat alone in our living room staring into the dark and sobbing her heart out as I wailed and screamed "for hours, literally hours," she said. Darkness shrouded everything.

Mama apologized to me many times, even when I was a child, for setting aside her better instincts "to follow that nutty book when deep in my heart, I knew better."

I remember myself as a little girl staring wide-eyed at her the first time she said she was sorry. I puzzled about how she could worry about something that happened when I was too tiny to remember, yet say nothing about the beatings, which, by age six, had built an impenetrable wall inside me. I remember the sting of the leather belt on my backside and thighs. I remember crying as I ran to lock myself in the bathroom. I remember tracing the welts, pressing a cold washcloth against the bloody stripes. I remember sobbing until I was convulsing for air.

My mother was generous in praising my accomplishments, but when I neglected to hang up my clothes or put away my toys, she would grab Daddy's leather belt and let me have it. He was at work when the "spankings" took place. It became a vicious circle. The more she hit me, the more frightened and rebellious I became, and the more reasons I had for blaming myself.

She had thrown out Watson's book before my sister Eileen was born, but she knew it was too late to undo the damage done in me. I remember her telling me many times, "The one regret of my life is how I raised you."

And I remember responding the same way every time, "It's OK, Mama. I'm OK."

But I was not OK. Years later when a psychologist asked me, "When did you lose your mother?" I startled myself by answering, "I never had her."

I stand up, walk to the window above my kitchen sink, and look out through wavy tears at our well-lit yard. Thanks to hard work in psychotherapy, I no longer suffer the panic attacks that plagued me into my late thirties, yet in recent weeks, writing the autobiography required for my sabbatical has stirred an anguished longing for Mama.

I can still see her sipping her coffee and flashing me a smile as we finish lunch in the carpeted dining room of Gimbels Department Store. I am six or seven. She, with so little money, had treated me—just me— to a ride on the streetcar to shop in downtown Milwaukee. A piano is playing and my legs are swinging under my chair as she talks. I see her dimples. She had the prettiest smile in all the world.

In my thirties, a dream brought insight into my ambivalence about her. My sister was sitting in a rocking chair holding her six-year-old, who leaned contentedly against her. Suddenly, the little girl leapt from her arms throwing herself to the floor in a snarling, screaming tantrum. My sister turned to me. "I have no idea what to do." I felt loving and calm in the dream, quite capable of helping the little girl. I asked the child why she was acting like this. She stopped. "One minute my mother loves me, the next minute she hates me! I don't know how to act!"

In my thirties, Mama once asked if I ever noticed how quickly she put away knives, never leaving one in view. In a recent flashback, she had seen herself as a terrified little girl huddled in a corner, watching her daddy chase her mama with a butcher knife. "He was drunk" was all she said. Then she added, "You will never know how much fear has damaged my life."

But I do know.

Her struggle to control me stretched far beyond childhood. She was furious with Vatican II reforms, especially changes in our convent life. Catholic Sisters, she insisted, should wear black habits and veils to set them apart from the world. My ongoing formation as a Sister, my Cursillo retreat, the Catholic Charismatic Renewal—rich spiritual movements that shaped me—she condemned as "from the devil." Phone calls turned into arguments. Visits became battles. I just wanted her to love me as *me*, but she snapped, "Thank God I have a photograph of you when you were still a nun!" I remember phoning to invite her and Daddy to my silver jubilee dinner . . . but the memory is too real. I still feel the jab in my gut as she sneered, "Your religious life is such a laugh!" I grip the kitchen counter as sobs jerk up from some inner chasm.

I cry and cry, one painful recollection flowing into another. My eyes sting. My gut hurts. I blow out the candle, grab another wad of Kleenex, and walk through the dark into the living room.

Mama often professed her love for me, and I have no doubt she meant it. I forgave her long ago. She died in 1990, crippled in a fetal position, her body in pain but her mind and spirit alert, mellow, and genuinely kind. As I drove home from her deathbed, I suddenly sensed her breaking into the fullness of Unconditional Love and turning with joy to bless us—Daddy, each of my sisters, and me. At last she was free to love us as she always wanted.

The living room is brushed with a glow from the streetlight. I lean back on the settee exhausted, tears rolling into my collar. What a painful Holy Thursday this has been, my own Garden of Gethsemane. But I am finally quiet enough to look again at Regina and David. "OK, God," I pray, "whatever it takes, but you've *got* to be there. You've just *got* to help me."

———————

I awake on Good Friday calm and rested. Something inside has settled.

At the breakfast table, I reach again for Psalm 77: "You stand beside us as we walk through our fears, the path to wholeness and love, though our footsteps are unsure. You send the Counselor as a guide to lead us on the paths of peace, of truth, and love." In the hazy quiet, I realize how I have been driving myself these three days just to keep my personal life at bay. Today I'm OK—not energetic, not ready to take on the world—but genuinely OK. I also realize how tired I am. Tired in a good sense. After last night's struggles, everything feels different. I no longer crave that Easter break.

Beyond the rose-tinted curtains, leafless branches hold up a misty, colorless sky. My great grandparents, immigrants from Ireland, would call this a "soft day."

If the one regret of Mama's life was how she mothered me, then surely she is praying for me now. I set down my empty mug and slowly lift the unlit gardenia candle to my face. I close my eyes to drink in its fragrance. Thank you, Mama.

Gardenias were her favorite flowers.

12

GOOD FRIDAY

Perhaps Regina sensed my need for quiet. She does not phone until well after ten.

Her voice is listless. "Good morning, Sister. They move me last night. I'm in the Kenosha County Detention Center. Now I sleep in a big room, I don't know what you call in English . . ."

"It's a dorm. I hope this is better, Regina. Sister Ginny told me they might be transferring you. Yesterday when I remembered that she works as a chaplain in Kenosha County's jail and detention center, I phoned her. She said if you need anything, anything at all, just write her a note or ask the guard to call her."

"A Sister come to see me yesterday, but not that one—Sister Jean. She ask if I want my pastor to visit, so I say I want Sister Josephe Marie Flynn. She says she knows you."

Jean is all heart. Once a week, the former school principal helps Ginny make her rounds. "Yes, Sister Jean answered the phone. She was surprised to hear why you are in jail."

According to Jean, no one in the chaplaincy office is told if an inmate is an immigrant or a criminal. Unless the person volunteers something about herself, they have no way of knowing.

"But jail personnel will obviously assume she is a criminal," I had objected.

"Confidentiality is a strict policy. I'm just glad you called. Hang on, I'll get Ginny."

"She's not only innocent, Ginny, she's terrified. No trauma survivor should ever be locked in with criminals. I'm worried about her."

"I'll see her as soon as I can, but Josephe, did you know that as a religious, you qualify for pastoral visits on weekdays? Just fax me a letter of authorization on letterhead from Regina's pastor, OK? Include your Social Security number, date of bith, and driver's license. By the way, I think they will transfer her to the detention center, where visiting times for families are better. In the jail, inmates get only ten minutes per week or less, based on the severity of their crimes."

She described the Kenosha County Detention Center (KCDC) as newer, brighter, and surrounded by open fields. "It's a better place, built for inmates with lesser offenses. Don't worry, Josephe. Regina will be in a dorm of thirty women. I'm pretty sure they'll send her there. It's where they send most of our immigrants."

"Most of our immigrants? Ginny, how many immigrant detainees is Kenosha holding?"

"Well, they come and go, but on any given day, in jail and detention center combined, I would say about one hundred."

The number had stunned me.

"Are there other immigrants in your dorm, Regina?"

"Leticia is here and Norma, too, and another woman, Emma, come from a different jail."

"How is Norma?"

"She just worries about her little boy is all. Leticia and me, we tell her to get a lawyer, but she is depress."

"And Leticia?'

"Leticia has strong faith. But I don't understand how they can deport her, Sister. She has her green card. She's married to her husband twenty-five years and has two American children. Their son, twenty-three, is over there fighting in Iraq. What they gonna tell this boy—while you are fighting for this country, they deport your mother? How can they do something like that?"

"She must have done something wrong."

"She says it's some paper her immigration lawyer told her to sign before he filled it. Then later he filled something false, but she did not know. The judge knew it was the lawyer's fault, but still they gonna deport her. *Why?* I say, if she really did something wrong, OK, give her jail time like anyone else, but do not deport her! This makes no sense. It's cruel to her family.

"Emma, too. She came from England when she was fourteen, and her mother marry an American. Emma is maybe thirty years old. She, too, marry an American. But she stole some money from her boss, so she was in jail for five years. Now they want to deport her. Why? She finish the five years. How can they deport an American citizen?"

"Can she show a certificate of citizenship? She might think she became a citizen by marriage, but marriage qualified her only for legal permanent residency, not for citizenship. There are only three ways to become a citizen—being born in America, being born outside of the country to at least one US parent, or going through the process of naturalization."[1]

"These are good women, Sister. They don't deserve to be deport. Why can this happen?"

———

Later online, I am shocked to learn that, according to DHS statistics, on any given day in 2005 America is holding 22,000 immigrant detainees.

In 1994, the daily count was 7,444. Why the ballooning numbers? Further research leads me to legislation in 1996.

As I read, my uneasiness sinks into anger. Emma and Leticia may be legal permanent residents, but their offenses, though nonviolent, are considered "aggravated felonies."[2]

Introduced as a rider to the Anti-Drug Abuse Act of 1988 (ADAA), the term "aggravated felony" originally designated three categories of serious crimes as separate grounds for deporting noncitizen offenders—murder, drug trafficking, and trafficking in firearms or destructive devices. However, legislative acts over the next eight years quickly expanded both the definition and its penalties. Finally came the harsh legislation of 1996.

A key part of the Antiterrorism and Effective Death Penalty Act of 1996 (AEDPA) said that the judge can no longer weigh countervailing factors against deporting an aggravated felon—good moral character, family unity, length of residence, military service, job history, community service, etc.—ways of showing the person to be an asset to his or her community. AEDPA reduced the judge's role to simply signing the deportation order—a rubber stamp.

Five months later, the Illegal Immigration Reform and Immigrant Responsibility Act of 1996 (IIRAIRA or IIRIRA) added many more crimes to the aggravated felony list, including certain misdemeanors that carry a one-year prison sentence—even if the original judge commutes the sentence. Worst of all, for an aggravated felon, deportation now means permanent exile from the United States. Neither Leticia nor Emma will be allowed to re-enter, not even for a brief visit.

IIRAIRA also ordered certain provisions to be applied retroactively. That's why, when it went into effect in 1997, detentions rocketed. Well-established legal permanent residents with growing families and productive jobs, having lived here an average of fifteen years, suddenly found themselves facing permanent deportation for a single indiscretion committed years earlier for which they had already served jail sentences: Xuan Wilson forged a check for $19.83, Olufolake Olaleye shoplifted baby clothes worth $14.99, Sal DeWitt faced marijuana charges. Within nine years (1997 to 2005), 672,593 noncitizens once convicted of crimes were deported, 64.6 percent of them for nonviolent offenses. Thousands of families were, and are, destroyed by the indiscriminate overreach of this legislation.[3]

Even legislators who voted for these laws later expressed regrets. Their public bills over the next ten years (three in the House, three in the Senate) tried to restore fairness, but only one of the six even made it out of the committee process.

Late this afternoon, I answer a second call from Regina.

"Sister, we can have visitors for one-half hour on Sunday afternoons between one and three o'clock—two adults and two children. I wrote down you, David, Lydia, and Christopher."

"Great! We'll be there on Easter Sunday, Regina."

"David's phone is still block. You please tell him about the Easter baskets, OK? I put them under a blanket in the back of the minivan. And for Easter, Lydia has her new dress, the blue jumper. And tell David to put the white socks and her black shoes. For Christopher, he has new pants and the blue shirt with the green lines."

"Sure, Regina, I will tell him, but you can talk to him yourself tonight. I'll have him bring the kids over before eight."

Patchy skies are giving way to a colorful sunset. Regina seems less the frightened prisoner, more the concerned mother busying herself with her children's happiness.

13

In Good Times and in Bad

"Christ our Light!" chants Deacon Bill Goulding as he hoists the newly lit Easter candle high into the air at the entrance of our dark church. "Thanks be to God!" we all sing in response. Row upon row of pews radiating from three sides of the sanctuary quickly fill with the hundreds who flood in ahead of him carrying small, unlit candles. We've just come from the drizzly cold where we huddled together in the dark—friends, families, kids, teens, elderly—to watch the priests kindle the new fire then light the Paschal candle. Attendants with candles now pass the Easter flame to others until hundreds of amber lights are dancing on faces, gilding the massive cedar beams, and glittering off the twenty-five-foot-tall windows. All are caught up in glory.

So begins the ancient Holy Saturday Easter Vigil, high point of the church year, when Catholics pull out all the smells and bells to celebrate the full power of the Risen Christ.

After the Liturgy of the Word, I stand at the ambo (lectern) calling our RCIA candidates forward. They and their families pour out of the pews to join our pastor and me in a procession to the baptismal pool. The congregation knows it's the last time for both of us. Months earlier, when Father Art told our large staff about his transfer, we all wept with him. Tonight his voice is firm, his stride is happy, and he is fully engaged in the prayer. But part of me backpedals. I don't want to leave this ministry. My heart is full. My heart is broken.

I remember the Easter Vigil when David was among those I called forward. He looked great in the same tan suit Grégoire had given him for his flight to new life. I bite my lip. Tonight he tosses and turns in their king-size bed while miles away, Regina shivers sleepless in a jail dorm, each wrestling the unbearable horror of losing the other again. I remember . . .

After telling me how his friends smuggled him into America, David leaned back on the couch. Regina came in from the kitchen and quietly took a chair opposite me. The window behind her held the fading glow of a once sunny day.

"So, David, it was two and a half years since you had seen Regina. How did you know she was in America? When you got to the Brussels airport, did you phone Uncle Basil?"

He wrinkled his forehead. "No, Sister, you do not understand. Nobody knows what happen to Regina. Maybe she is not even alive. When I get to Belgium, I don't think of Regina's uncle. I just think how I can find the right plane to save my life."

"Well, did somebody give you her phone number? How did . . ."

His voice dropped. "No, Sister. I did not think I would ever see Regina again."

The poignancy in his voice stopped me.

Regina spoke quietly. "So how did we find each other? It's God, Sister. It's all God. Remember I told you that after the judge deny my asylum, I was *very* worry. I just pray God to help. That's when I met Émile, the man who live in New Jersey."

As far as she could remember, Émile had come to Greensboro for some big Congolese event, perhaps a funeral, and at some point they happened to be sitting next to each other. After some introductions, Regina told him it had been more than two years since she had seen her husband, David Bakala, who was still somewhere in war-torn Congo.

"Barbart?" he exclaimed. "We called him 'Barbart'! I grew up with him!"

"You know David?"

"Yes, yes! I remember him very well. We went to elementary school together."

As the conversation continued, he asked if there was anything she needed, any way he could help.

Émile not only got her an appointment with Attorney Lybeau, he also funded the long bus ride, drove her there, and afterward phoned now and then to see how she was doing. In November, he called with *big* news—David was coming to America. If all went according to plan, he would arrive the next day, Saturday, November 15, at Newark Liberty International Airport. He wanted Regina to be there.

"I was very, *very* happy, Sister! Every day I was pray, pray, *pray*. Then, I get this call!"

"This stranger! How did he know this? Was he in David's party?"

David shook his head. "No. He called his friends and mine in Congo—that's all we know."

"We don't ask more, Sister. All these things are secret from us."

Regina traveled all night by bus.

Realizing it would be too dangerous for David to travel under his own name, she asked Émile what name he was using, but he had forgotten to ask. Nor did he know the airline David was on nor the time of its arrival.

"But he knows where the international terminal is. So we don't know anything, Émile and me, we just go. We get there, go to the international area, look at hundreds, maybe thousands, of people. But David is not there."

In 1997, Newark Liberty International was moving an average 84,783 passengers per day. Terminal B's spanking new International

Arrivals Facility accommodated thirty-four different airlines serving sixty international markets and boasted of being able to clear some three thousand passengers through Immigration and Customs every hour.

"We walk *forever*. We look through the *whole* airport, Sister—*everywhere*. We go back to the international terminal. He is nowhere."

David had entered the massive, new International Arrivals Hall almost two hours earlier. He cleared customs without a problem, but when he emerged into the main airport where visitors waited, there was no one giving him the "V" sign, no one holding up his name or searching for his face. He waited awhile, but when no one came toward him, he began wandering through the streaming crowds looking for a face—any face—that might be looking for him.

"I was very nervous," said David. "I even walk outside to look for people. I don't know what to do. Finally, I think I must phone the motel number the guy gave me in Brussels. But . . . tsk." He swirled his palms. "I cannot speak English! What I gonna do?"

After an hour and a half of searching, Regina and Émile were also at a loss. They came to a standstill to study the streams of busy travelers. Suddenly Émile jutted his finger toward a thin man standing beyond the flow of people, about fifteen to eighteen yards away. The man's back was toward them. "Look! There he is! That's Barbart!"

Regina briefly studied the stranger. "*Nooo*, that's not David."

"Yes! Yes, it is! That's Barbart! See the shape of his head, his hair, short neck, thick shoulders—that's him!"

"No. I know my husband," she objected. "That's not David."

As the stranger began walking farther away, Émile did not wait. He ran through the crowd, calling, "Barbart! Barbart!"

Regina was right at his hip.

Just a few feet from the stranger, Émile shouted, "Barbart!"

David spun around.

"I saw Émile, his arms open to me. I reach to hug him, but then I see . . . Regina! Just like that, I have her in my arms!"

Nobody said anything for a few moments.

When she spoke, Regina's voice was gentle. "He was so thin, Sister, just bones. I was shock when I hold him. He has many bruises, and his eyes were in so much pain." She paused, gave her head a little shake, then smiled. "After we hug, he would not let go of my hand." The smile gradually became a chuckle. "Can you believe? All that day, wherever we go, even on the all-night bus ride, he hold on to my hand."

Sometime during their story, the sun had set and the sky had muted.

David did not smile. His eyes were bright, but his voice was somber. "I would not let go. I *could* not let go." The words lingered in the air like incense.

I looked from one solemn face to the other—their words so simple, their life experience so far beyond what I could imagine.

After a while, Regina leaned toward me, her brow furrowed. She spoke in a near whisper. "But, Sister, I still have this problem—what if he reject me? I am too scare to tell him about the rape in Kinshasa. I know I must, but not right away." She gave her head a little shake. "Beside that, I still feel too scare to be with a man. Not even with David. It is just too much for me."

A psychologist once told me that when someone with PTSD uses the phrase "too much for me," she is struggling to keep from firing up the trauma again.

For refugee women who have suffered rape, the refusal to tell their husbands is common, especially among those from cultures where speaking about sex and sexuality is taboo. Their terror outweighs even the anguish of keeping themselves and their husbands in lonely isolation. While many manage to cope with a sexual relationship, a large percentage of these women will never again experience the spontaneous enjoyment of normal sex. This has proven true across all cultures and all levels of education.[1]

"I want to tell him, but I cannot do it yet. All the time I was riding the bus to come to New Jersey, I worry . . . worry and pray. Finally, I decide I will say—with me being Catholic, you know—we must have the church wedding before we can sleep together."

"But that was an excuse?"

"Yes. I use that to give me time. He can sleep in the bedroom and I can be on the couch."

"So you actually did that?"

"For seven months. After he was baptize in May, we talk with his minister about our big church wedding. Then I know I cannot wait longer. We come back. We are sitting at the table. I say, 'David, I have something to tell you. I am sorry it take me so long, but I was too afraid until now. I was rape again by soldiers on my way into Kinshasa.' When I look up, I see David's face. To my surprise, he look relieve. Then he said, 'Thank God! I thought you had another man.'"

I gasped.

Her face softened. "Then he just say to me, 'Regina, it's OK. That's all in the past. Now we start again.' I am so relieve, Sister." She looked lovingly at him.

David returned her sweet gaze.

"Then I tell him everything how it happen, and he tells me all about the jail and what happen to him."

"You didn't know?"

"No. He said nothing about what he suffer. And I did not ask."

"I wasn't ready," said David. "My mind was too much in pain to talk about these things."

I knew how fear could paralyze a child or ignite fury in an adult—my sensitive digestive system still carried the effects. But nothing like this—such deeply wounded people hanging onto each other for dear life yet too terrified for months to share their hearts, to tell their truth to the one person they trusted in all this world. I leaned back in my chair, covering my mouth with one hand. I was beginning to understand how multiple rapes had affected Regina, and how her silence, in turn, had deepened David's terror.

She, imprisoned by her shame; he, by his fragility.

Two outspoken advocates of freedom—totally silenced.

14

EASTER

Easter arrives all decked out in robin's egg skies with organdy clouds, but this afternoon when I open my door, I'm greeted by a slap of icy air. It's a strange Easter, just a promise really—bits of bright green pushing up through dirty snow.

I'm uneasy as I drive to the Bakalas'. Visiting at the Kenosha County Detention Center starts at 1:00 and Kenosha is forty-five minutes away, yet David doesn't plan to leave Milwaukee until 1:15. I don't like the late start. I remember being an eighteen-year-old candidate for the School Sisters of Notre Dame when we were allowed visitors one afternoon a month. Most families arrived hours early and picnicked on the motherhouse grounds while waiting, but my folks, living just thirty minutes away, typically came hours late. I worry that Regina will feel hurt when we're not there on time.

I park my car behind an unfamiliar green Nissan in front of the Bakala home and walk to the back carport. It's 1:10 but no one is outside yet. Lydia throws open the kitchen door. "Happy Easter!" Christopher jumps up to hug me. The kids dance around me, chattering nonstop about going to see Mommy, Easter presents, church, Christopher's cough, and Uncle BasKELL.

"Who?"

"Uncle BasKELL!" shouts Christopher.

Lydia plants her hands on her hips. "You don't know Uncle BasKELL?"

A well-built young man in navy pants, tan polo shirt, and brown suede jacket comes from the hallway, smiling, his hand extended. "Hi. I'm Pascal, a friend of David."

I like his strong handshake. Amid the patter of the preschoolers, Pascal and I get acquainted. He has Caribbean roots and speaks fluent French. "I will be going with you, Sister. David asked me to drive the minivan. When I see Regina, I want to surprise her," he says, his face bright. "I plan to give her my French Bible to use while she is in jail."

I smile, but my shoulders tighten. "Pascal, I'm sorry—maybe David did not understand—but Regina is allowed only two adult visitors and two children. She listed David and me."

His shoulders momentarily sag, but he recovers quickly. "That's OK. David can give it to her for me." He hands me the new, leather-bound, soft-covered Bible with ultra-thin pages and gilded edges. The inscription inside reads, "To Pascal from your mother. Happy birthday." I wonder if Regina will see it also as a gift from *her* mother.

"Maybe they'll let you and me take turns," I say.

After quite a while, I glance at my watch—1:40. My shoulders tense again. KCDC authorities won't let us see her if we're not there by 2:30.

While the kids bounce around showing Pascal and me the Easter cards they made for Mommy, David calls from the front closet where he is looking for Lydia's coat and hat, "Remember, Pascal, first we have to stop at a gas station."

Again I look at my watch.

On our way to the freeway, Christopher stares quietly out the car window for a few moments. "Daddy, look. The trees are moving."

David chuckles. "That's what I said to my father when he carried me on his shoulders to Grand-pére's village. We took the train, then a taxi, but the last part . . . yeah, he carried me."

KCDC is a sprawling, one-story, tan complex set back from the road. Across County H are the back acres of the Kenosha Regional Airport. As we drive up, I push my watch up my sleeve so I can't see the time.

Not bad for a jail. Two rows of dark brown bricks run the length of the facade, one near the top, the other near the bottom. Windows, high off the ground, are accented in bright blue trim, as is the glassy entrance under its own triangular, blue roof. But the side of the building is drab concrete, no windows.

We walk into a shiny-floored, sky-lit lobby, empty except for a table with visitor forms. To our left is a low-ceilinged alcove with a few rows of empty chairs bolted to the floor, bus-station style. Two walls hold rows of safety deposit boxes for visitors' use. The picture window on the third wall looks into an empty visiting room with narrow counters on opposite sides, each with a thick Plexiglas barrier from counter to ceiling running the length of the room. Small protruding panels partition off six visiting stations on one side and five on the other, with two phones and two steel stools anchored in front of each. At the far end of each prisoner side is a locked steel door, its window reinforced with imbedded chicken wire.

We approach the desk. The female officer, a businesslike brunette in crisp blues, asks the prisoner's name, checks a list, inspects our driver's licenses. No, Pascal cannot come in, not even to switch places with me. She gives David and me papers to fill out, then hands each of us a safety deposit box key for wallet, keys, purse, etc. Pascal asks if David can deliver his Bible.

"No. You cannot give her anything. If you want her to have access to it, you must give it to me, and then it becomes the property of KCDC." She reaches up and accepts the leather Bible. "I will give this to the chaplain's office, and the inmate can request to use it." As she runs her fingers over the buttery leather, her gray eyes soften. "Are you sure you want to do this?"

Christopher leans against the L-shaped desk and stares up at Uncle BasKELL.

Pascal hesitates, then says a firm yes.

She looks apologetic as she takes out a scissors. "I hate to do this, but no strings or ribbons are allowed." She carefully clips off the silky bookmarks.

David takes out a check for twenty dollars to deposit in Regina's prison account so she can buy stamps, envelopes, miscellaneous items.

"I'm sorry, sir. You'll have to send that by US Mail. We are not allowed to accept anything for prisoners at this desk."

He opens the large brown envelope with the kids' Easter cards and drawings along with the children's photos that Regina begged him to bring.

"No, sir. You'll have to put those things in the mail, too. Nothing comes into this facility without going through the mailroom."

Lydia pulls back from the desk, all eyes and triangular mouth. She huddles against Daddy's leg. Christopher just stares at the woman.

I butt in. "Well, maybe you could . . . please . . . take it to the mail-room for us?"

"No. That's not allowed."

As David pushes the kids' drawings back into the envelope, I put my arm around Lydia. "Please tell us where the mailroom is. We'd be happy to take the envelope there ourselves."

She looks at me through hooded eyes. "No. That is not possible. You must mail it." She rattles off the regs: "Nothing is given to an inmate unless it is mailed through the United States Post Office. And remember, no packages are allowed, only letters, cards, that kind of thing."

"Nobody told us any of this."

She does not look up. "Well, now you know."

David takes out a few blank checks. "Excuse me. This is very impor-tant, please. My wife and I have separate accounts. I need her to sign these today so I can pay the big bills this week."

"No. That is impossible."

"Officer, please," I say, trying to sound gracious. "This is an *urgent* need. We're talking credit card, car payment, utilities, mortgage, bills that must be paid by Wednesday. Could you please . . ." I glance around at the locked office door. "Could you or maybe some other officer, please just get her signature for us?"

Hooded eyes again. "I'm sorry, but you'll have to send them through the mail."

"Send blank checks through the mail?"

The officer picks up a phone to notify a guard that Andes Imwa has visitors.

After David puts the checks back into his wallet, Pascal offers to take our belongings. David and I help the kids out of their jackets. Each of us passes through the metal detector, waits for the electronically locked steel door to open, then enters the visitors' room. We stand scattered around the middle of the room, glancing from one chicken-wired window to the other.

Finally, the door on the left opens. She is in prison orange from neck down—oversize sweatshirt and bulky gym pants—and, on her feet, brown plastic scuffs. Her hair is slicked flat against her scalp. The moment she sees David and the children, she throws up her hands. Her face contorts in agony. We can hear her wailing through the soundproof glass. She grabs the narrow counter nearest David and doubles over in pain. He yelps, then plunges toward her, sobbing as he grabs the counter on our side. He, too, doubles over, mere inches between them.

The children and I stand back, stunned.

Gradually, she pulls herself to the nearest stool—her eyes streaming, open mouth turned down, quivering. She leans in toward the glass, her arms trying to scoop her children closer. As Lydia and Christopher venture near, she mouths the words, "Don't cry! Don't cry!" but she herself cannot stop. She wipes her eyes and cheeks with the cuffs of her sweatshirt, then picks up her phone. David gives each child a telephone, but neither speaks. As she talks to her little ones, Regina's wet face gradually takes on some light. David and I hear nothing until the children start to answer her questions: "Yes . . . yes . . . no . . . yes."

Christopher uses two hands to hold the heavy phone. "I got a Scooby-Doo video from the Easter Bunny! You gonna come home soon, Mommy?" Lydia's demeanor is more tentative, but her message is the same. "I want you to come home now." Christopher hands his phone back to Daddy.

Regina frowns at David as she gestures toward Lydia. I can read her lips: "Where is her good Easter dress?" Lydia, still listening on her phone, is wide-eyed. David fumbles a bit, then switches languages to Lingala. Gradually Regina's face goes from concern to laughter, back to concern. Lydia hands her phone to Christopher. As David talks, Regina nods.

I sit down on one of the stools, and Lydia leans into my side. I put my arm around her and press my cheek against her head. Christopher hands me his phone, climbs onto the other stool, then wants the phone back. He interrupts to tell Mommy to tell Daddy to let him watch his Scooby-Doo video when they get home. Regina breaks into a smile.

When it's my turn, I try to be upbeat and reassuring. I tell her about Pascal's Bible and remind her that if she needs anything, she should ask Sister Ginny. As I talk, Lydia, who has not smiled once, quietly leaves my side to nestle against her daddy. She never takes her eyes off Regina. David puts his arm around her as he continues talking in Lingala.

When the guard signals that our time is up, each of us takes a final turn on the phone. Regina bites her lip, stands, and shuffles out the steel door. After she is gone, we wait for the heavy clunk of the visitors' door being unlocked. A different female officer enters to usher us through.

Christopher is first. Suddenly he stops, looks up into the officer's face, and demands, "You let my Mommy out of jail now! She did not do something wrong!"

The woman's eyes widen. Her mouth falls open. After an awkward moment, she gives him a sweet smile. Her voice is kind. "No, I'm sorry, but I can't do that."

"Yes, you can! You are a police officer. She did not do something wrong."

She gazes helplessly at him, then looks to David and me, both of us as speechless as she is. Finally, she bends down to Christopher and says in a gentle voice, "I'm sorry, but I did not put your mommy in jail, so I cannot get her out."

Christopher mulls that over, gives her a simple, "Oh," then turns and moves on. The rest of us follow proudly in his wake.

As we leave Kenosha, Lydia returns to her normal kindergarten self, talking about her friends, begging to stop at McDonald's, saying she wants to be a doctor when she grows up. Christopher wants to be a lawyer so he can get Mommy out of jail.

David's face is drawn, but the mask stays in place.

I wish that somehow he could still feel the strong shoulders of his father carrying him.

15

"It's Hard to Be Here"

The *Milwaukee Journal Sentinel,* Tuesday, March 29, 2005: "20 Illegal Immigrants arrested in Wisconsin: All defied orders for deportation, agency says." I set down my morning juice, scanning the rest: Most arrested at home. Ten with criminal records—drug dealing, bank fraud, assault. No personal names, but the Democratic Republic of Congo heads the list of eleven countries of origin. All are part of an eleven-day sweep.

My heart sags. Regina—taken seven days ago—is *not* a criminal.

The phone rings. A recorded message from Correctional Billing Services. My phone line will be blocked until they receive $130.51.

What? For one week of Regina's collect calls? I punch the number for customer service.

"That's right, ma'am," says a perky voice. "I'm seeing fourteen calls. The rate is $3.95 to connect and 69¢ per minute with a fifteen-minute maximum. Your credit card number, please?"

Whoa! Four bucks to connect? "Never mind," I mutter. "I'll wait till my bill arrives."

Phone rings again. Attorney Lybeau whips into legalese.

I grab a pen: *Mot'n to Stay Execut'n of Ord of Removl rec'd in Chicago; bond top priority! only Atlanta img jdg can set bond. <u>Need affidavits!!!</u> from R re rape/clinc details; <u>R's boss</u> & <u>me</u> re charactr, no flight risk; wants to chg venue > Chicgo; <u>Hurry!</u> need Midwst lawyer!*

So much for the first half hour of day two in my retreat week.

My heart calms this afternoon when I see Regina come through the door with the chicken-wire window, but her first words unsettle me: "Sister, how is Lydia? I saw how she hang onto you or David on Easter, just look at me, so quiet. Christopher seem OK, but Lydia, no. I worry about her. When you see her, tell her a special message, 'Mommy love you very, *very* much.'" Her eyes burn each word into my memory. "'You are Mommy's *very* special angel. Mommy will be home . . . pretty soon.'" Her voice drops but loses none of its intensity. "Sister, my children need me. If they deport me, I must take my kids with me."

I pull back in alarm, my mind scrambling. "Yes," I venture, "yes, of course, you would want this . . . but"—I lean closer—"Regina, isn't it too dangerous? Think what could happen . . ."

"No!" she blurts. "They *must* be with me! I saw Lydia's face. These little ones need their mother!" She moves forward on the stool, gripping the phone with both hands, her eyes pleading. "I am so afraid they will suffer emotional scars for their whole life. And David, Sister, he could not handle this. Congolese fathers do not have this job to care for the children. Only women do this. Besides, he still is too much hurting from Congo."

I know what she means. For years I've suggested David interact more with his kids. He loves his children, but he seems emotionally unavailable. It's Regina who nurtures, engages, and enjoys them. Like Regina, I worry about his relentless PTSD. With her in jail, a stable routine is about all he can manage. If she is deported, I doubt he could parent them alone.

"But Regina, Congo is not safe! Your children . . ."

"If something happens to me in Africa, remember, they are United States citizens, they can come back to America. Tell David to get passports for them." Pausing, she adds, "Just in case. But don't worry, Sister. I gonna be out soon. God's gonna do it."

I try to move on. "Regina, Attorney Lybeau just filed a motion to stay your deportation. She expects the 2002 BIA decision today, but she needs you to write a detailed affidavit about the Kinshasa rape and your visit to the clinic. It will be hard emotionally, but it's the only way she can persuade them that your fear of returning to Congo is reasonable. Remember details—the size of the clinic building, was it wood? Concrete? Did you receive medication? The first rape, too. Describe the soldiers' uniforms, the hut they took you to, the jail. Details, details, details."

She stops me, her face suddenly awash with weariness. "Sister, my memory, it is not good now. You explain in a letter, OK?"

"Sure." I lean back, trying to change the tone. "Why don't you tell me about your dorm."

She describes one half as a sleeping area with fifteen bunk beds, the other as a day room with movable tables, stacks of plastic chairs, and a TV high on one wall. Her bed is lower bunk 1, located where the low dividing wall opens into the day room. Nearby, a female guard sits at her desk next to the steel door. On the far end are open showers, toilets, and sinks.

"We go to a dining room for meals. The food is not very good."

Fluorescent lights illuminate the dorm twenty-four/seven, and the incessant TV presides from 9 A.M. to 10 P.M., when most lights go off. All night, she is repeatedly jolted awake by the roaring flush of high-pressure toilets and the *blam!* of the steel door, "making me crazy."

When I ask about outside exercise, she says, "Not for the women."

The men, held in four similar dorms, have access to a gym, but women are confined to their windowless dorm. Two small skylights frame flat patches of sky, but there is no way for them to see spring's tender grass or budding trees. Nothing to nurture hope.

The DHS *Detention Operations Manual* states: "Every effort shall be made to place a detainee in a facility that provides outdoor recreation.

If a facility does not have an outdoor area, a large recreation room with exercise equipment and access to sunlight will be provided."

When I later ask Captain Gary Preston about the lack of outdoor exercise, he says such "luxuries" are mandated only in the federal system. The gym? "It's mostly used for storage."

"There is nothing to do here," Regina complains. "Most women sit around playing cards or coloring cartoons to send to their kids. Mostly, they just watch TV."

According to the Kenosha County Sheriff's website, KCDC offers "Life Skills and other practical programming . . . as an alternative to unproductive time in custody," but Regina says these are open only to criminals. There is no in-house volunteer work (encouraged by DHS standards), nor can she qualify for a day job under Wisconsin's Huber Law for convicts. Life in jail is noisy, depressing, tedious, and lonely. For people like Regina, it can also be terrifying.

"I'm in a *big* dorm—thirty-two women. Two must sleep on the floor. Not the immigrants, no, because the United States government pay for our beds."

"The federal government pays for your beds?"

"Yeah. They rent the beds for the ones being deport."

Captain Preston later tells me that Kenosha County gets about $70 per immigrant per day. He also confirms Sister Ginny's estimate of 100 detainees daily. At $2.6 million a year, no wonder KCDC plans to expand.

By 2009, America will be holding an average of 32,000 detainees daily at an average cost to taxpayers of $141 per detainee per day.[1] With immigrants the fastest growing prison population in America, county jails quickly become addicted to the handsome revenue. Since the 1996 laws and especially since September 11, detention of immigrants has also become a federal cash cow for huge construction companies and private prison corporations.[2]

––––––––––––

"It's hard to be here, Sister. I keep to myself. I don't talk much, just pray, pray, pray."

"How many immigrants are in this dorm with you?"

"They come and go. Many stay only one night. But now? Just three, because Immigration come last night, take one to Broadview—someplace near Chicago—before they put them on the plane to deport. But it's OK, Sister. This one, she has family in Mexico." She leans forward, frowning. "I was scare last night, Sister. Maybe they gonna take me. On Thursday nights, everybody sleeping, that's when they come. Maybe four o'clock in the morning." She leans to one side, taps an imaginary woman, then crooks a finger for her to come. "That's how they do. In the morning, it's 'Where's Maria?' . . . Always on Thursday nights the immigrants are scare."

I recoil. I will later learn that ICE also frequently transfers detainees out of state to remote rural areas, hundreds of miles from their lawyers, family members, and local pastors. "Regina, our phones should be unblocked soon. Be sure you call me *every* Friday morning, OK?"

After mutually encouraging each other, I suggest we close with prayer.

I spread my fingers against the thick Plexiglas and she matches her hand to mine. With closed eyes, we both open into a silent awareness of God's presence. I feel the heat from her hand pulsating through the glass. When I finally look up, her face is tear-streaked but serene.

Later she phones. "Remember, Sister. Tell David to get passports for the children."

One minute into the call, Correctional Billing Services cuts the connection.

16

"MY CHILDREN NEED ME"

During Easter vacation, the kids are with Regina's cousin Belinda Msese in Illinois. David, Pascal, and I have gathered around the Bakalas' kitchen table for what David calls our evening briefing. Energized, we decide it's time to spread the word about Regina's situation. I agree to write a one-page insert for St. Mary's church bulletin. We name others—like Regina's boss—to tell more personally.

As Pascal and I stand to leave, David pulls his reading glasses down from his forehead and opens a wrinkled paper with a Chicago phone number. "Sister, I want you to call Tonton, a translator at Chicago Immigration Court. He watches the lawyers, how they are in court. Belinda says he knows the best ones."

He is smiling. "Tonight is good. We move forward."

Tonton speaks slowly, his voice strong but gentle, his diction clear—a sharp contrast to the noisy laughter in the background. "That's Belinda's family you hear." He speaks louder. "First of all, I would try Attorney Donald Kempster. The judges respect him. He is intelligent, thorough, and good with African immigrants."

I copy down his phone number. "We have no money, Tonton."

"That doesn't matter. Just explain Regina's situation. See what he says. If nothing else, he will have good ideas to help you."

In the kind concern of this stranger, I feel myself begin to relax. "Thank you, Tonton."

"If there's anything more I can do, please call me." He gives me his work number. "May God bless you, Sister. Thank you for helping this family." Then he adds, "I am praying for you."

Tears come to my eyes.

The week ends without my reaching Attorney Kempster, but having left voice mails Thursday, Friday, and again Monday, I'm in no mood to hear his receptionist say, "I'm sorry, but I have a stack of at least a hundred messages . . ." I cut in. "Well, three of them are from me! And I'm about to give you another one, which you are going to put on top of that pile!"

Midway through our parish staff meeting, Kempster calls. After discussing the case at length, he suggests we try for withholding of removal on a derivative basis. However, he's too swamped to handle it. He refers me to the Midwest Immigrant and Human Rights Center. "MIHRC— Mirk—uses pro bono lawyers from some of Chicago's top firms, including ours," he says.[1]

Maria Bernal of MIHRC returns my call Wednesday morning. Attorney Claudia Valenzuela, who assesses detention cases, will be back from Europe on Monday. I agree to send Regina's full file—all of it confidential—by express mail, including the transcript of her hearing and a cover letter giving a detailed overview. She promises to have it on Ms. Valenzuela's desk Monday morning.

"Hi, Regina! I'm so glad to see you." It's Friday afternoon, tens days after my last visit. "Ooh, who did your hair?"

"Just one of the women." She shrugs. "The one who do my hair is nice to me, but the others, they look down on the immigrants."

"What?" I wince, but seeing the sadness in her eyes, I sit up tall. "Well, I have some hopeful news. We might have a lawyer."

I tell her she's to call Attorney Valenzuela collect on Tuesday for an interview. After having her repeat the phone number several times, I launch into the rest of my list, ending with this weekend's church bulletin insert. She listens intently. When I get to the line, "In Congo, Regina had been raped and jailed for months for advocating democracy," she jerks back.

"Sister! People will know I have been *raped!*"

For a moment I cannot speak. "Oh, Regina, I'm so sorry. I should have asked you first."

"You know in my country, rape is a great shame for a woman."

"Yes. I know . . . but, Regina, that is not true in America. We do not look down on people who have been raped; we look down on the ones who raped them." My voice is firm. "You have nothing to be ashamed of. We blame them. Not you."

She searches my face.

"St. Mary's people love you. They will feel terrible that you have suffered so much."

Seeing her nod, I know she believes me, but I regret not being more sensitive.

Suddenly, I see beyond this small exchange—her colorless affect, her talk about avoiding others, the sadness in her eyes. Her anxiety level is considerably higher than at last week's visit. "Regina, are you working on your affidavit for Attorney Lybeau . . . writing about the rapes?"

Her face turns suddenly somber. "Yes. It is very, *very* hard." Her voice is almost a whisper. "It is the hardest thing for me to do."

"Oh, Regina. I'm so sorry that—"

She quickly switches topics, back to an earlier discussion. "Sister, if they deport me, I have to take my kids. They need me. I cannot leave them, Sister. Be sure David gets their passports."

"He's already doing that." I hesitate, then speak gently. "You're not thinking clearly, Regina. Surely you do not want Lydia and Christopher in danger." I look into her perplexed face. "You do realize that the United States is asking the Congolese Embassy for your passport, don't you? That means the Kabila government will know you are being sent back as a failed asylum seeker. What do you suppose they will do to you?"

Her eyes widen. "I cannot think for that right now."

"But if Congo is so dangerous for you, why would you take your children there?"

"No! They need me! If something happen to me, they can come back. But they *cannot* be without me." She taps her own chest. "Remember, Sister, I was an orphan. All my life I long for my mother. I don't want my children to suffer like me. No!" She wipes back tears. "I will never forget when they brought my mother's body in the casket. She was wearing her wedding dress."

When Regina was nine, her mother suffered a heart attack. Her father, Dieudonne ("God's Gift") cherished his wife. He flew her four hundred miles to the best hospital in Central Africa, Kinshasa General. She improved rapidly, but the day before her release, she handed her husband her house keys, saying they were for his other wife. When he asked why, she told him to entrust the children to her. Then she closed her eyes and died. She was thirty-nine.

"They put the casket on my parents' bed. I remember us standing around the bed—my father, Aunt Véronique, Uncle Basil, Uncle Constant, Grand-mère Gabrielle, us children—we was eight children. But nobody wants us. I remember that, Sister. In Congo, because fathers do not take care of children, when the mother die, the mother's sister is to take her kids, but Aunt Véronique, my mother's only sister, she say no. My father, he say my mom wants us to live with his second wife. But Uncle Basil says no, it's not right. Everybody was crying. Then Uncle

Basil said he promise my mom if anything happen to her, he will support her kids, so he propose to pay Véronique. My mother was also raising her little boy. But Aunt Véronique will take only her own son." Regina scrunches her shoulders. "I was so scare. I think, what's gonna happen to me?"

I lean closer to the heavy Plexiglas. "I'm so sorry, Regina."

"Finally, Uncle Basil says he will take us."

When Basil arrived home in Kinshasa with eight more children, his wife, Julienne, was not happy. She already had five. (More would be born later.) Julienne instructed the servants not to tend to the needs of the Imwa children. The oldest, Marie Angel, eighteen, was about to begin university studies, so she was exempt from chores. The next two, Celestine and Lucién, fifteen and fourteen, were boys, and in Congo, boys don't cook, do housework, or take care of little kids. Chores and kids—ages six, four, two, and not yet one—all fell to nine-year-old Regina.

Her shoulders sink; her voice gets quieter. "My cousins, the children's chauffeur come, take them to the private Catholic school, but we have to walk to the public school. If the chauffeur gets sick, I have to go on the bus to get another chauffeur, pay him to take her kids, because Aunt Julienne, she does not want them riding the public bus."

"Did your father ever come to visit?"

"Sometimes. But he lives far away. He died three years after my mom. My brothers went to the funeral. I did not go."

When it came time for Regina to enroll in secondary school (grades seven to twelve) where she would also begin preparing for a career, she took her uncle Basil aside.

"I say, 'I study hard because I want to be a teacher like my father. Now I want to go to Lycée Matondo Catholic Boarding School in Bandundu, the one run by the nuns and the principal is the cousin of the King of Belgium.' He was surprise. He say, 'The public school is not good enough?' I say, 'The Catholic school in Idiofa was better.' When he name another school, I say no. But I was surprise. He listen to me, then he say, 'OK.'" She flashes a wry smile. "I was scare, but I just do it."

Basil later sent his own children to the same school, but when her cousins got food and money from home, Regina got nothing.

"I feel like a charity case. Many times I cry for my mother. I miss her all the time."

"Let's pray, Regina."

I spread my fingers against the glass, and she matches her hand to mine. With few words, we are drawn deeply into God's presence. In the stillness, I suddenly have the sensation of Regina's mother behind me. With the energy of Regina's hand rippling through the glass and the gentle encouragement of her mother at my back, my eyes fill with tears. After a while, I take a deep breath and open my eyes. Regina is wide-eyed with concern.

"I'm OK, Regina. I felt your mother's presence encouraging us. It was beautiful."

Tonight I arrive early at David's house. After telling him what happened as I prayed with Regina, he says, "Ah, I want to show you something," then disappears into the master bedroom. When he comes out, he hands me a badly wrinkled wallet-sized photo—a black-and-white head shot of a beautiful African woman in a three-quarter pose, perhaps in her twenties. Her head is slightly tilted, her expression soft and simple. The silky scarf wrapped around her head like a tall turban lends an air of royalty. "This is Regina's mother—the only picture her family has."

I hold the fragile relic under a nearby lamp. "David, she looks exactly like Regina."

He laughs. "Exactly."

"David, may I please borrow this for a few weeks? I promise nothing will happen to it. My friend Sister Caroline does photo restoration."

He jerks up his eyebrows and his chin. "Ah, wonderful."

By Sunday morning, St. Mary's is abuzz with talk about Regina. School parents received copies of our flyer on Friday; others found them tucked into the church bulletins. Many stop me after Mass.

"How is Regina? Do we know any more? Several of us parents are beginning a rotation of hot meals for the family three times a week."

"Sister, at today's Liturgy of the Word for Children, the kids made cards for Regina."

"My husband and I are sending letters to President Bush, Senators Kohl and Feingold, congressional reps Gwen Moore and Paul Ryan. We will enclose copies of the bulletin flyer."

"Could we set up a fund at a local bank?"

"Sister, if you need help with anything . . ."

"If there's more we can do . . ."

I come home from church with an Easter heart.

17

"THEY ASK ME WHY I CRY SO MUCH"

"Sister, thank God your phone is unblock! It's been *too long*. David, too, I can never reach. Leticia and Norma, they tried to get their husbands to help, but nobody knew what to do."

My line has been inaccessible for two weeks, David's for all three. I feel a wave of guilt, having been secretly grateful for the emotional and financial reprieve. Her constant anxiety is hard to bear. Meanwhile, David's phone company, accessible only during business hours, insists on him being present to authorize my speaking to them.

I hear her sigh. "God told me it would be hard. I had a dream my second night in jail. I was climbing up some stairs to get on the plane to go back to Congo, but David grabs my hand. 'No, Regina! Come with me!'" She describes descending into a basement of sorts. "It's very hard to know where to go, what direction. David holds my hand, and we are like running and climbing over rocks. We knew we was gonna be late, but that was OK. We just keep going." Her voice sounds solemn.

"Sister, I think God is saying it's gonna be a long, hard struggle to get to court."

My mind latches on to the word *long*, as though a three-week-old dream promised us time enough to get her case reopened. I tell myself not to read hope into someone else's dream, especially one with no resolution. Nonetheless, I begin breathing easier. Maybe week four will bring us a lawyer.

"I'm sorry, Sister," says Attorney Mirna Adjami from MIHRC on Wednesday. "We have decided not to take Regina's case. After studying the documents and interviewing her, we have concluded that Attorney Lybeau is probably best suited to help you."

"No! You don't understand! It was Anne Lybeau's negligence that got us into this mess."

"True, Regina could have had better representation, but ineffective assistance of counsel requires a very high level of proof and is probably not provable. Furthermore, Sister, her case has too many layers. Attorney Lybeau is familiar with it and has already submitted the motions, so we really cannot do anything."

I stop breathing. My mind races pell-mell for something, anything. "Attorney Lybeau herself is eager for us to get a Midwest lawyer."

She says nothing.

I pinch my eyes closed. "OK, Ms. Adjami. Tell me honestly—what are the odds of our getting Regina freed?"

"Well, Sister, the substance of the case is very, *very* difficult to overcome. First, in my experience with Congolese cases, because of dramatic changes in the Congolese government, the US is very reluctant to look at past persecution cases now."

By "dramatic changes" I presume she means the UN-brokered transitional government of President Joseph Kabila and four rival vice presidents. I bite my lip. Their uneasy coalition is slated to end as soon as a new constitution is approved and free elections are held, supposedly this

June—a flimsy proposition since it's already April and no preparations have been made. Each is vying for power. In fact, two of them lead the largest rebel militias in the Congo war, which—peace accord or not—continues to rage. How dare we consider that country safe?

"Second, the basis for her 1997 denial was the number of inconsistencies in the case." She continues, "Third, pro bono attorneys are regular lawyers who help simple, indigent cases, so there's also a money issue. I recommend you hire another lawyer."

So that's it. She doesn't want to saddle a pro bono lawyer with an urgent, multilayered case she fears is a loser. I want to object—*Look, inconsistencies are not lies, mistranslations were not Regina's fault, and for crying out loud, she was beaten and raped!*—but her mind is made up. I take a deep breath. "Ms. Adjami, may I ask one more thing? To get Regina released, Attorney Lybeau wants her boss and me to submit affidavits of support for a bond hearing and—"

"Unless and until the BIA reopens her case, there will be no telephonic bond hearing."

I freeze. Is Anne Lybeau ahead of the game? Or learning as she goes?

"Frankly, Sister, if you want to make a difference for asylees, mobilize your community to oppose the Real ID Act. Congress is cracking down, making asylum increasingly harder to get."

"Thank you, Ms. Adjami, for your time . . . and for your honesty."

After hanging up, I slump down in my chair, depleted. Tears start. I've known it all along. Regina's case is just too messed up. What lawyer in her right mind wants a complex case, especially one this urgent? I swivel my chair to face the tall, hand-carved Indonesian sculpture on my side table. The stylized mother giraffe rises seamlessly in muted green from its base. Her neck arcs slightly toward her brown calf, but her face looks outward. The little one stands close, its head turned up toward hers.

"Do not be afraid, Sister. There are many other lawyers," says Tonton, a smile in his voice. "God is with you." On the phone, he sounds as gentle and unhurried as a wise old monk. "You've lost a battle, yes, but you certainly have not lost the war. Another attorney you can ask is Chicago's Mark Davidson. He's smart and aggressive."

I discover on his website that Davidson has been a conference speaker on asylum law for other lawyers. He also probably costs a fortune, but I brush that thought aside. My call catches him as he is about to leave for court. To my relief, he agrees to consider the case. Another call to MIHRC assures me that they will immediately deliver Regina's documents to his office.

This evening, I return a call from a man named Bob Mutranowski.

"Sister, my daughter Karly is in Lydia's kindergarten class. Today we got word through a school flyer in Karly's weekly red folder about Lydia's mother. My wife Amy and I can't stand to think of a kindergartner not being tucked in at night by her mommy. I will help you, Sister."

"It's very nice of you to offer, Bob, but I'm not sure what you can—"

"Well, I've got a lot of connections, including an attorney at Foley & Lardner, a circuit court judge in Chicago, and some media people, too. But I thought first I could talk to our senators and Gwen Moore, congressional rep for Milwaukee, to get their advice—what do you think?" His voice is gentle, determined but not pushy. "Would you have time to write a more thorough summary so I have more background? And how about a photo of Regina?"

Suddenly the load feels lighter. "Sure! Gee, thanks, Bob. I really appreciate your help."

The telephone jars me awake. After staying up until 3 A.M. to compose the four-page summary for Bob Mutranowski, my eyes are puffy and raw. I squint at my watch—9:17 A.M., Thursday. Thank God for a flexible work schedule. I bound to my feet, rush into the next room, and grab the phone on the third ring. I clear my throat a few times and try to sound cheery. "Good morning, Regina!"

"Hi, Sister."

Something's wrong. Her voice is tiny, wavering.

"Sister, I've been writing about the rapes, the details that I can remember."

Each breath sounds short. Is she crying?

"My mind is tired. All the time I forget things, even little things."

Last week she returned the power of attorney document without the notary public's signature or seal despite my careful explanation and sample copy with instructions in bright red.

"The weeks I could not phone you or David was so hard. Now I am afraid all the time. It's very, *very* hard every day. At night in the nightmares, someone is chasing me. I'm being attacked. I dream about blood and dirt. I wake up in a panic."

O dear God, what do I say? How can I possibly help her?

Post-traumatic stress disorder creates a psychological torture all its own. When the trauma is severe enough to rupture the normal bubble of invulnerability, it traps survivors in a Catch-22. While their psyches struggle to "master" the overwhelming stimuli of the trauma, they can never quite resolve it, "forget" it. Any reminder can trigger extreme anxiety, even panic. Waking or sleeping, they keep reexperiencing the trauma, over and over.[1]

"I write the affidavit in French so nobody can read what I write, Sister, but sometimes I cry so hard, it's very hard to breathe."

Back in 2001, it had taken months for her to tell me that she had been raped. Later, she would describe the second incident that precipitated her fleeing the country, the one in the flashback. But this first attack, nine months earlier, is what first threw her into trauma.

It came out tentatively. "I was raped . . . by soldiers."

We were in my kitchen, just the two of us. Clouds had earlier elbowed out the sunlight, but now it was dappling my table.

I reached over to take both her hands in mine. "Oh, Regina . . ."

"It happen two times. The first was in October, just five or six weeks after our wedding."

After returning to Idiofa to help PALU, she had notified the chief of Elom, her mother's home village, that she would be speaking Saturday at 10 A.M. in their soccer field. Soldiers had disrupted past meetings five times in Elom and other villages. "But most of the time they do not come. When they do, they threaten me, tell me to stop, that's all. This time I am speaking to about fifty people when I see four men in camouflage and black berets coming behind the group. My heart was pounding, but I try to speak in my normal voice."

Suddenly they barged into the gathering. Two grabbed her and her helpers. The other two swung clubs: "Out! Get out! Don't listen to this liar!" People ran screaming under their blows. The soldiers quickly tied Regina's hands and secured her two male assistants, then marched the three of them ten minutes down a dirt road to the gray hulk of an old truck, where they ordered them onto the truck bed. Two soldiers stood guard while the other two returned to loot and pillage.

Regina remembered the sweat pouring down her body as the sun beat down on the metal truck. Hours later, the two returned and piled into the cab with their spoils while the guards climbed up with their prisoners. By the time they rumbled into Idiofa's southern outskirts, daylight was almost gone. They drove through the city and past the outer limits, then stopped.

"The two in back order me—just me!—to come with them. I was shaking. What they gonna do to me? My PALU friends look very scare for me, but they did not move."

Within seconds, Regina heard the truck lurch away behind her as the two soldiers, one on either side, jerked her toward an abandoned hut.

She pulled back. "Please," she begged, "don't do something wrong to me!"

"If you scream," hissed one, "we will kill you!" The other smacked her butt, kicked open the door, and thrust her into the dark. Pointing to the scar near her hairline, she described how she plunged forward, smashing her head into the wall as she fell. "I remember how they hit and kick and yank—everything violent, everything by force. They tear my T-shirt apart down the front, yank down my jeans. I am screaming . . . screaming . . . I cannot breathe. . . ."

When one man finished, the other moved in.

I watched Regina cover her face, drop her hands to her knees, then straighten up, taking a deep breath. "They say to stand up, we have to get you to jail. I am crying hard . . . too hard to get air . . . tears down the sides of my face, my hair . . . I try to breathe . . . I cannot get air. I cannot think. I cannot move. The big one, he grab my arms, yank me to my feet. Everything hurts. I am shaking . . . too weak . . . dizzy . . . I have trouble trying to get on my legs to stand by myself."

"Who's gonna want you now?" they taunted.

"I struggle to pull up my jeans, but my hands was shaking so bad. I fold over the two halves of my T-shirt." It was then she saw the great splotches of blood feathering down her shirt from her throbbing head. Her body quaked wildly. "The tears would not stop. Everything that matter was gone—David, my marriage, my dignity, my life—all was gone."

The younger soldier spat on the ground, "Keep your mouth shut or we will kill you." Each man grabbed an arm, forcing her down the dark road toward the army camp.

During the forty-five minute walk, Regina gradually got hold of herself. In a surge of anger, she thought, "Why I didn't stop them? Why I didn't just say, NO! STOP! Then I think, no, they would not listen. But it's *my* fault. If I did not do this political work, none of this would happen to me. But no, it's *not* my fault. I made the right decision to help these poor people. But I was angry . . . very, *very* angry with this military, so angry I want to kill these men."

The women's jail was a separate building surrounded by a high fence topped with rounds of electrified wire. They shoved Regina into a tiny intake room, then stood by as the prison guard gestured her toward the little bench across from his desk. When she sat down, the kerosene lamp illuminated her bloodied face and shirt. He was alarmed. "You're hurt! What happened?"

Regina said she straightened up but kept her eyes down as he came around the desk, then dipped a clean cloth into fresh water and gently cleaned the gash. "I will write this in my report. A doctor will examine you tomorrow." He gave her some clothes and pointed to a tiny room with an outhouse-type toilet. She came out in a long, gray sleeveless dress with flip-flops for shoes.

"I give my jeans, T-shirt, and tennis shoes to the guard. He put in a plastic bag, then he gives a bamboo mat and one blanket."

He lit another lamp, unlocked the steel door on the back wall, and took her inside. As he raised the lamp, Regina saw three sleeping women, each on her own mat. The windowless room was about twelve feet by eighteen feet with a cement floor. After she was settled, he left. Hearing the heavy clunk of the lock, Regina sat up and pulled the blanket around her battered body. She could not sleep.

In the morning, the doctor came—"a kind man"—but she did not want him touching her. When he asked what happened to her, she looked away, wanting no record of her shame.

The prison was lit by a skylight. Near the corner sewer hole were scraps of newsprint and a bucket of water. A locked door led to the prison yard where once a day they were allowed to walk for a half hour. They ate two meals a day, usually cassava leaves or a little fufu made from cassava root, a Congolese staple similar to potatoes. October. November. December.

"Most of the time, I just think about David. I worry, *Is he gonna reject me?* I pray a lot."

Almost three months later, near the end of December, the guard shone a flashlight in her eyes at 5 A.M., signaling Regina to come with him. Her handed her the plastic bag with her clothes, minus her tennis shoes, and pointed to the tiny changing room. When she emerged in jeans and her blood-stained, torn shirt, he said, "Now you must stop."

"'Stop what? What I do is legal. I teach the people.' But he say I must stop trying to change people's minds about our political system. He look very hard at me. 'I warn you. If you want to stay alive, go back to your regular job. You won't get another chance like this.'"

Regina walked an hour barefoot through the cold, unlit streets of Idiofa until she reached the familiar fenced yard of her childhood. When she tapped on her cousin's window, the woman welcomed Regina with tears. Thanks to pressure from Amnesty International, Mobutu had freed political prisoners all across Congo.

"Sister, I was scare, *way* too scare to tell anyone I was rape." Regina's eyes gathered me in with an immediacy that pulled me deeper than her words. "At the same time, I know I cannot keep something like this from David."

With no phones or reliable postal service, she sent a carefully worded letter with a lorry driver, saying she had been in jail, had much to share, and would be home "in a little while."

The "little while" stretched into five more weeks.

Finally, one morning in early February, Regina arrived before dawn at their apartment in Masina Zone—a two-room unit in what resembled a small motel. Shared cooking and bathroom facilities were outside. She knocked, then heard footsteps. He opened the door just a crack, but seeing her, flung it wide. He threw his arms around her, both of them laughing and crying at the same time—he in bare feet and pajamas, she in sweaty T-shirt and jeans after a two-day lorry ride.

"Then he do like he always does, he hold my hand and take me inside. We talk, get cleaned up, then after breakfast, I said, 'I have something to tell you, but I'm not ready yet.'"

That evening after supper, she asked, "David, do you still love me?" He looked stunned by the question. "Yes!" he answered.

"I say, 'Do you trust me?' He say, 'Yes, I trust you.' I was so scare, Sister. I talk in a very quiet voice, like a whisper. I say, 'OK, I gonna tell you something. I was raped.'"

David jerked upright. "WHAT!"

"I could not look at him. I could feel his eyes staring at me. But then, Sister, he just did like this." She reached across the table and rested her hand gently on mine. "He said, 'It's OK. I am still your husband.'" Her face softened. "David really loves me." She withdrew her hand, then frowned. "But, the next thing he says is, 'Now I want you to stop this political work. You could be killed.' But I say 'David, I *can't* stop. These people need me.'" She pursed her lips. "David was not happy."

She honored his wishes through March, staying home while David worked weekdays and was gone most evenings and weekends. Gradually, she again brought up Idiofa, convincing him to let her recruit her replacement. Two months later, on her way home, she was raped again.

I remember both of us weeping as I hugged her.

I remember, too, the fear roiling my gut—could she ever fully rebound from such trauma?

———————

Detention in Kenosha is a test.

"Sister, I don't have words to tell you how I am—so nervous, so anxious, I cannot stop shaking. It's like somebody is burning me, but I cannot die. There is no solution. I just sit on my bed and cry. Sister Josephe, I tell you the truth. I never cried like this in my whole life."

According to Craig Haney, PhD, the trauma of prison life carries its own psychological risks—loss of self-worth and self-initiative, distrust, social withdrawal, hypervigilance. But for someone like Regina who has suffered prior victimization and abuse, it can trigger long-term, disabling psychological reactions. Moreover, effects worsen the longer the person is detained.

I close my eyes, asking for wisdom. What comes to mind is 1 John 4:18, ". . . perfect love casts out fear," the scripture I used in my thirties to help myself through panic attacks. I steady my voice. "Regina, you are encircled by love. I hold you always in my heart. And David—David *deeply* loves you. And, of course, your beautiful children cherish you! Everyone here . . ."

"I know," she says quietly. "I got cards from people at work and at the parish . . . but, Sister, it's so hard. At night, I'm too cold to sleep, and every time the toilet flush, I jump in panic. In the day, I am so tired and cold, but they won't give any blanket. I just sit on my bed, shaking. Then I write. When it's too hard, I read my Bible, but I can't concentrate, Sister. I have to stop when the words—they like jump all over the page. It is very, *very* hard. The people here, they ask me why I cry so much."

———————————

On my morning walk, I am haunted by Regina's pain—but not only hers. I recently discovered that thousands of asylum seekers—many fresh from trauma—are shackled and jailed the day they arrive in our country.[2]

The 1996 legislation—the Illegal Immigration Reform and Immigrant Responsibility Act—radically changed how we process arrivals. Since April 1, 1997, every person arriving without valid documents is subject to *expedited removal*.[3]

An initial inspection by a US Customs and Border Protection officer takes less than a minute. Anyone asking for asylum or raising suspicion is sent to a second set of inspectors who ask more questions, search luggage for anything betraying a purpose different from the incomer's stated intent, study her documents, etc. Since international law forbids returning anyone to a country where she would be in danger, the CBP officer is required by US law to ask four questions to determine if she has a "credible fear" of being sent back.[4]

Though this *threshold screening interview* may be the only opportunity for an asylum seeker to present information to a government official, it is not monitored by outside sources, nor does US law require the presence of an interpreter. The foreigner is not read any Miranda rights, even though the questions are not merely administrative but go to the heart of the asylum case. As the only record of this secretive process, each answer recorded by the officer *can and will* be used against the foreigner either at that moment or later in an immigration courtroom.[5]

If the inspector decides there is *no* credible fear, the asylum seeker is refused admission and put on the next flight back, preventing any opportunity to have her case reviewed by a trained asylum officer, much less heard by an immigration judge. The foreigner is given no access to waiting relatives or community nor to any legal help. No appeal is allowed, and the person is barred from reentry for five years, twenty years following a second or subsequent removal.[6]

If the inspector decides there *is* credible fear, the asylum seeker is handcuffed, shackled, and taken to prison, where this psychologically vulnerable person is expected to prepare her case. Many, not understanding what is happening, are terrified.

According to the United Nations High Commissioner for Refugees (UNHCR), the detention of asylum seekers is "inherently undesirable." The UNHRC allows governments to hold them in a nonprisonlike facility only long enough to establish identity, determine credible fear, deal with destroyed or fraudulent documents, and assess whether the person poses a danger to the community. Should an exceptional case warrant longer confinement, use of a prison is to be avoided. If separate facilities are not available, the person is to be housed in a section apart from criminals.[7]

As I turn the corner nearing home, Regina fills my thoughts. I quicken my pace. *Dear God, how can I help her?* On Sunday, she'll see David. She once told me that after his marriage proposal, she felt protected. Back home, I leave a message for him to ask to get off work early so we can get his phone unblocked. There's a comfort and strength only he can give to his wife.

On Friday morning, her voice is bright. "It was so good to talk to David and the children."

I open my drapes. Spring is coming in fits and starts, mottled snow piles are shrinking, and in our yard the crazy, old magnolia tree, against all common sense, insists on budding.

This evening Bob calls. "Congresswoman Gwen Moore urges us to 'shine a bright light,' to use the power of people and the media to raise consciousness about Regina's situation. It's a David and Goliath story about fighting the system, you know?

"Sunday I'll finish copying 150 e-mail addresses from the school parents' directory. Then I'll shoot out an e-mail asking everyone to saturate cyberspace with pleas for prayer and letters to their senators and congressional reps. Today, after talking to Gwen Moore's office, I called Mike Anderson at Channel 12, the local ABC affiliate. He is very interested, so I sent him a copy of your four-page summary. Tomorrow, I'll send the photo. If 12 picks up Regina's story, *Oprah* may be interested, so I talked to one of her producers who also asked for the summary and photo. She's meeting with the executive producer this weekend."

I am speechless.

"Oprah?" Regina exclaims on Saturday morning.

"I don't know, but get ready! The school families are determined to get you freed."

"Oh, Sister! God really love me." Her voice drops. She hesitates. "Sister, I don't know, but whenever I pray now, I shake. I think it's the Holy Spirit, but the people here ask me what's wrong, why I am shaking. It happens all the time now. I can't stop the shaking."

The muscles in my shoulders tighten.

"When I shake, I feel God is with me . . . I know God is with me. But I feel cold, too. All the time, I'm cold. It's the air conditioning, I think . . . but the shaking . . . maybe it's God."

Regina tends to spiritualize everything. As she talks, I feel myself being sucked deeper into worry. I close my eyes, trying to surrender— *You love her, God, far more than anyone.*

"So what do you think, Sister?"

"It's a good idea to check it out. Is there a nurse on staff?"

On Monday, she reports, "My blood pressure is too high. The nurse did not give me medication, no. She just says to be calm. So, I don't know . . . I am trying to be calm."

"Be calm? That's all she said?" My shoulders clench.

"Yeah. Just to watch TV or play cards or something."

I cringe. How could this possibly help a traumatized rape survivor about to be sent back to her torturers? If that nurse had any idea . . . I take a deep breath. If KCDC doesn't even tell their personnel who ICE detainees are, I doubt her training covers trauma. Besides, the DHS *Detention Operations Manual* says psychological care is generally limited to suicide watch.

"Did she say anything about seeing a doctor?"

"No. Just to be calm."

I'm the one who needs to be calm. "Regina, if you still don't feel all right or if you need medication, promise me you'll ask to see a doctor, OK?"

When I tell her about tomorrow's appointment with Attorney Davidson, she says, "God's gonna do it, Sister. Remember my dream? It's a long, hard struggle to get to court."

"Yeah, I get the long, hard struggle part. What I need to know is do we get to court?"

"I don't know. The dream just ended with us struggling to get there."

"Well, for cryin' out loud, Regina, please go back to sleep and find out what happens!"

She laughs. Thank God, she laughs.

18

DID SHE TELL THE TRUTH?

"This is an impossible case," Attorney Davidson begins, his long fingers paging through the inch-high stack of Regina's documents. It's Tuesday, April 19, week five. He sits at the head of the polished conference table in a camel suit, cream shirt, and patterned tie. Behind him is a wall-to-wall bookcase of handsomely bound tomes. Fair-complected with brown hair setting off a high forehead, he looks to be in his late forties, early fifties. His face is creased in worry.

Complicated, yes. Difficult, yes. But impossible? I jot down the word in my notebook.

No one sits in the chair closest to him. I had directed David there, but he took the second chair, Pascal the third, and I the last. Celeste sits on the far end, with her husband, Theo, directly opposite me, three empty chairs between him and the frowning lawyer.

Celeste and Theo are good folks, retired professionals whose opinions I trust. The large windows behind Celeste frame the top floors of

Chicago's neighboring skyscrapers against a bright azure sky, a blue that muddies as it sinks toward Lake Michigan, where the line between water and sky is hopelessly smudged and undefined.

Still poring over Regina's papers, Davidson says, "I've carefully studied her documents, and I have to be honest." He raises his furrowed brow to look at each of us in turn. "This is a horrible record. It doesn't even list her husband." His eyes linger on mine. "She applied as a single person, but now you claim she was married in 1994 in Congo?"

Holding their Congolese Certificate of Customary Monogamous Marriage, he leans toward David. "Was this a tribal marriage or a government marriage?"

Hunched over, his hands wadded between his knees, David seems bewildered, withdrawn. He hikes his shoulders. "I do not understand."

As Pascal leans closer to David talking quietly in French, I answer, "Both."

"So it was a legal marriage," Davidson says, leaning back on his chair and shaking his head. "What you've got here is a Catch-22. In order to get this case reopened, you must allege new circumstances. The relevant new circumstance is the arrival of the husband who was granted withholding of removal, so now you have to prove beyond a reasonable doubt that they were married before he arrived. But in order to do that, you must say she lied. And that's exactly what the judge said—the case is fraudulent, she lied."

"In Congo, marriage happens in stages," I say, my words calm, but my heart stuttering.

"Sister, she was either married or not." He picks up the transcript. "Then there's all the discrepancies—the omission of rape and imprisonment from her affidavit, yet she signed it; the mix-up in dates for her arrest; her inability to name the clinic and date she was treated."

I pipe up again. "Mr. Davidson, she was traumatized in court. Women who have been raped have trouble remembering under pressure."

"What I am saying is that if she was not totally truthful about her marriage, how can the court be expected to believe what she says now?"

He glances around, catching the eyes of each in turn. "We have no way of knowing what else might not be entirely factual."

I feel the blood draining from my face. "Mr. Davidson, Regina's lawyers botched this case from the beginning. No one prepared her for court." I clear my throat. "Look, I know this couple well. I've worked closely with them for five years. They trust me and are always honest with me, even when it involves matters they'd rather not discuss."

"That may be, Sister," he says, sounding judicious, "but our judgment, too, can be clouded. Things are not always what they seem." His eyes linger on mine. Then he straightens up and sets down the transcript. "In any event, what's done is done. You can't reopen a case on evidence that should have been presented in the first place."

I feel a chill race through me.

After another go-around on discrepancies, someone raises another reason for reopening, "changed country conditions."

He looks sympathetic, but the frown never leaves. "You have to prove—100 percent—that this particular woman would be harmed if she is sent back to Congo now." He turns again to David. "Can you prove that?"

After consulting Pascal again, David answers, "Not 100 percent. No."

"Right." Davidson tightens his frown. "It's been *nine years*! It is almost impossible."

"But the government—right now!—is targeting her political party," I object. "PALU is pushing for elections that the UN slated for June. Today's government is using the same strategy to silence them as Mobutu did—killing the grassroots organizers. That's what Regina is, Mr. Davidson, a well-known grassroots organizer for PALU."

Davidson speaks calmly. "To prove that she is in danger today, Sister, you would almost have to have a document from the State Department listing her as a target."

My heart sinks. I did not expect this man to flatly discredit our every argument.

He pauses. "As far as new evidence is concerned, the arrival of her husband and his subsequent favorable ruling are still your best option." His frown persists as he studies the polished wood, saying nothing. Finally, he turns to David. "Was there any mention of the marriage in your court record?"

I brighten. As David looks to Pascal, I interject, "At the beginning of David's hearing, Attorney Block inserted information into the record about David's wife and children."

Davidson says nothing for a while, then jerks his head. "Do you realize that if David had been granted asylum, she would qualify for asylum on a derivative basis?"

"But my lawyer, he appeal the asylum part," says David. "Not the decision for withholding of removal, not that. Only the asylum part."

"Well. That's good. Has the BIA ruled on it yet?"

"No," says David. "Not yet."

Davidson stands up to search the shelves behind him. "I found a paragraph in a law book, kind of a back door that might be useful. Now if I can just remember . . . ah, here it is. In withholding of removal cases, while the law does not specify inclusion of the spouse, in some cases, it allows the judge to use his discretion." He opens the photocopier behind David's chair. "Perhaps David's lawyer knows this, but it may prove helpful if the BIA refuses his appeal."

He expects Hal Block to take over. I manage a smile as he hands me the photocopied paragraph, but inside, I feel cut off. *Dear God, where else can we turn?*

Pascal asks, "Can Regina ask to go to another country?"

"Not at this stage."

"Can David go to another country, then eventually petition for her to come?"

"Yes. The US and Canada have some agreement about honoring each other's rulings on asylum, but since David was denied asylum based on the one-year filing deadline . . . Well, you'd have to contact an attorney in Canada to be sure that he could apply."

As Pascal explains this option to David, the attorney hands me the name of a Canadian firm. "You can find them online—either in Toronto or Vancouver."

I try to sound encouraging. "That's not a bad idea, David. Canada is not far from here."

"Just north of Wisconsin," says Theo.

"They speak French in Toronto," adds Celeste.

I see David hunch down, looking from one to another with blank eyes. We're all trying to focus him on Plan B. "Let me come back to Regina, Mr. Davidson. What do you recommend?"

His frown deepens. "The case is very flawed, full of inconsistencies. First, you would have to get all the new facts straight. It would take a ton of work with a full staff to figure out ways to overcome all of that. Worse, she's in deportation proceedings, so everything is urgent. I'm sorry, but all our lawyers are busy on other cases." He packs up Regina's documents in the original box, then stands. "*If* you can somehow overcome the marriage problem and all the inconsistencies . . ." He stops, shakes his head. "What can I tell you? It's an incredible long shot."

As we leave, he hands me the box. "I admire you for wanting to help, Sister, but . . ."

I thank him for his time and his honesty. Celeste adds the careful attention he has given to this case. We all echo her words. Beyond the kindness in his eyes, I see his concern . . . or is it caution? At the moment, I am too discouraged to care. It's been a month since Regina was taken. We are out of time and out of options.

In the long elevator ride down, David stares at the floor. No one speaks.

In the foyer, we stand in a loose circle. Someone suggests lunch. Celeste remembers a nearby deli . . . but no one moves. David is crying. We close in tighter.

"What can I say to Regina?" he blurts.

Pascal puts an arm around him. None of us can hold back our tears.

Our evening briefing in the Bakala house is glum. David is drained. Pascal is worried. I'm beat.

"When Regina called, she ask what happen with the new lawyer." David's mouth turns down. "What could I do? I had to tell her. She was not happy. She want to know all what happen. I told her you will come tomorrow, Sister, and explain. In the end, she say God gonna help."

"I'll ask to see her privately, David." I push a few papers across the table. "The Canadian law firm is not far—in Toronto, near Quebec Province, which has many French-speaking people."

He shakes his head. "I think no, Sister."

Pascal explains, "David and I were talking earlier. He has decided not to go that route."

"Would you prefer Europe, David? Belgium? France?"

His eyes pierce mine. "We just bought this house, Sister. I have a job. My children are American citizens. Why I should think now to go?"

"Well, you could inquire . . . just in case Regina gets deported."

"Now? No, Sister. Not now."

I nod. At this point, I have no heart for consulting with Canadian lawyers, or any lawyers.

"For maybe just two, three days after ICE take her, I was too depress to fight," he says. "But now? Now I just think how to get Regina out of jail."

"Of course. Well, then," I bumble, "it looks like we're stuck with Anne Lybeau."

"I don't like this lawyer," says David.

"Well, neither do I," I admit. "She sent a fax yesterday. The government is opposing her motion to stay the removal, and the Atlanta judge told her he cannot set bond for someone in deportation proceedings. I don't know what that means, except"—I stop short of voicing the obvious—"except that Regina is not coming home anytime soon.

Meanwhile, what choice have we got? Kempster and Davidson seemed to be really good lawyers, and even they said no."

"There must be someone . . ." he says, his voice trailing off.

"For four weeks, Lybeau has been filing motions and working hard . . . at least until now," I say. "She asked for payment two weeks ago. David, did you know that Regina never paid her?"

"Nothing?" His voice drops. "*Tsk.* I did not know."

"Regina probably presumed that Émile had paid the attorney. He paid her travel expenses to New Jersey, remember? Anyway, yesterday Lybeau faxed an itemized bill for close to $2,000 saying she will not do anything more until she gets at least *some* payment."

Pascal frowns. "But why should he pay the lawyer who got his wife into this mess?"

"Yeah. But she's all we've got right now."

David looks frightened, lost. Pascal's arms are folded.

"Look, she's not a bad person. She was quick to admit her neglect. She's been filing motions and working hard these weeks. Besides, it bothers me that she's never been paid." I look into their troubled faces. "Lybeau said her next move is to file for habeas corpus in federal court. Habeas corpus is an internationally recognized way to get someone like Regina out of jail."

Their eyes brighten.

"I've got a parishioner willing to cover the bill for her past work," I add. "So what do you think?"

They nod. "But keep looking," adds Pascal. "There's got to be a better lawyer out there."

———

Tonight I toss and turn, too worried to sleep. Sunday I didn't get to bed till after two. Monday it was three. I plump up the pillow, turn over, and try to think of only the good stuff.

The next thing I know, the morning sun is pestering me.

After breakfast, I get permission for a one-time, face-to-face pastoral visit with Regina for Father Dominic and myself. Dominic Caldognetto is an Italian-born Xaverian missionary whose many years in Bangladesh severely damaged his health but also broke open his already warm heart. Our immigrants light up when they see his glittering eyes, big nose, and full head of wavy black hair. St. Mary's help-out priest has become family, especially to the poorest and those suffering injustice.

After I phone him to synchronize times, I call Celeste to keep her and Theo apprised.

Her greeting sounds a bit flat. I rattle on about today's plans, but she says nothing. I feel a flutter of worry in my stomach. "Celeste? Is there something wrong?"

She is uncharacteristically cool. "Sister, are you sure you want to be involved in this?"

I feel suddenly dizzy, weak. Outside, a gust of wind sets a tangle of branches trembling against the gray sky. Just yesterday she and Theo were ready to help me take on the world. I take in a quick breath and sit down. "What are you saying, Celeste?"

Her voice is calm, reasonable. "I can understand their predicament, Sister. Regina and David are immigrants. They're scared." She carefully lays out her words. "People who are scared tend to say whatever will help their situation. I understand that, but it seems pretty clear that . . ."

The treetops are being yanked around by the sporadic blasts.

"Wait. Are you saying that Regina lied?"

"Well, they were either married or they weren't, Sister. This business about three stages of marriage did not convince this lawyer. You heard him. If she lied about something this basic, why should we believe that other inconsistencies in her testimony were due to trauma?"

"Regina is not a liar, Celeste. She's always been honest with us, and—"

"Well, Davidson is obviously a good lawyer, Sister. He studied her case thoroughly."

"Yes, but he doesn't know her."

"Didn't you see his face when he was talking to us? Even though, with David sitting there, he had to guard his words. Didn't you catch what he was trying to tell you?"

The room feels suddenly cold. "Yes, but—"

"Well, please think it over, Sister. This whole thing could easily backfire on you. Theo and I have decided to pull back."

I come away from the phone badly shaken. Something in me cowers. I feel no protection, no assurances to cling to, nothing to hold me until I can make sense of the fear rearing up inside.

From the very beginning, Celeste and Theo have been wonderful friends to David and Regina. To lose them is . . . Suddenly, fear grips me. *O God. What if they're right?* What if Regina has not been truthful? The most miserable periods of my life were when I got tangled in deception—being sucked into my mother's anti-Communist paranoia, championing the cause of a woman who was actually a pathological liar, referring needy friends to someone I should not have trusted. I can't bear to think of those who were hurt because of me. I try breathing more deeply.

How do I know if she's been honest? At times I have had to question her about discrepancies. Then again, it's usually because I filled in missing information with my own presumptions. But what if this time . . .

I tell myself to get a grip. Regina was ripped from her family, taken in her pajamas, and treated like a criminal, all because of a lawyer's neglect. Even if she lied years ago, this is flat-out wrong. She at least deserves a chance at justice.

I glance at my watch. In an hour I've got to be at the Xaverian Missionaries House to meet Father Dominic. Why can't I shake this fear? What's at stake here? My reputation? I grab my shampoo and towel from the bathroom and head for the kitchen sink. So what? Did Jesus worry about his reputation? I test the water, then stick my head under the faucet.

Brrr-ing!

Maybe it's Regina. I turn off the faucet, whip the towel around my head, and scramble to get the phone before it goes to voice mail.

"Good morning, Sister. This is Mike Anderson of ABC, Channel 12."

I draw in a sharp breath. So much for my reputation.

"I understand you've been working with a woman named Regina Bakala, an immigrant from Congo who is currently in jail. Well, we would like to do a story on her for Sunday night's extended coverage. Could I set up an interview with you this afternoon at one o'clock?"

"I'm sorry, Mike, but I will be out of town this afternoon."

"Where will you be?"

"Kenosha."

His voice rises. "Kenosha? Are you visiting Regina?"

"Well, yes, but—"

"Ah! That would be great! What time will you be there?"

"No, this is a special visit, Mike. A private visit. We got some bad news yesterday, and I need to talk to her about it."

"Bad news?" He's caught the scent. "You're breaking some bad news to her?"

"This is a private visit, Mike."

"Yes, well, I wouldn't want to interfere with your visit. We'll interview you before that. Do you think we could also interview Regina?"

"I really don't know, but I doubt it. I had to get special permission from the prison."

"That's OK. We'll interview you, then our cameraman can get some shots of the detention center. When will you be there?"

"I should be there by one-thirty," I say, though Dominic and I plan to arrive by one.

"Thank you, Sister. We'll see you there."

My mind races. What should I wear? Maybe my gray pantsuit. And what can I do with this hair? My dying curly perm is at Albert Einstein stage. I hurry back to the sink and thrust my head under the full flow of the faucet, and the phone rings again . . . what if it's Regina?

"Hello, Sister. This is Chandra Cooper from CBS, Channel 58. I understand you have been working with an immigrant named Regina Bakala. We would like to interview you this afternoon at one o'clock."

"Could we make it later, Chandra? I'll be visiting Regina in the early afternoon."

"Oh, great! We'll interview you in Kenosha."

"No, you don't understand. Channel 12 will be there and—"

She pounces. "Oh! Then we'll be there for sure!"

Of course. Silly me. I tell her to meet us at one-thirty, then head back to the sink. But before I get the faucet turned on, the phone rings again. I forget the towel.

"Josephe. This is Carolyn. You need to get into the parish office right away. FOX News, Channel 6, will be here in fifteen minutes to interview you and Jeanne Siegenthaler."

Water dripping down my neck, I pronounce a definitive, "No, I am washing my hair!"

"But, Josephe . . ."

"Tell Channel 6 they'll have to make an appointment. Maybe late this afternoon. I'm being interviewed by 12 and 58 in Kenosha at one-thirty."

"Oh, boy. Well, at least they can talk to Jeanne."

"Why the school principal? She doesn't know anything more than what was in the flyer." I decide to let the hair drip. "Connect me with Jeanne so I can brief her."

Thank God I finally get my hair washed. I apply some conditioner, set the timer for thirty seconds, and . . . The phone rings again.

"This is Correctional Billing Services. You have a collect call . . ."

By the time Regina hangs up, my thin white hair is pasted to my skull and I have only ten minutes. I throw on my suit, charge back to the sink, rewash the hair, dab on some mousse, scrunch and pouf and tweak as I blow dry, then hold it in place with a few spritzes of hair spray.

Father Dominic and I pull into the KCDC parking lot at 12:50.

"Thank God, we beat them here. I need some time to put my thoughts together."

Dominic looks in his rearview mirror. "I don't think so. . . ."

Before I get a chance to groan, two gigantic black cameras are at my window staring like one-eyed monsters poised for attack, their masters twisting the lenses to get me in focus. As I struggle with the minivan door, it suddenly opens, sending Bible, notebook, purse, and umbrella tumbling every which way. With both massive contraptions eighteen inches from my face, I slide from my perch and scramble to pick up my stuff. Neither cameraman smiles. Each has one eye behind the lens while the other stares deadpan at me. I jerk back; they move closer. I pull to one side; they follow. I try smiling; they don't.

I crane my neck to locate the reporters. They wait with solemn faces, notebooks in hand, about fifteen yards away, neither anywhere near the other. With both TV cameras recording my every facial wrinkle and tortured curl, I make my way against the cold wind. Suddenly, a mighty gust plasters my jacket against my body and whaps me across the face—*shhhwa-foom*! In a split second, whatever hairdo I had is literally gone with the wind.

I think I hear God laughing.

The officer at the front desk stares open-mouthed as we enter—ordinary me flanked by cameramen and followed by two local TV personalities.

The interviews go well. When Chandra Cooper asks why I got involved with Regina's case, I am surprised by my tears. "Regina, who was orphaned as a child, told me years ago that she felt her mother sent me to help her. My name is Josephe. Her mother's name is Josephine." The same thing happens when Mike Anderson asks a similar question. Of course, that will be the ten-second blurb that makes it onto CBS 58 this evening.

After the cameras leave, Father Dominic and I sign in and pass through the metal detector. We enter an automated steel door, wait in a small area for a second steel door to open, then step into the barren, windowless hallway where a male guard waits to accompany us.

Regina stands five yards away in a small entryway to the glassed counseling rooms. I hurry to throw my arms around her, but her hug is reserved. Is she deeper in depression? As Father Dominic hugs her, I notice her eyes dart toward the guard. Maybe it's fear.

The guard ushers us into one of the soundproof rooms that line each side of a small corridor. Each has a metal table, two or three chairs, and an intercom phone to signal the guard. Two rooms are occupied, one with a dour orange-clad woman listening to a man in a rumpled black suit, the other with a male inmate and a young, well-dressed lawyer using a laptop. The guard locks us in then walks back to the entryway, where he keeps an eye on all three rooms.

Now that she's alone with us, Regina's face is serene. "I'm glad you come."

Father Dominic begins with spontaneous prayer. As he nears the end, he adds, "Dear God, after freeing your people from slavery in Egypt, you did not send them back there again."

Regina, eyes closed, smiles and nods. When we ask how she's doing, the smile continues. "Fine. Father Dominic said it, God's not gonna send me back into slavery. I'm gonna be OK." She turns to me. "David told me about the lawyer, Sister. Why he say no to my case?"

I'm taken aback by her strange serenity. I try to be sensitive as I spell out Mr. Davidson's response, but she remains calm—so calm that I fear she's not getting it. "Regina, I know you think you're going to be freed, but this all might turn out very differently than we hope."

Her smile is gentle, her words firm. "I know that, Sister. But God loves me, and God is gonna be with me no matter what happen."

I explain the Canadian option, cautioning that it would take years to reunite their family.

She pauses. "Sister, I pray all the time, and I feel very close to God. Now all these people write to me, they send me cards, they pray for me—people from St. Mary's, people from my work. Sister, I tell you the truth. This is my family God give to me. I have never been loved like this in my whole life! Never." Her eyes are radiant.

"I'm so glad, Regina. This must be wonderful for you. But—"

"Sister, I have never experience love like this. Not in Congo, not in Belgium. This is my home. God show me in the Bible, Joshua 1:4, before I come to America, 'Wherever you put your foot shall be yours.' All I want is to be a citizen of this beautiful country where God sent me."

"But, Regina, if it turns out that you must leave—"

"I am not afraid, Sister. God is my father and he love me." She peers into my troubled eyes. "I hear you . . . maybe I be deport. Even while you say these words, I try to think how that would be." She crosses her hands over her heart. "But in my heart? In my heart, I have peace."

As Dominic repeats the what-ifs, she rests her hands in her lap and remains unfazed.

I throw in more bad news. "The government is refusing Anne Lybeau's motion to have you released. But we may have to stick with her as your lawyer." I can't hide my worry. "Regina, if the best attorneys are saying this is an impossible case, I don't know what else we can do."

"Remember my dream, Sister. It's a long, hard time to get to the court."

"Regina, it's April 20. Four weeks have passed. Five attorneys have said no."

She pauses, studies her quiet hands, then shakes her head. "No, Sister. I'm not gonna be deport. I know that in my heart."

After an hour, the three of us join hands to pray. I feel her warm, vibrant spirit.

We end our visit with hugs. In her embrace, I discover that what I mistook for reserve seems to be an inner quiet. I don't know what to make of it. Less than a week ago she was in turmoil. I remember praying for her to feel loved, but today's tenor feels unreal.

Father Dominic holds her by both shoulders. "Just remember that God is with you, Regina. No matter what happens, God is with you."

"I know that." She smiles.

At our evening briefing, I report that—at least for now—Regina is peaceful and full of faith. This brings visible relief, but David's expression quickly reverts to a frown and down-turned mouth.

"What is it, David?"

"Something happen today. I don't know . . . Theo called me at my work. He say he's not gonna pick up the kids anymore. Every day he and his wife take them to McDonald's, things like that, take care of them until I come home from my work. Now they stop."

I wince. "Did he explain why?"

"No. He just say they not gonna do it. I was scare. He say it's OK for today, but after that, they not gonna do it. I don't know why he just say like that. What am I gonna do? So I went and got the kids, bring them to my work to wait for me. Why he do like this? Why?"

Darn it. At least Theo could have been up-front about his reasons. I take a deep breath. "I know why, David." I blow out my frustration. "Celeste called me this morning."

As I explain, his eyes widen. "They think Regina lied? No!" he shouts. "How can they think that? Can we do something?"

"I don't think we can change their minds, David."

"But they are *wrong*! They know Regina is not like that. Regina is a very good person."

"They're afraid, David. Remember, until yesterday, they knew nothing about her struggle with lawyers, the marriage, what happened in her hearing. A lot of this frightened them, especially coming from this attorney."

Pascal says nothing. His worried eyes study his friend.

David's shoulders sink. His voice quiets. "They don't know Regina. I thought they knew us, but they don't." His eyes widen. "Sister, I don't want people to think this about my wife!"

"Don't worry. Celeste and Theo are good people, not the kind who would spread this around. I think we can be confident that they will keep quiet about their fears."

"We have to give it to God, David," says Pascal. "All we can do is trust God."

David nods, his eyes glistening. "This will hurt Regina. How can I tell her?"

One of the greatest fears of torture survivors is that others will not believe them. Yet I myself have been struggling since this morning's call. When David leaves to answer the phone—calls keep coming since the evening news—I ask Pascal, "Regina's case was new to you, too. What do you think? Was she telling the truth?"

He shrugs. "There's no way to tell, Sister. All I know is that two little children are without their mother. If she is deported, this family will be broken apart . . . maybe forever." His eyes are clear, determined. "In my mind, what matters now is this family, these little children."

By the time I get home, neighborhood windows are dark. I brew some decaf tea, wrap a throw around my shoulders, and sit in the dark. The only sound is the sigh of a passing car.

The trouble working with immigrants is that no matter how forthright we are, we easily end up with entirely different understandings. It's not just language but cultural assumptions. I remember questioning Regina, "How old were you when your mother died?"

"Nine."

"But in the past, you've said ten. So which is it, Regina, nine or ten?"

"It depends on the country. America celebrate the birthdays, but not Congo. Here I was nine because my mom, she died before July 15, my tenth birthday. But in Congo, everybody turn one year older on New Year's. When the year change, your age change. So in Congo, I was ten."

Tribal customs, tribal rivalries, marriage customs, polygamy, hospitality, the importance of family/community over time/tasks, religious faith, mysticism, reverence for their elders, honor for ancestors, sense of time, history of colonialism—Congo's inbred, ancient ways are easily misunderstood or dismissed in our more pragmatic, fast-paced, individualistic culture.

Then there's the matter of "filling in the blanks," hearing more than what was actually said. When Regina leaves gaps in a story, I too readily fill them with my own assumptions. I remember embellishing what she said happened after the Kinshasa rape. Our initial conversation:

Regina said, "I go to my family in Kinshasa. They took me to a doctor for treatment."

I was confused. What family? Hadn't she once said that her brothers and sisters had all left Congo? But I didn't want to interrupt. Besides, I knew she had two sisters in Africa now, so I figured I must have misunderstood the timing. The others had left, but the two who remained in Africa were probably still in Congo.

"We decide because I was targeted, it's too dangerous to stay in Congo."

"How did you escape?"

"In the middle of the night, we cross the Congo River."

So I wrote in a letter:

> The soldiers gang-raped her and sent her *home* traumatized. Her *sisters* took her to a *medical facility* for treatment. Realizing that their *family* was being targeted, the *young women* made plans to quickly escape then *to split up later, each going to a different country.* Not long after making plans, *they* fled by night across the Congo River.

She didn't use the word "home." She said nothing about "sisters" nor a "medical facility." I presumed that her sisters, who—another presumption—settled in different African countries, had left with her. Wrong. When Marie Angel married years earlier, she and her husband adopted her youngest sister, Fezza, and moved to Cameroon. All the others went to Belgium with Uncle Basil. The only person with Regina when she crossed the Congo River was the fisherman.

Sadly, I repeated my fictional version on several occasions until Regina herself overheard me and strongly protested, "Where you hear that, Sister? I never said that!"

Regina's struggle for asylum was fraught with presumptions and misunderstandings from all involved, starting with herself. She trusted a student's translation, expected her lawyers to help when none had heard her story, and signed official papers without checking their accuracy.

Not only did her attorneys fail her, but so did Judge Cassidy. In his reasoning, the omitted incident became an outright lie—what kind of logic was that? His oral decision leapt from one error to another, all the while ignoring his primary presumption—that rape survivors can testify to details of a time when their brains, ablaze in panic, dissociate from reality.

I set down my tea. Standing at the window, I tick off the facts: Put Regina, a non-English-speaking rape survivor fearing for her life, into a complex immigration process involving an adversarial, one-time-only hearing with a judge who has life-or-death authority over her. Start with well-meaning advice from people who don't know the system. Toss in a student translator, an overworked lawyer (make that three, none of whom listened to her story nor checked translations), a shrewd government attorney, and a flustered courtroom translator. Give her no preparation, which of course will kick her into post-traumatic stress. Then call her a liar.

I know Regina. She told me that her biggest "sin" was using false papers to flee Congo. Despite the minister's assurance and my protests, she recently decided that her suffering in jail is sufficient punishment, and she promised God she would never do it again.

I replenish my tea and sit down. So what about applying for asylum as a single person?

I imagine living in a culture where rape is an act of war, where victims are ostracized by society and their men will not touch them. I put myself in Regina's place.

What would it be like to be double-raped within the six weeks of my marriage? What if my husband "forgave" then warned me, but within months I was raped again? I stop. If it were me, I would not want my husband to be hurt any further. Better he think I am dead than that I didn't love him.

After I flee for my life, I must decide: am I married or not?

Presumptions again take hold: My marriage is over—I "knew" this waiting for the second lorry. I will never see my husband again, and if I do, he will surely spurn me. In fact, I fled Congo to spare us both that pain. If I say I am married, America will insist on proof, but it's too risky to write for the certificate. Besides, what does it matter now? What we had is gone. The crowning event, our church wedding, did not even happen.

So when is a marriage not a marriage?

I decide not to ask my lawyer. He does not care about my story. My best friend says it's time to start all over again. She advises me to file for asylum as a single person.

All the houses have gone dark; only the streetlights remain lit. I swallow the last of my tea.

Regina confides in me. She tells me things she's not shared with anyone else. We pray together. And David? He was too frightened to share anything in 2000. Now, outside of Regina, I am probably the only American to whom he has confided his whole story.

These immigrants have deeply honored me with their trust. I choose to trust them now.

PART III
MOBILIZING FOR ACTION

19

SAVE REGINA

"When I saw David on the TV last night, I was surprise," says Regina in her morning call.

"Channels 4 and 6 had your story last night; Channel 12 plans longer coverage Sunday. More good news. Today the *Milwaukee Journal Sentinel* featured an article with a big photo of David and the children. And tomorrow David, Pascal, and I are meeting with others to organize a public effort to get you out."

"Wow." She pauses. "It's God, Sister."

"Everyone is praying for you, Regina. And did you know the Priests of the Sacred Heart are holding your job in the Development Office for you?"

"Sister, before I come to jail, I am a little bit too lazy to pray. Here is different. Every time I pray, I am filled. I know God is with me." She lowers her voice. "Last night I have a dream. God was showing me all the people here in the jail, what they was saying about me, Sister. Some were laughing at me."

My brow tightens. "Regina, not everybody—"

"Don't worry, Sister. God show me not to be angry with them. *Nooo.* Just to be careful."

"Regina, maybe—"

"God showed me who not to trust, Sister. I do not talk to them, just be nice, that's all. I spend most of my time alone sitting on my bed, praying and trying to read my Bible."

————

After her call, I answer a long ribbon of e-mails and phone messages at home, skip lunch, then sail into the parish office. A woman on her way out calls, "Nice job on TV, Sister! Did you hear Charlie Sykes this morning? Regina was the hot topic."

I spin around. "Talk radio?"

"Charlie Sykes on WTMJ and Mark Belling on WISN—both are supporting Regina."

I swirl past Carolyn, the assistant administrator, who hands me two messages and warns of a slew of voice mails—Senator Feingold's office needs more info; Ecumenical Refugee Council offers to start petitions; black talk show host Eric Von of station WMCS-AM wants an on-air interview at 5:00. I boot up my computer—dozens of e-mails.

In a long one, Maria Flores offers help. Maria is co-chair of the immigration task force of WISDOM, the largest faith-based advocacy group in Wisconsin. Five months earlier, the task force had supported Terwinder Singh, another mother of two who, like Regina, had not been notified when her appeal was denied. She was also labeled a fugitive and imprisoned. Despite petitions, rallies, vigils, protests, prayers, and last minute legal motions, less than six weeks later, Terwinder Singh was deported.

Tonight in my follow-up call, Maria says, "Terwinder lived in Congressman Jim Sensenbrenner's district, but she got *no* help from him! Right now we're trying to stop him from pushing his Real ID Act through Congress. Real ID will make things even worse for asylum seekers."

"That's the bill requiring proof of legal residency before getting a driver's license, right?"

"Yes. But the license requirement just distracts from the more controversial sections. Real ID stacks the deck against asylum seekers. First, it requires corroborating written evidence of their torture. How can victims fleeing for their lives ask their persecutors for records? Second, it entitles the judge to deny asylum if a person looks suspicious—how arbitrary is that? Would the judge know how women from some cultures interact with authority figures, especially when they must talk about personal trauma? What if an Asian avoids eye contact because to him it's an act of aggression? Third, any contradictory statements, under oath or not—a mixed-up date, a misquote, even stuff unrelated to the case—can be used against the asylum seeker. Fourth—"[1]

I glance at my list of calls. "Sorry to interrupt, Maria, but my concern is Regina."

"Sister, the Real ID Act threatens Regina's case! Number four is the biggie: it restricts those in deportation proceedings from having their cases reviewed by a federal judge. She would not be allowed to apply for a writ of habeas corpus."

"But habeas corpus is guaranteed by the Constitution."[2] It's also Attorney Lybeau's next step to free Regina. The "Great Writ" of habeas corpus, a bedrock of Western common law, requires a judge to order the one responsible for the detention—in her case, ICE—to bring the petitioner into court so the judge can determine whether the detention itself is legal.

"Maria, are you free at 3:30 tomorrow? A few of us are meeting to brainstorm next steps."

"I'm not available, but I'll send some WISDOM reps."

As I arrive Friday afternoon, Carolyn hands me a phone number. "A young man, Darryl Morin, stopped to see you about Regina—very well dressed."

I reach him on my office phone. He and his wife, Angela, want to donate a website. He also has connections with influential folks in Washington. My mind is suddenly doing somersaults.

As I head toward our meeting room, a tall, tan, muscular guy in khaki shorts, sleeveless white T-shirt, and scruffy sandals rounds the corner. "Hey, Sister, how's it goin'?" He flips up his Ray-bans onto spiky, gray-brown hair and stretches out a hand. "I'm Bob Mutranowski."

"So this is the mover-and-shaker behind those phone calls and e-mails."

His brown eyes are warm, his handshake firm. "Actually I'm just a big Polish guy who'll do anything to help kids." Bob's aw-shucks demeanor hides the savvy entrepreneur I later discover he is. "Hope you don't mind, Sister, I invited a few others. One is a local activist, Leon Todd."

I recognize the name of Milwaukee's former mayoral candidate, an African American known for his political activism.

He continues, "Leon's a rabble-rouser. He's got integrity, you know? He's also a smart guy with connections in the African American community as well as in city government."

Meanwhile, David and Pascal arrive with two Congolese friends I already know: bright-eyed Patrick Ntula, a recent college graduate, and teacher Tshimankinda Kadima-Kalombo, president of the local Congolese Community Association. I admire how the younger Africans defer to the graying leader, calling him Papa Kadima.

Two bright-eyed women and a wiry, middle-aged man, representatives from WISDOM's immigration group, appear in the doorway. After welcoming them, I see Bob and Leon coming down the hall on either side of an attractive blond. Bob introduces her as Tracy Borgardt, head of St. Mary's Home and School Association, who worked for years in local television. She tucks her sunglasses into her tousled hair and thrusts out her hand. "Hi, Sister. I've got a lot of good connections in the media."

Leon Todd is tall and trim with thinning gray hair. He peers gently at me through his bifocals, then, smiling, extends his hand. "Perhaps I can help, too, Sister. I'm Leon."

After welcomes, handshakes, and an offer of fresh coffee, I lead an opening prayer then explain the seriousness and urgency of Regina's case.

"The first thing we all need to agree upon is this," says Bob, his eyes sweeping from one to another. "Our whole purpose is positive. We're here to free Regina, and we are going to do it."

There is no shortage of ideas.

Leon, the activist: "Use the court of public opinion. Dramatize the situation. Stay upbeat. Write open letters to Senators Russ Feingold and Herb Kohl and Congresswoman Gwen Moore, appealing to their humanity. Use paragraphs they can lift as quotes. Sister, write a detailed account of Regina's plight for them. Include specifics on how the lawyers messed up. We'll also need talking points the rest of us can use."

Patrick, the young grad: "I can write about the dangerous political situation in Congo so people understand what could happen to her."

Leon: "Good. I'll also put that out on *The Digital Drum*, my e-mail newsletter."

Bob, the guy who started it all: "We need a rally, the sooner, the better. How about it, Sister? Would you ask Father Art if we can use the church and the gathering space? Let's get local politicians to speak. How about the archbishop?"

Me: "Great idea. But I doubt Archbishop Dolan will be available."

Pascal: "Invite him anyway. If he can't come, maybe he could send a written statement."

Bob: "How about next Sunday, May 1, 4:00?"

Heads nod.

Papa Kadima: "I will invite the Congolese community. They will surely come."

Tracy: "Count on me to get the media here. I'll also set up interviews and take care of all details for press conferences."

David, hunched over, says nothing. His drawn face merely moves from one to the other, brightening only when someone catches his eye or asks him a question. He's tired, but . . .

Leon: "We should paper the metro area with posters. In all communication, stay clear about the goal. Emphasize the positive: Regina wants to become a US citizen. She's imprisoned in Kenosha. Threatened with being sent back to almost certain death. We can save her!"

Pascal leans closer to David, translating Leon's ideas sotto voce. David shifts in his chair, his eyes fixed on the tabletop. He nods, flashes Leon a smile, then goes blank again.

I've read that the most damaging part of torture is not the pain itself but being powerless to stop it. Our brains, action-oriented, direct us to respond quickly. When we can't stop the trauma, we either freeze, explode, or do something irrelevant to what's occurring.[3] David freezes.

I remember him doing this both times Regina and I sat with him outside the Immigration Court waiting for his asylum hearing. Each time, I breathed a sigh of relief when circumstances dictated that it be postponed for another year. I don't know how he steeled himself that third year through seven hours on the stand. Looking utterly spent afterward, all he could say was, "I did my best." The more I know about post-traumatic stress, the more I realize David's best is heroic.

WISDOM activists, their faces animated, raise the issue of the Real ID Act. "A protest on behalf of Regina can galvanize public outrage," one woman says.

"Regina's situation showcases the fragility of immigrants trying to work through our system," adds another. He leans forward, his eyes intent. "Remember, if Real ID passes, Regina will not be allowed to appeal to a federal judge. In fact, many immigrants will be hurt."

"But wasn't Terwinder deported just *days* after your protest?" I ask. "I'm leery of—"

"There are other ways, too," says the woman, "like your rally on Sunday." She looks at her watch. All three need to leave, but they say WISDOM is willing to help in whatever way we decide to use them.

After they've gone, the other seven volunteers turn to me.

Bob is the one who speaks. "They're nice people, Sister, but their mission is not ours. Whatever we do, we must not politicize this effort. It's our job to gather people across a spectrum of positions to stand with us for the sake of this one woman—Regina."

All heads are nodding.

"Now wait a minute," I object, raising my hand like a stop sign. "I read about the Real ID Act. It will hurt Regina's case. It could prevent her from getting habeas corpus."

Their heads are shaking, and Bob is clear. "No, Sister. We cannot risk dividing people against Regina's cause. Let WISDOM lobby against the Real ID Act, not us. We have only one goal: to save Regina."

"I see your point, but this is a prime opportunity to show how government actions can have dire consequences in the lives of real people."

"Not now, Sister," cautions the more experienced Leon. "It will probably get politicized later by other people, but at this point, we are gathering support for a purely humanitarian cause: to save this one woman from being sent to her death."

Bob leans in. Pascal is nodding. So is Patrick. It's eerie. Not one of them is on my wavelength. David is studying my face. Tracy's eyes have darkened. Kadima's jaw is set.

"OK, we won't link the two." I watch their faces relax. "But at the rally, I say we at least put out flyers about the Real ID Act, OK? I'll also mention it . . . just a little."

One corner of Bob's mouth goes up. "Just a *very* little."

Tonight, Sunday, I flick on Channel 12's hour-long newscast to see the extended coverage reporter Mike Anderson promised. The teaser shot of Regina's face is from a family photo, but her pleading voice jolts me. "Please help me, Mike! Please help me!" My eyes quickly well up. I find out later that Mike had been interviewing David when her serendipitous phone call came.

Dear God, you sent us talented workers and great media coverage. After thirty-three days, it's time for the attorney. This time I'm asking for the best . . . one tailor-made for Regina.

20

IT WAS A DARK AND STORMY NIGHT...

The woman's voice on the other end of the phone is gentle but precise. "You don't know me, Sister, but I'm a friend of a parishioner. I prefer you call me Grace. I am not an immigration attorney, but I once worked for Immigration and Naturalization Services before it was divided. The government prefers I not talk to people like you, but I have been watching Regina's case."

It's Tuesday, week six. A menacing night storm growls and spits against the windows next to my desk, but she has my full attention.

"On Channel 12 last night, you said Attorney Lybeau is now countering the government's argument against her motion?"

"Yes. I originally thought that the BIA had *rejected* it, but apparently not. You see, I'm new to all this, but—"

"As I said, Sister, I am not an attorney, and I make no claims to expertise." Her words are measured. "However," she pauses, "I know what the government looks for in making a decision on an immigration case. If you have a copy of Lybeau's motion, I would be willing to take a look at it. If it seems inadequate to me, I could pass it on to an immigration attorney friend to get his opinion. His office is just down the hall from mine. This could prove helpful."

"Yes, of course. I can loan you a copy, but I will need it returned." I glance at my watch. It's almost nine. "How can I get it to you fast?"

We decide that I will drive it to her secretary's house tonight. While she calls ahead, I find the three-page document, grab my jacket and umbrella, and head downstairs to my landlords, salt-of-the-earth types who treat me like family. "Hi, Pam. I have to deliver a document in an unfamiliar neighborhood. Is Dave home? I need some brawn to accompany me."

As Dave and I race to the car, a streak of lightning with chest-rattling thunder unleashes a downpour, pelting our faces, drenching our clothes. What in the world am I doing hauling my landlord out on a night like this? The noise, the deluge, the empty streets—to hand over a confidential document? To someone whose name I don't even know?

Turning off the main street, we enter a narrow canyon of huge elms. The headlights poke two bright funnels into the driving rain. Older houses perch shoulder to shoulder on steep front lawns, but all is so murky and the rain so fierce that we cannot make out any addresses. Dave sees it first—a two-story clapboard house with its porch light on.

With the wind too strong for an umbrella, I pull up the hood of my spring jacket, and we dash through the downpour. We plunge up the steep, wooden porch stairs, ring the bell. And wait. The drapes open a crack, then close. Shortly after, the top of a man's face peeks up through the tiny window high in the door. I shout my name over the pounding rain, but his eyes are riveted on the dripping "brawn" standing with me. "And this is Dave, my landlord." I offer my nunniest smile. He finally undoes the deadbolt and lets us in. I hand over the envelope, jabber some about the weather, and we leave.

As we pull away from the curb, I begin to laugh. "This is crazy, Dave. I must be nuts."

He holds up both palms, stick-up style. "I'm not sayin' anything!" he croons.

This morning Grace calls again. "As I suspected, Sister, Ms. Lybeau's brief is not going to cut it. With your permission, I'll send it to my lawyer friend for a more professional opinion."

Months later I will learn that Grace is an unlicensed immigration consultant, commonly known as a *notario*. When offering her services for hire, she is operating outside the law.

Notarios may genuinely want to help needy immigrants fill out forms without giving legal advice, but many are not reputable. The Spanish title *notario publico* is often used in the United States to deceive the Spanish-speaking into thinking they are hiring a lawyer with the same elite expertise that the title conveys in Mexico.[1] How to know the difference? US notary publics notarize documents for free. For other services, they charge nominal fees set by the state (one to ten dollars). *Notarios*, however, charge fees that can run into the thousands.

I later got the woodshed treatment from a woman working in an immigration law office familiar with Grace's track record. "We've been trying to shut her down for years. You're lucky. *Notarios* are known to scam immigrants out of money—a *lot* of money. They operate under legitimate titles—bookkeepers, paralegal services, immigration advisors—to target immigrant communities, including Eastern Europeans, Asians, Middle Easterners. In our office, at least one client a week comes in with issues caused by a *notario*. Many are beyond help because their paperwork was filed fraudulently. Sister, *notarios* have ruined people's lives."

This afternoon, Grace's attorney friend calls. He takes a good hour discussing the case, but when I ask if he'll take it, I hear an audible sigh. "Sorry, Sister. I don't have the time, but I recommend Attorney Don Chadwick in Illinois. He has extensive experience in African cases."

"I'm familiar with the Congo situation," says Chadwick, but after an hour discussing the case, he says, "I might be willing, if only it weren't so complicated and so very urgent, but . . ."

My throat tightens. "No, Mr. Chadwick. Please don't refuse me. You're the seventh lawyer I've asked. She could be deported at any time. Please!"

His voice is calm. "Sister, I cannot devote the time and energy that this case demands. It would be unfair for me to pretend otherwise." He pauses. "But I'm going to suggest you try Mary Sfasciotti. She's aggressive—the kind of lawyer who just might grab this thing."

I hang up, take a deep breath, and dial Ms. Sfasciotti's office in Chicago. Hours later she returns my call. As I explain the case, she shoots out barbs—"This is a chamber of horrors!" "That third lawyer is an idiot!"—then quickly takes over. "First of all, these lawyers have each deprived her of due process. I would investigate what went wrong, each specific thing. Lybeau has already admitted her utter stupidity. She could not have cared less about this client, then she used her mother as an excuse?" Sfasciotti harrumphs. "It was her *obligation* to inform the BIA!"

"Well, she's genuinely sorry," I say. "Recently, she told me not to be discouraged because there were lots of ways for a new lawyer to go, including to go after her."

"Indeed! That's the first thing I would do."

My heart is wild with hope.

"However, the case is not only urgent, but obviously complicated—too much to absorb in a phone call. I will need to study it more thoroughly before deciding."

Feeling almost giddy, after we hang up I grab my jacket and rush to David's, late for our briefing. When he swings open the door, I exclaim, "I think we've got our lawyer! She's a pit bull!"

It's well after 9 P.M. I'm working on rally signs in the kitchen when the phone rings.

Ms. Sfasciotti apologizes for calling so late, then begins, "Regina's case is a mess. Before anything else, I would serve Anne Lybeau with notice that she was ineffective. I'd also have to send a complaint of Lybeau's failures to the New Jersey Bar Association to prove to the Board of Immigration Appeals that the misconduct was serious."

Her voice gets more forceful. "Here's why it was so serious, Sister: The BIA's 2002 order gave Regina a chance to appeal her case to a federal court or to leave the country voluntarily within thirty days of their decision, but none of this was possible if Regina did not know about the decision. What's worse, she lost the ninety-day period to file a motion to reopen based on newly discovered evidence. This was tragic. Since she did not leave voluntarily, the May 2002 order became a deportation order. Now a late motion must show changed circumstances from when the case was last heard in court, but this is narrowly interpreted. It's tough to get a case reopened, even within the allotted ninety-day time limit, but to get it reopened *late* is *very* tough!" She pauses. "Yet it's the only way to stop her deportation. So, number two, I would file a motion to reopen, alleging ineffective assistance of counsel and naming the very specific ways Regina was deprived of due process. I would also study changed conditions in Congo and . . ."

Dear God, she's already structuring the case! I can hardly breathe.

". . . I would thoroughly examine David's case. To grant him withholding of deportation, the judge had to have found it *more likely than not* that he would be persecuted in the DRC. Imagine what that same regime would do to his wife! Does the United States want to send his wife back to get raped some more, simply because of a ninety-day limit on motions to reopen?"

I like the anger I hear.

"All this must be included in the one big motion to reopen. However, the board will deny it, so at the same time, I would . . ."

"Wait. Did you say you *expect* the BIA to *deny* it?"

"Sister, there is a rule of finality to every court decision. For her case, it's been three years. *There may not be a way to reopen.* The BIA ruling usually constitutes the final order. Many times, it's all the immigrant can get. You see what I mean?"

"Yeah, most lawyers won't even *try* to get it reopened. But none of this was her fault."

"In immigration cases, the substantive standard for assessing whether counsel was effective or ineffective is derived from the courts' reading of the statutes and regulations in the Immigration and Naturalization Act. Ultimately, they resort to only the Fifth Amendment's due process provisions. Were this a criminal case, they'd have the usual other safeguards in play. So for an alien—even one in a deportation proceeding—the fact that judicial review may have been denied or forfeited doesn't necessarily mean the equivalent of what would be a procedural, constitutional due process violation."

"Whoa!" I interject. "If she's in our country, she is protected by our Constitution."

"Sister, federal courts have tended to look for violation of INA regulations, then violation of statutes. They have rarely found the US Constitution to have been violated over a proceeding involving the INA. So, even assuming that Regina's former attorney is found to have prevented her from asking a federal court to review the BIA's decision, this alone would not necessarily cause the board to reopen her case."

"That's insane," I spout. "If Regina had stolen a sweater from K-Mart, she'd be entitled to all kinds of justice. Why should criminals get more protection than an innocent woman whose life is on the line? She fully cooperated. She sent in every address change. She called her lawyer regularly. One mistake by a lawyer years ago could send her to her death? No American would call that just!"

"And reopening is not the only problem, Sister. Think about how terribly complex this case is. Not only was the board's decision final, but they agreed with the judge that Regina was not credible, that her story about being abused was untruthful. Had she been able to appeal her case to a federal court, the federal judge would *not* have overturned that ruling unless there was no evidence at all to support it. Now it turns out that, although she listed herself as a single woman on her asylum application, she was married at the time in a customary African ceremony. Cultural customs aside, that inconsistency is enough to suggest that she lied about everything." Her tone softens. "This poor African woman. Reading the transcript of her hearing, I could see her falling more and more into hopelessness." Her voice turns angry. "Sister, that judge paid no attention to the fact that she was raped. He treated her being raped as if it didn't matter. Now she's in anguish not understanding why Immigration is treating her so badly. She was raped in Congo, now she's being raped in this country!"

Dear God, please let her agree to take this case.

"Everything in this case is urgent. They could whisk her off any day. So in order to crank down the urgency," she says, "you would have to take two roads at once: first, get the BIA to grant—or, more likely, to deny—the motion to reopen, and because ICE cannot release her unless the case is reopened, second, you file for habeas corpus to get her released, in hopes of . . ."

My heart stops. *She changed pronouns.* Until now, it's been, *I* would do this, *I* would do that. "Wait," I say, crouching in over the phone.

She stops.

I straighten up. "Attorney Sfasciotti, tell me you will take this case."

Silence. Then, "Oh, God. I knew you were going to ask that."

I say nothing.

"Sister, I'm exhausted. My workload is overwhelming. I have three huge briefs due in less than a week, and that's not the half of it. I don't see how I could do it."

I close my eyes and grip the phone with both hands.

"I mean, you'd just have to pray like mad for me to somehow find the energy to—"

"*Pray?* Mary Sfasciotti, you're talking to a *nun.* A nun who's got the backing of a huge parish plus a lot of others, including my Notre Dame sisters."

"Sister, you need to know: This case is beyond urgent, and given its complexity and the fact that the decision made years ago is so final, it would require nonstop work by myself and my colleague. Such immense work will cost a lot of money . . . with no guarantee of success."

I ignore the anxiety in my stomach. "I'm not worried about the money. Families in our parish school set up a fund five days ago. Regina's story has been all over the local media. Next Sunday, we're having a big public rally, we'll be signing petitions, and our new website will be up. You *will* be paid, Mary. I promise." My whole body tenses.

Silence again.

"All right," she says, her voice low, but firm. "On one condition— apart from money. You must ask God to give me strength, because right now I don't have the strength to deal with this."

I muffle my tears. "Thank you. Thank you so much!"

The rest is a blur. Something about interviewing Regina this week-end then hiring a top-notch forensic psychologist—the fee makes me gulp—to independently determine whether Regina's halting testimony at the hearing was due to reliving the trauma of an actual rape or an indi-cation that she was lying. Women very rarely lie about being raped—just the opposite, she says, they try to hide it, repress the awful memory, have problems recalling specifics. Either way, Dr. Val will know. Mary quotes her own retainer and hourly fee. I bite my lip.

She rattles on: Atlanta's federal appeals circuit court is tough— remember Elian Gonzalez? The judge ordered him returned to Cuba. Also, sexual abuse is rarely grounds for asylum, so far only in cases of female genital mutilation and of Muslim women persecuted for not wearing a veil. Regina's judge was very calculating; he set her up, did not take her rape seriously. Need to transfer to Chicago. Wants to include in her motion as much of the original case as possible. . . .

"Sister, I can't emphasize enough how difficult this case is."

I repeat my promise of prayer.

21

THROWING
GARBAGE CANS

St. Mary's is a flurry of activity. An array of baked goods waits on carts as women spread white tablecloths. Others struggle with the huge banner. The media is setting up. Helpers abound.

As rally time nears, a concerned school mom pulls me aside. "Sister, did you notice that Bob Mutranowski is wearing jeans?"

I brush it aside. "He's been moving tables. I'm sure he'll be changing." I look around. Darryl is in a crisp navy suit, the other men in dress pants, shirts, and cardigans, the Congolese in bright-colored traditional shirts. The women wear dresses or pantsuits.

Later, as I swirl into the office workroom, I run into Bob, still in jeans and a white T-shirt. Hmm.

"Hi, Bob. Umm, you *are* going to change for the rally, aren't you?"

"Hi, Sister. No."

"No?" I look for the twinkle in his eyes. "You're kidding me, right?"

"I'm not kidding."

"All of us are dressed up, Bob. You've got time. Please, go home and change."

"No, Sister."

"But Bob, you're the emcee."

"So?"

I'm back in my twenties, dealing with a just-dare-me fifth grader. "It's not appropriate," I say, my eyes locking on his.

His face softens. "But it's a *rally*, Sister. This is how people dress at rallies."

"It's in *church*, Bob. Go home and change."

"No."

"Yes," I snap. "Now."

The fifth grader digs in his heels. "No."

"Don't argue with me." I spin on my heels and head down the hall. "Just do it."

"No."

I retreat into my office, rattled and furious—more with myself than with this darn kid. Who cares how he dresses? Today is about Regina! I lean against the closed door. Dang, I don't even have time for self-pity. *Please, God. I'm so exhausted. Please help me.* I close my eyes, take in a deep breath, then slowly exhale, repeating Psalm 46:10, "Be still and know that I am God." Inhale . . . exhale, "Be still and know . . ." Again and again. Finally, I open my eyes.

Bob is waiting for me in the main office. "I called my wife, Sister. She's on her way with a sports jacket. Is that OK?"

"Perfect," I smile. "Please forgive me for being such a hardnose."

"Me, too." He puts an arm around me. "We're good."

Above the animated voices in the crowded gathering space, I pick up a flutter of piano music: "Sometimes I feel like a motherless child. . . ." The words catch in my throat, but I keep moving. As a reporter from Channel 4 stops me for a follow-up to an earlier interview, a nearby cameraman remarks, "We're *all* here—a first in Milwaukee history—all six commercial TV channels plus radio and press. He estimates 250 to 300 in attendance. On all counts, the Save Regina Rally quickly becomes a success. Donations will total $2,012.

After Bob revs up the crowd, I tell Regina's story, announce that we have a new lawyer, add a bit about the Real ID Act, and ask them to sign Save Regina petitions and, above all, to pray.

Our much-loved village president, Jim Ryan, is the only politician to speak. Father Art reads a letter of support from Archbishop Dolan, Patrick explains Congo's volatile political situation, and popular black talk radio host Eric Von strikes a chord when he says through quiet tears, "I'm so ashamed of my country." Finally, David thanks the crowd, and we sing our closing song: "Who will speak so her voice will be heard? O-oh, who will speak if we don't?"

As folks begin leaving, David's brother, Samson, who had arrived a few days earlier, asks to say a few words. Patrick translates. "This week I came from Belgium to support my brother David. He is the only member of our family in America. I was afraid because he was alone."

Those in the aisles turn to listen.

"But today I come *here!* Today I see *you!*" Samson stretches wide his arms. His face is beaming. "You give my brother wonderful support. Thank you from all in our family!"

Leon tells me afterward that among those at the rally was a woman named Shelley. Her husband, José, had been arrested by ICE the same week as Regina but was deported within four days. Holding his photo during the rally, she could not stop crying.

I later phone her.

"Immigration treated us like garbage!" she begins.

Arrested March 21, the day before Regina, José was also held in Kenosha, but just four days later—as Shelley put it—he was "dumped" in Mexico. He later told her ICE had chained him around his waist and ankles like a wild animal. No one asked if he had money, a place to go, or anyone to meet him. They drove him across the border, took off the chains, and left.

"Sister, my husband is conservative, responsible, not tough, not street smart. He is forty-nine years old. He came here when he was a boy. What does he know of Mexico? Now he lives in a mountain shack with no running water or electricity. His whole family—all of us—are here."

José, a legal permanent resident, had come to America with his parents at age fourteen. He was deported thirty-five years later as an aggravated felon for a relatively minor drug offense committed eighteen years earlier. After serving his full three-year sentence, he had turned his life around. Yet on a Monday in March, ICE swooped in. By Friday, he was gone.

The list of remaining family members sounds like an obituary— besides his wife, José left behind his four American children, their spouses, his four grandchildren, both his parents, all nine brothers and sisters, their spouses and families.

José will never be allowed to reenter the United States, not even for a brief visit.

The purpose of human rights law is to define the rights of an individual as a protection against the coercive power of the state. Deportation—removing a legal resident like José from lifelong community and family ties—is an example of coercive state power.[1]

Countries of the European Union and many others honor their commitment to human rights by granting noncitizens an opportunity before deportation to raise four key issues in court:

1. Right to family unity
2. Proportionality of a crime to its punishment
3. Ties to the deporting country
4. Likelihood of persecution upon return

The United States does not.[2]

Shelley describes their final good-bye. Told that José would be allowed a twenty-minute farewell visit between 5 and 7 A.M., she, José's father, and his brother drove through an icy rain at 4 A.M. to the ICE processing facility in Broadview, Illinois. His mother chose not to come. Shelley brought the requisite small suitcase with phone numbers and $150 in cash for José. They would wire more later.

Shivering outside with twenty-five others, they were stunned to hear that each deportee was limited to *one* visitor and only two people could wait in the building at a time.

"Inside, it's like a small office and only two chairs. I put his bag on the table. The guard opened it but didn't go through it—maybe because I'm a neat-freak. When they call his name, I go in. My husband is standing behind a split door—you know, like a barn door with only the top open. The bottom has a shelf. Then the lady guard—*mean, really rude!*—says to just put his stuff on the shelf. Sister, I've seen my husband cry only once before, but now he has tears in his eyes."

"Could you hug him?"

"No! The guard says in a mean voice, 'Now! Back. Away. From. The door!' My husband said he loved me, I should not worry." Her voice wavers. "That was it. We were promised twenty minutes, but it was maybe two. Then she says, 'That's all. You have to leave.'"

That afternoon ICE dumped José in a country totally foreign to him. It was Good Friday.

Monday morning, May 1, the flowering crabapple tree outside my kitchen is ablaze in magenta blossoms, and Regina's voice is upbeat. "Sister, the new lawyer, Mary Sfasciotti, came to visit me, maybe three hours on Saturday and then again yesterday. No lawyer *ever* listen to me like Mary Sfasciotti. Now I have a *real* lawyer."

Mary herself calls this afternoon after talking with Attorney Lybeau and filing a formal complaint against her with the New Jersey Office of Attorney Ethics.

"Actually, Sister, Anne Lybeau seems like a good person."

"She *is* a good person, Mary, but she met Regina only once, back in 1997. How could she possibly understand her case? Same with Jeanne Wyuna, an overworked, pro bono . . ."

"Yeah." Mary sighs. "Been there, done that. But, Sister, the stickler in Regina's case is that, as I mentioned, sexual abuse is rarely seen as grounds for asylum. None of her lawyers seems to have understood the responsibility of taking on a case like this—positing rape either as political persecution or as persecution of those in a special class, women. To me, every asylum case is literally a capital case—a death penalty case—because my client's life depends upon my work.

"Regina, still facing a Congolese dictatorship intent on punishing those who do not comply, is now the subject of an outstanding deportation order. It's urgent that I find legitimate procedural obstacles to prevent the government from forcing her onto a plane to Congo. It's like this: Regina and I are racing down a dark alley with the government chasing us. If we can get to the light at the end of the alley, her life will be spared. As we run, I am throwing every legal garbage can I can find into the path of her pursuers, hoping and praying that one of those cans will be enough to stop them."

"Sister, we're going to have to study this contract before someone signs it," says Bob at Thursday's meeting. Tracy, Bob, and Darryl are the only ones who could make it on short notice.

"I estimate this will end up costing big bucks," says Tracy.

I feel my shoulders scrunching me inward.

Darryl agrees but then adds, "It's a good contract, Sister, not exorbitant for a lawyer. We just need to consult our attorneys."

Tracy looks at Bob. "Shouldn't David be the main signatory?"

I cringe. "David has no money."

"But it's his wife."

The men agree.

I flip to the last page. "What about the line that says, 'Co-guarantors of the legal fees'? Who would sign here?"

"Regina?" suggests Darryl.

Bob leans in toward me. "Don't worry, Sister. No matter who signs the paper, we're all going to be working together to get this fee paid."

Suddenly I recognize why I've been feeling so anxious. I sit forward. "Look, right now we're in this together, but what happens when a decision comes down on Regina's case and, win or lose, it's all over?" I look from one to the other. "My fear is that you'll each disappear into your own busy lives and it will all fall to me."

Tracy shakes her head. "Not gonna happen."

Bob leans forward, his eyes piercing mine. "We are with you, Sister. We will not pull out until Regina is safe and this bill is paid in full."

"Absolutely!" Darryl adds with an assuring smile.

"Furthermore, Sister, we want to take over more of the jobs," says Bob. "There are lots of others like us, you know. If it's OK with you, I'd like to call an informal meeting for volunteers, maybe do up a flyer for the school parents and for the parish bulletins. People can air ideas. We can ask for organizers to blitz other parishes with flyers and petitions."

Relief washes over me like a fresh baptism.

Saturday Regina reports a beautiful dream—flying through the air with someone in white blessing her. A Bible was turning pages, and when she looked up, a big door opened. Everything outside was clear, beautiful, open. "When I woke up this morning, I feel deep peace."

This afternoon, I learn why. I'm in Office Depot, trying to decide between white labels or the more expensive fluorescent ones to advertise our website on flyers when a melodious cell phone keeps trying to get a shopper's attention. Suddenly I realize that the music is coming from my own hip. I scramble for the new cell phone Darryl gave me.

It's Mary Sfasciotti. "The first big motion is filed, Sister—the Motion to Reopen based on Ineffective Assistance of Counsel and Changed

Country Conditions. I just FedExed the document to the BIA in Falls Church, Virginia. Your copy should arrive Monday. My colleague and I worked nonstop twelve hours assembling the exhibits. It's a good document, Sister, not perfect—we can make corrections and add the psychologist's report later—but it's well researched and thorough."

Her voice is animated. "Sister, I discovered something important in my research. Back in 1997 when Regina's case was heard, there were no human rights reports about women being raped in the DRC because, as a legal matter, rape was not considered a form of persecution. Therefore, the judge had nothing to substantiate her story and find her to be truthful because—get this—rape as a form of torture for political reasons was unknown. And remember, Regina based her asylum claim on 'political opinion.'"

"Rape was not considered political persecution?"

"Right. The first authoritative documents attesting to widespread incidents of rape in the DRC start in 2000 with reports from our State Department and from NGOs [nongovernmental organizations]. They list pages of incidents." Her voice escalates. "Because rape was the heart of her 1997 case, the judge gave her no credence. Think about that! He did not see rape as a method of coercing a woman to comply with a powerful dictator's regime. In his mind, rape was an ordinary crime, if that. Therefore, being raped had nothing to do with being persecuted."

I interject, "But everyone knows rape is a vicious assault, and Mobutu's regime was notorious for its brutality. The effects of Regina's rapes were happening right in front of the judge—the dissociation, confused memories, anxiety. How could he not put two and two together?"

"I uncovered a second thing. Rape was included in the 1975 Convention Against Torture, but it was not prosecuted in international courts as an act of war until the International Criminal Tribunal for the Former Yugoslavia and the International Criminal Tribunal for Rwanda."

"So rape was off the judicial radar screen."

"Yes. But in the United States, the women's movement generated strong public criticism of judges for being too lenient with rapists. So where has this judge been?" She pauses. "You see what's happening here? We're dealing with outdated accusations of women falsely crying rape. How could Regina defend herself when this judge was deaf to her claim?

"Worse, here is a woman from Congo where rape is a weapon to suppress women, and he did not believe she was raped due to her political opinion—political activities. What we're talking about is the status, or lack thereof, of African women who assert rape as persecution in an immigration proceeding. This is devastating for rape survivors who claim to be persecuted on one of the grounds for asylum."

"Mary, if Judge Cassidy already knew, going into this hearing, that there were no international judicial precedents regarding rape nor any corroborating country reports, why—"

She interrupts. "Was he setting her up for failure? Or giving her a chance to prove, by her own credibility, that she deserved some form of protection? We'll never know. Then again, if the case is reopened because there is now corroborating evidence of rape as a tool of persecution, he might be more amenable to changing his mind about Regina's truthfulness and find her credible . . . *if only* we can get her case reopened. I've heard he's tough, but maybe he could fit her case within the Convention Against Torture, another remedy she did not have in 1997."

"This gives me hope," I say.

"If only we can get the BIA to reconsider her case quickly. Their backlog is enormous. They deny about two-thirds of all appeals by issuing summary affirmances, a single sentence, 'We agree with the judge.' I'll be working on habeas corpus next week."

On Monday, a bulky envelope arrives in my parish mailbox. Peeling back the tear strip, I pull out an inch-high stack secured on top by a double-pronged paper fastener and divided neatly into four sections with labeled tabs for each and numbered tabs for the twenty-three supportive documents—four-hundred-some pages. Mary based her motion on changed circumstances: Regina's husband was granted withholding of removal, her current detention and removal are due to ineffective assistance of counsel, and she will be exposed to certain death if forced to return.

Besides citing Attorney Lybeau's failure to notify the BIA of her address change, Mary criticized her 1997 brief appealing Regina's case and her most recent motion to reopen: in challenging the judge's findings, Lybeau failed to cite any authoritative rule or case law to substantiate Regina's claim of persecution, failed to research and cite relevant cases granting asylum for women like Regina in similar situations, failed to request that the board remand the case for consideration of Regina's claim under the Convention Against Torture, failed to provide evidence of country conditions in the Democratic Republic of Congo, etc.

She also attached five US State Department reports on Congo from 1995 to 1999 stating, "Rape is believed to be common, but, there are no known government or NGO statistics on the extent of this violence." Eight 2000 to 2005 reports from the State Department, the BBC, other major news organizations, and human rights groups extensively document a pattern of rampant rape and torture specifically directed at women in the DRC.[3]

She cited relevant cases: the Third Circuit of the Court of Appeals made specific findings that rape can constitute torture; the Second Circuit held that an adverse credibility finding, while adverse to an asylum application, does not taint a claim under the Convention Against Torture; the Sixth Circuit said that country conditions can justify a claim to the Convention Against Torture.

I rest both palms on the hefty document and close my eyes. *Dear God, thank you, thank you, thank you. You sent us the best attorney.*

22

TEAMWORK

A chilly Lake Michigan breeze ruffles the grass at Veterans Park on Milwaukee's lakefront as a small crowd gathers, unfolding lawn chairs and spreading blankets for the annual Mothers Day for Peace family rally. A few teens set up my Save Regina table with baskets of buttons, donation boxes, flyers, and petitions. From my chair near the tented platform where sound technicians are setting up, I watch children dart and play like bright-colored balloons, their happy squeals mixing with the occasional squeaks and squawks of the loudspeaker. I am last on the program—"five to ten minutes," they said. I feel honored to be here.

Antiwar songs, testimonies, poetry, and short speeches stir the crowd. Finally it's my turn.

"This Mother's Day, though she's done nothing wrong, Regina Bakala will not be allowed to hug her two little children, but must talk to them from behind bulletproof glass."

The crowd is still, their faces intent. While I talk, Save Regina clipboards pass from one to another for signatures. Afterward, knots of people cluster around my table, taking flyers and buttons and stuffing donations into the Lucite box.

"Your cause is in the great tradition of Joshua Glover," says a craggy-faced man with gentle blue eyes. "Glover was a runaway slave who was freed when five thousand Wisconsin citizens used a battering ram to break down the door of Milwaukee's courthouse jail in 1854."

"Really!"

"Sherman Booth, Waukesha editor of the abolitionist newspaper the *Freeman*, was arrested and convicted for his role in aiding Glover's escape. Booth was later freed when the state supreme court made Wisconsin the *only* state to declare the 1850 Fugitive Slave Act unconstitutional."

A woman named Joyce hands me her phone number. "Call me if you need someone to muster a large protest. I've got lots of people who will stand with you."

I come home happy, tired, and content . . . until I open my e-mail.

Bob to Darryl, Tracy, Leon, and me: "Please see the attached article. Darryl, we have to put this link or the whole article on our website. Our friend Mark Belling says it very well!!!"

Our *friend* Mark Belling? My heart sinks. I can barely tolerate Milwaukee's haranguing talk radio host. I hit the link, read the article, and dash off my own e-mail.

"Sorry, but I'm not for posting a link. Besides errors about the Bakala family and things like Congo being a Muslim country—it's 70 percent Christian, mostly Catholic!—Belling's criticism of other immigrants is cruel. He condemns the Hmong—our Vietnam allies from dirt-poor refugee camps—whom Catholic Social Services helped resettle, then lumps these *refugees* with the undocumented, claiming they all just want to 'hop on the welfare gravy train.' Huh? He even rants about 'tens of thousands of *legal* immigrants' getting 'immediate' welfare. This is not true. I don't want our website entangled with Mr. Belling's distortions."

I hit the "send" button, then sit and stew.

Refugees are the *only* immigrants qualifying for immediate welfare. By international agreement, the United States provides transitional resettlement assistance through contracted nonprofit groups, mostly churches, charging them to use federal, state, and local aid as well as private assistance to provide food, housing, jobs, health care, clothes, and so on to help refugees resettle.

For other immigrants, federal assistance is limited to two things: public education through grade twelve and emergency health care to protect society. In fact, United States law requires every immigrant to be sponsored either by an American employer offering the prevailing wage for the position as determined by the US Department of Labor or by a citizen or legal permanent resident who can demonstrate sufficient financial resources. To prevent any immigrant from needing public assistance, INA section 213A requires the sponsor to sign an affidavit of support, a binding contract that the federal government will enforce if need be. The contract lasts for ten years.[1]

Mark Belling certainly did not do his homework.

The United States began opening our golden door to refugees after World War II, when we welcomed 250,000 displaced persons with nothing but the clothes on their backs. Under a series of successive refugee programs, we took in large groups fleeing Communist regimes—Hungary, the former Soviet Union, the former Yugoslavia, Korea, China, and Indochina. Finally, Congress passed the Refugee Act of 1980 to systematize entry and to standardize our resettlement services. Historically, we have accepted more refugees for resettlement than all other countries combined.[2]

After September 11, numbers fell drastically, but the Palestinian refugee crisis, Sudanese genocide, and wars in Iraq and Afghanistan have generated a new surge.

Tragically, nowadays many countries are more intent on curtailing migration than in guaranteeing the basic rights of persecuted people. During any given year, less than 1 percent of the world's refugees get the chance to build a new life in a safe country. The rest, hundreds of thousands, are either warehoused—kept totally dependent in refugee camps, sometimes for decades with limited or no freedom of movement—or are hiding somewhere in urban populations.[3]

Today's challenge is to look anew at the world's displaced people to find better, more nimble solutions. Global patterns are shifting. Families are fleeing not only persecution (qualifying them for refugee status) but also natural disasters, government collapse, and extreme poverty.[4] We are the richest country in the world. This is no time for us to begrudge welfare to the statistical handful who have legally made it to our shores.

———

Bob to Darryl, Tracy, Leon, and me: "Sister JM, while I understand your concerns, this is and always has been about getting Regina out of jail and freed from deportation. Families helping another family. No politics, no agenda except that focused goal. Having said that, Belling is on our side! To provide access to his point of view for our side helps, especially given his rather wide audience. That's all. We need as much exposure as possible. We need $$. I'd like you to reconsider. Conservative, liberal—it just doesn't matter."

In a morning e-mail, Tracy chimes in. "I agree with Bob. I see the article as really positive to our position. (Disclaimer—I am a Belling fan.) I don't agree with the 'politics' of many others; however, they are helping Regina. The nice thing is that we are of varied political backgrounds and so are the people covering her story. That we can all come together is awesome. Belling reaches about 250,000 a week, mostly upper middle class, white-collar conservatives who also have access to what we need, *money!* Let's balance writers so we won't appear to favor one over another. Bottom line—we are all fans of the human cause: getting Regina out of jail and keeping her here."

Me to the four: "I am also grateful that talk show hosts Belling and Sykes support Regina's cause, but we agreed to stay nonpartisan. This position, though difficult, is paying off. Let's thank Mark Belling and suggest he create a link to our site where his listeners/readers can help Regina."

Late tonight Darryl joins the discussion. "The issue of immigration is very personal to me. I believe Regina's case was a calling from the Lord for us to be active in the ongoing immigration debate. I understand concerns about endorsements from people on either end of the political spectrum. They have personal agendas and are prone to taking liberties. That said, I am for posting the Belling article for download under the heading, 'Mark Belling issues support for Regina Bakala.' Viewers would need to download it . . . and most who do will be Mr. Belling's fans—offending few, and hopefully motivating many. I would also favor posting articles from the liberal side. In the end, the one thing all sides agree on is that a grave injustice is being perpetrated on Regina and her family. Both conservative and liberal public figures have their constituencies who can assist in our efforts and whose resources we will need to be successful."

I'm concerned that Leon, who lives on his computer, has said nothing, and David, Pascal, and Patrick are not even in the loop. Our meeting is tomorrow.

I write, "Darryl, please do not post any articles until we discuss this together and come to consensus as a team. Thanks."

Bob, responding to my report of the peace rally, is already taking another tack: "Let the woman who wants to muster a protest muster! We can use as much exposure as possible to keep this on the evening news."

Citing Terwinder Singh's case, I write that I fear it's too risky right now.

Bob e-mails the volunteer flyer he designed to advertise an upcoming meeting for volunteers, adding, "P.S. Mark Belling loved it!"

Darryl dashes off a late-night idea: "Who would like to write all the updates? Do we know someone who can? I'm willing to review and make suggestions, but we need a powerful, moving writer with a consistent style and the ability to write updates on a timely basis."

Hey? What about me? I've been doing this for weeks! Cool it, Josephe. He's trying to spread the jobs around. Doing business by e-mail is like trying to steer a team of wild horses.

———————

We've barely gathered around the familiar maple table for Tuesday afternoon's meeting before Tracy throws us into the thick of things. "My uncle who's a missionary priest says that nuns and priests tend to be more liberal while people in the pews are more conservative."

Bob's turns to me. "Is that true?"

"Well . . . yeah . . . I guess it is."

"Why is that?" he asks.

"We are deeply concerned about people, especially the poor and those who are hurting."

I want to say a lot more: that government has the obligation to protect society's most vulnerable, that social justice is at the core of Jesus' mission . . . and ours. I want to quote Mahatma Gandhi: "The best test of a civilized society is the way in which it treats its most vulnerable and weakest members." But I bite my tongue. Sounding all preachy won't help. Better that I treat each of these good people (whom I hardly know, for heaven's sakes) with a large dose of humility.

Gradually we come to consensus: we will post links to many articles, including Belling's.

Bob points to my curly white head. "Listen up, guys. Everything about Regina's case is in this one head. Got that? Therefore, nothing happens without her approval. OK?"

Everyone agrees. My shoulders relax. The wild horses will race together.

I thank them, assuring them we will always seek consensus. We sail through the rest of the agenda. My suggestion—that their names be linked with mine in the media—they all reject, insisting, "It's not about us." David agrees to sign Sfasciotti's contract. Various others volunteer to research fundraising ideas, incorporation as a nonprofit, Paypal and "Contact Regina" options for the website, and stepping up PR. I will continue to write the updates, one-page letters for mass use.

"By the way," Bob adds, "Oprah's producer is asking to view tape segments from Channel 12, their ABC affiliate."

Smiles break out around the table.

"Sister, it's time to get you to Washington, D.C., so you and I can discuss Regina's case with some high-level people," says Darryl. "Don't worry about the cost. I'll take care of expenses."

After some cajoling, I agree, and Darryl says he'll start getting plans in place right away.

"One more thing," says Bob. "You should all know what the school kids are doing—raising money, writing letters to Regina, other stuff, too."

"Kids have posted signs and held classroom fundraisers bringing in $300," adds Tracy. "All the school kids are praying for her. By the way, I said our initial deposit from Jeans Day was $2,065, but the final amount was a whopping $7,632."

"The point is, we gotta plan something to thank the kids," says Bob. "Take an ice cream cart around to all the classrooms on a Friday afternoon or something."

We all agree, and Bob promises to discuss it with the principal.

As Tracy and I head for our cars, we cross paths with one of my friends.

"How's it going, Josephe?" says Paul.

After introductions, I laugh. "Well, what can I say? God sent me an outright fabulous committee, Paul, but I realized tonight . . . they're a bunch of Republicans."

"Don't laugh," says Tracy. "I've got a shrine to George W. in every room of my house."

Paul turns to me. "And I suppose Josephe has a dartboard?"

"That's it—I have a dartboard!"

At Wednesday's evening briefing, David brings news: Dr. C. Lumana Pashi, leader of PALU in America, offers his help, as do Émile in New Jersey and other East Coast Congolese. All are praying for Regina. He hands me a long e-mail being circulated by Regina's paternal uncle in France, Attorney Jérôme Akiewa, who explains what will happen if she is deported.

Those who come back under these shamed "conditions" are received as fresh fruits at the airport, led to dungeons, tortured to death for having the audacity to denounce, during their demand for political asylum, the Congolese government's distortion of the justice system and denial of human rights through persecution and rape.

David's troubled eyes meet mine. "This is why I don't tell Regina's Uncle Basil and Aunt Julienne in Belgium. Her family would worry too much. But Regina's brother Lucién, he calls every day from France to see what is happening with his sister. Every phone call, he cries."

Our "Save Regina" effort grows bigger every day.

Thursday, May 12, 9:20 P.M., Mary Sfasciotti calls. "Can you believe it? I was in federal district court yesterday to file for habeas corpus when the clerk stopped me. President Bush had signed the Real ID Act while I was getting ready to go to the courthouse. It had gone into effect immediately."

I moan. "Yeah, I saw the signing on last night's news."

"Why does Congressman Sensenbrenner insist on meddling? Our asylum system is already among the toughest in the world. He used the War on Terror to justify setting up new barriers to justice for a whole class of innocent people. But why? Not one of the 9/11 terrorists got into this country on an asylum application. Nor were they here illegally. They each used one or more of our twenty-two types of temporary visas. Why not focus on that? Or on the most crucial element of all—good intelligence? Why in the world did he target asylum seekers?"

While the Real ID Act did not create new standards for asylum, it set the stage for dangerous confusion in current practice. Asylum seekers have always borne the burden of proof for their own cases: (1) establishing that their claim fits one of the grounds for asylum, (2) producing corroborating evidence when possible, and (3) demonstrating their own credibility. But in its clumsy attempt to codify existing case law, regulations, and agency guidance, the Real ID Act actually created potentially dangerous ambiguity in these very areas.

For instance, prior to the passage of the Real ID Act, judges, who often have no training in psychology and know little about the social mores of a particular culture, might have hesitated to trust their own reading of an asylum seeker's affect (or lack thereof) or to attach meaning to the person's demeanor. The Real ID Act now *requires* such interpretations to help determine credibility. In a system plagued with arbitrariness, Real ID further jeopardizes the safety of those most in need of protection.[5]

"Bear in mind, it's already a very uneven system," says Mary. "Some judges grant asylum 40 percent of the time, others only 2 percent. Instead of deterring terrorists, Sister, the Real ID Act makes it more difficult for asylum seekers to get protection."

"How could 100 senators and 435 representatives approve something as flawed as this?"

"Well, Sensenbrenner found a way," she says. "He tucked it into the must-pass federal budget appropriations bill for our soldiers in Iraq and Afghanistan and for the tsunami victims, that's how. There was no meaningful discussion on its provisions."

My shoulders are in knots. "So Regina remains in imminent danger of being deported."

Having followed online warnings of the American Immigration Lawyers Association (AILA), I presume that habeas corpus is now out of reach for Regina. Only later will I find out I am wrong. The Real ID Act transferred habeas jurisdiction from the lower district court to the higher appellate level. Restoring it to the Circuit Court of Appeals was part of a larger effort by Representative Sensenbrenner to restore all judicial review to the appellate level, including the review of constitutional claims and questions of law that AEDPA and IIRAIRA had stripped away. The Conference Report on the Real ID Act makes it clear that the intention of lawmakers was to restore judicial review for every alien as it was prior to 1996.[6]

"Well, yesterday I also filed a motion with the Board of Immigration Appeals to stay her removal," Mary assures me. "And now I'm studying the legislation, determined to get her case into federal court. You see, Sister, most people put all their energy into Plan A. Not me. I never take for granted that we have a victory until we actually do. I am already working on Plans B, C, and D."

"Looking for more garbage cans, huh?" I grab a pencil. "How can we help?"

"It's time to lobby the top guns—Lori Scialabba, chairperson of the BIA, Wesley Lee, acting national director of ICE's Office of Detention and Removal Operations, and Alberto Gonzales, the attorney general. I sent you their contact information earlier. Call their offices. Send petitions, e-mails, letters, especially from big names. Let them know we are watching."

23

"I Want to Help"

Outside my window, young maple leaves backlit by the afternoon sun flutter like small, translucent flags. No one should be locked in a window-less concrete dorm on a day like this, least of all Regina, who comes from a startlingly beautiful land—lush forests, flowers, fruit trees, teeming rivers and lakes—where neighbors share their lives in the glorious outdoors.

"Ah, Sister. We miss many, many things in Africa," David once told me. "Every day you wake up, the sun is there, and, in the evening when it goes down, the sky—it's *so* beautiful! Nights, too, because the moon and stars are so bright the children can read and do their homework out under the stars. *Everything* is like that. People enjoy their life. There is not a sad day, because the sun is there and we are together—all of us—caring for each other."

I turn back to my computer. Letters to immigration's "Big Three" must be ready tomorrow for St. Mary's pastoral team to sign. I urge myself to use concise, clear reasoning while, in my gut, I want to grab these bureaucrats by the throat and rattle them until they *feel* Regina's tragedy. An hour later, the phone rings. I'm so intent that when I look up, even the leaves have morphed into a bunch of ragtag protestors.

"You have a call from the Kenosha County Detention Center . . ."

Regina never calls on a Sunday. Her weekly visit with David seems to be enough. I clear my throat and offer my usual cheery, "Hi, Regina! How are you?"

"I'm good, Sister!"

"Good?"

"Yesterday the psychologist, she come to see me. And, *ohh*, Sister, she was *wonderful!*"

Dr. Graciela Viale-Val had met with her for five hours. In addition to listening to her story, Regina says she also administered several psychological tests.

"For the first time in my life, I tell someone official my *whole* story—being an orphan, the rapes, the jail in Idiofa, my marriage, my pregnancies, my babies, everything. It was the hardest thing I did in my whole life. My head was so hot, like burning. After that, I took a cold shower. My head was still pounding, but I finally fell asleep." She pauses. "But today . . . today, I feel different, Sister. Like a whole new life!"

"Oh, how wonderful. I'm so glad for you!"

Mary Sfasciotti had assured me that Dr. Val from the Department of Psychiatry, University of Illinois–Chicago, had impeccable credentials. She would know from the interview and test results whether Regina had actually been raped.

Her voice drops further. "*Ohh*, and Sister, she *believe* me. She listen to everything, and she *believe* me." I can hear the tears in her voice. "She tells me that when I get out, I should get more counseling."

"I can recommend an excellent counselor, Regina."

Later I will have the opportunity to read Dr. Val's lengthy psychological report, and I, too, will weep, not for joy but for the depths of Regina's inner struggles and constant fears. She has taught herself to function well in her various roles, but, like David, she wears a mask.

"At the end, Sister, she tells me I am a very brave woman and strong. She says, too, when I get out of jail, maybe I can talk to other women—you know, to help those who have been rape."

As she talks, the setting sun dabs all the leaves with gold.

Two cardboard boxes crowd David's kitchen counter, each filled with canned goods, cereal, fresh fruit, groceries.

I plop my notebook onto the yellow tablecloth. "Been shopping, I see."

"Not me!" he laughs. "That's from the kids, from Cara and her friends."

I wrinkle my forehead. The name sounds vaguely familiar.

"Cara D'Amico. She's Lydia's big sister."

"Big sister?" Not working in the school, I don't know much about day-to-day operations.

"The kids in kindergarten have big sisters and big brothers from the seventh grade. Cara came with Mrs. Ambord yesterday to bring all this food from the seventh graders."

"Who is Mrs. Ambord?"

"I don't know. She is from St. Mary's, got three little kids. Couple weeks ago, Cara sent her to ask, what do I need? What can the kids at St. Mary's do to help me—babysit, mow the lawn, clean the house, what? I say I have no time to buy groceries." He lifts his shoulders, laughs sheepishly. "So they bring all this."

"This was Cara's idea? People love your family, David. They are eager to help."

"Look! The hot meals, too." He swings open the refrigerator. "Tonight lasagna leftover for tomorrow, carrots from two days. Salad and jello, too. For weeks, many people do this. Three times a week." His eyes glitter. "The people at St. Mary's, they love us too much . . . *too* much!"

It's a treat to see David happy.

Christopher, barefoot in blue and yellow pajamas, bounces into the kitchen. "I got a new jacket! Look at my new shoes!" Sporty black Skechers with orange and white trim tumble to the floor, leaving him clutching the jacket.

"Those are really cool shoes!"

He thrusts the green and black jacket in the air. "And this is a really cool jacket, too."

David shakes his head. "Christopher, not now. Now is time for bed."

The little boy gives me a big hug, scoops up the shoes, then heads across the hall. That's one amazing thing about the Bakala kids. When it's bedtime, they go without a fuss.

David explains, "Mrs. Ambord, she ask, 'Do the kids need clothes?' So, what can I say? Yes, they need shoes, Christopher has no jacket. So yesterday, when they deliver the food, they take the kids to buy new shoes, a jacket for Christopher and jeans for Lydia. Then Mrs. Ambord and Cara take them all—my kids and her three—to Chuck E. Cheese's for supper. She got the money from other parents." He drops his voice. "Cara bring me this envelope, too, with money—more than $300— from the seventh graders, not from their parents. They save for weeks to give this to me for my family." He shakes his bowed head. "How I can thank these people? They love me *too much*."

I remember once asking David and Regina, "What do you miss most about Africa?"

David's face had opened in a great smile. "Community! In Africa, we live in community, Sister—everybody outside, talking, laughing, sharing food and conversation. Everybody cares about everybody around them. Not like here in America. Here everybody stay in the house, go to work or visit with their own family or friends. It's not like that in Africa."

Regina agreed. "You never stay inside your little house, Sister. You cook outside. You share your food. You need somebody to watch your kids? You don't have to ask, they just do it. Everybody is like this. It's true, Sister. You travel anywhere in Africa, need a place to stay? They take you in, even if they don't know you."

David chuckled, threw open his arms. "It's who we are, Sister— Africans! Congolese are poor, but they are very happy people—singing, dancing, laughing—even when they don't know what they gonna eat the next day. We help each other. Even in the middle of the big cities, they plant the fruit trees next to the boulevards and streets, so the poor have food and anyone can eat. This is what I miss most about Congo—how we take care of each other in our communities."

I hope he sees some of Africa's splendid spirit in St. Mary's care.

I arrive home late Tuesday afternoon, week nine, with my mouth frozen and a handsome, new permanent bridge anchored to my lower jaw. What I feared would be a scary ordeal had turned into a welcome break. I even fell asleep in the dental chair.

Among the usual ads and solicitations in my mailbox is a letter from my friend and former colleague Barb Searing addressed to: "The Regina Fund, Sister Josephe Marie." I slit it open to discover a check for $10,000. I can hardly breathe. *O my God!* I stare at the check from the estate of her aunt Emily, then grab a tissue to swipe at the tears tumbling down my frozen face. Money continues to come in, not only from towns in the Midwest but from as far away as Edinburgh, Scotland.

After supper, I head to St. Mary's for our gathering of volunteers. As Bob arranges the tables into an open square, a petite, fair-complected blond in jeans and lavender T-shirt introduces herself.

"Hi, Sister, I'm Theresa Ambord, the kindergarten mom who coordinates the hot meal rotation."

"Ah! David told me what you also did for his kids."

Bob interjects, "Theresa's the one who e-mailed all the kindergarten parents as soon as your flyer came out. That's how Amy and I found out. Let's get her on the committee."

"Fine with me."

Twenty folks come. After I read aloud the list of donations, I lower my voice. "God is with us. God is really with us."

Our discussion tonight quickly focuses on enlisting the help of other parishes, staffing a "Save Regina" table to solicit signatures on letters and petitions after weekend Masses. More ideas for our grassroots movement: buttons and donation boxes.

"This will take a lot of work," I caution. "I can compose letters and pulpit announcements, but then there's photocopying, phoning pastors for permission, making onsite arrangements, recruiting folks to staff tables, organizing packets of materials, arranging for pick-ups, and so on."

A slight woman with intense blue eyes and brown corkscrew curls tumbling around her face volunteers. "I'm Teresa without the *h*—Teresa Lee, an office manager who's great at organizing."

Everyone agrees to help.

I'm edgy this Friday morning until the phone rings at 9:21.

"I'm still here, Sister. Last night they took one of my Mexican friends, not Leticia. This one has family in Mexico, so she was OK with being deport." She sounds upbeat. "Sister, I had another dream not long ago. My mother came to me. Her face is different, but she has the same tattoo, so I know it's my mother. She say she is coming to help me get out of jail and go home."

Home? Heaven? Milwaukee? I hesitate to ask what she means.

"I feel so peaceful, like she is comforting me with this good news. I gonna be out of the jail to be back with David and the children. I just know it."

Monday afternoon, after collating the first batch of letters from St. Mary's parents and folks of eleven other parishes, volunteer Teresa Lee spins around from my office side table. "I have an idea. Let's send a pack of letters to the chairperson of immigration appeals saying, 'Dear Ms. Scialabba: Enclosed find sixty signed letters on behalf of our dear friend, Andes Imwa a.k.a. Regina Bakala. In the days ahead, a box of approximately 1,700 more letters will be arriving by regular mail.'"

I burst out laughing. "Perfect!"

"Then, let's add this: 'We are sending the same number of letters to Attorney General Alberto Gonzalez and another box to Wesley Lee in the Office of Detention and Removal. We are deeply concerned that Andes Regina Imwa finally receives justice. It is urgent that you move quickly.'"

I break into more laughter. "Amen, girl! Amen!"

"And we'll do the same with next week's batch."

This evening after standing in line for twenty minutes in Milwaukee's twenty-four-hour airport post office, I pull my luggage cart up to the counter, hand the clerk three cardboard express envelopes, and begin hoisting the heavy boxes. "These are letters to help Regina Bakala's case."

The clerk stares at me for a moment, then lights up. "That woman with the little kids? The one they want to deport to Congo?" Her eyes take on a sparkle. "Our church is praying for her."

I hand her a "Save Regina" button. "Keep praying."

With big windows and glass doors framing Wednesday's sunshine, the near end of St. Mary's cafeteria is quietly abuzz with twenty or thirty kids in after-school care. Lydia spots me and comes running.

"Stir Zhsseff!" My name is a whir of two syllables.

I bend down to hug her.

I haven't seen the children in a while. Though I spend every night meeting with their daddy and "Uncle Baskell," the kids are usually asleep when I get there. A few weeks earlier when I arrived early enough to kneel with them at their bedside, Lydia directed that daddy pray first, then herself, then Christopher, then me. After the Sign of the Cross, her prayer was almost a mantra: "Dear God, please get Mommy out of jail soon. Please, dear God, get Mommy out of jail. Dear God, please. And bless DaddyandChristopherandmeandSterZhsseff and please, God, get Mommy out of jail soon! Dear God, *soon*. Amen."

As I look into her piercing eyes now, I remember how, as a baby, she had eyed me with suspicion, burying her face in her mother's neck until that glorious RCIA session when I was sitting across from her parents at the big maple table in our former parish office and she was crawling on the brown carpet. Suddenly I felt a little hand on my thigh, then a second one. Talking softly to her sweet little face, I gently picked her up and set her on my lap where, to my delight, she had promptly curled up and fallen asleep.

"Lydia, honey! How are you?"

She pulls back a bit, says nothing, her stunning dark eyes wide under long, curly lashes.

As I look up, the after-school teacher mouths the word "sad" over her head.

"Are you feeling sad?"

She nods, eyes like a lost fawn.

"I know, honey. I'm sad, too." I touch her silky cheek. "This is taking such a long time to get Mommy out of jail."

Suddenly jerking herself up to full height—all three and a half feet—she announces, "I want to help!"

As my mind scrambles for ideas, she continues, her voice loud and insistent, "Stir Zhsseff, *I can do it! I can help you!*"

I remember her determination as a baby. One day she had pulled herself up against a parish office chair, turned to look at us, then propelled herself full tilt, squealing with delight, across a six-foot span into Mommy's arms. She was just eight months old.

Now she is leaning forward, fists thrust straight down, eyes urgent. "I'm a *good* helper!"

Suddenly, I feel my throat tightening, the pent-up tears mounting behind my eyes. I hasten to reassure her, "Yes, honey. Yes, I'm sure you are. Yes, I need your help with . . . with . . . Oh, I know." I snap my fingers. "The flyers! We need to paste bright stickers on a big stack of posters to give out in the parishes."

The five-year-old bounds forward. "Let's go! Let's do it!"

"Whoa! I'm not ready yet. I've got the stickers but I still have to print them. I'll get my part done, then I'll bring the project down here tomorrow for your part, OK?"

She flashes a big grin—"Yes!"—then bounces back to her table.

As I head toward the stairs, I blow out a stream of relief, grateful for the grace that whipped that idea to mind.

Regina talks to her children every night. She told me that in one conversation Lydia had asked, "Mommy, what food do you eat in the jail? Do you drink your wine?" Then after a little while, she said, "Tell me what your lawyer says because I can tell Daddy. . . . Mommy, I'm gonna save your life."

24

LET MY PEOPLE GO!

The distant, intermittent ringing speeds toward me like an approaching train, then blasts me into consciousness. I bolt out of bed, race into the dark office, flick on the blazing light, and in a split second I have the phone to my ear.

"This is Correctional Billing Services. You have a collect call . . ."

My heart is hammering wildly. I squint at my watch—4:47.

Her voice is quiet. "Sister, the guard give me just one minute to talk. I have to take a quick shower because they are taking me to a judge in Chicago at 5:00. But don't worry, I know in my heart he's gonna release me. I think Mary Sfasciotti knows this."

My whole body goes cold. For a second I cannot speak. "Regina, if Mary knew anything, she would have told you. They're not taking you to a judge, they're getting ready to deport you."

"No. I'm not gonna be deport, Sister. My faith about this is firm."

"Regina, if they send you back, contact a priest in Congo. The Church will help you."

"You call Mary Sfasciotti, OK?"

"Yes! Right away!" My every muscle is on high alert. "Regina, remember, do not say anything or sign anything without Mary. I'll call her immediately."

"Don't panic, Sister. Call David, too, OK? The guard says I have to go now."

"OK. Call me again if you get a chance. I won't leave the house. We'll be pray—"

Click.

O God, this is it! It's up to me! I struggle to breathe. My whole body is shivering. I fumble for Mary's numbers. Her home phone rings forever. No answer, no voice mail. Cell phone, same story. I can't wake David with this news. He'll be up by six. I pace through the dark, praying. After ten minutes, I dial both Mary's numbers again. Nothing. I call every twenty minutes. It's futile.

At 6:30, I finally get hold of David. "The kids are here," he says calmly. "I'll come over after I get them to school and day care."

"No, stay there, David, in case she tries to phone you."

I answer a second collect call at 7:32. At the sound of her voice, I begin to calm down.

"Don't be scare, Sister. I'm not sure where I am, but I'm OK. Maybe it's Broadview—the place near Chicago—because I saw the mean guy, the one took me from my family, but today he did not talk."

ICE had transported eight detainees from Kenosha, seven men belly-chained together plus Regina in handcuffs and leg irons. She and a Chinese woman who speaks no English are locked in a tiny room with two chairs, a toilet, and a telephone. The window in the door is covered.

Twenty minutes later she calls again, worried that I've not yet reached Mary. I remind her of all who are praying for her. She recounts her earlier dreams. We buoy each other's spirits. Another twenty minutes—another call. Her voice is shaky. We tell each other not to worry.

Over the next hour, I wash, get dressed, and call all Mary's numbers, including her office. No answer. Pour some juice and try again. Nothing. Poke at my cereal, try again. Nothing.

At 9:10 Regina calls. ICE moved her and the Chinese woman to downtown Chicago, where they're sitting in a similar room on a hard bench with another Chinese woman who speaks a little English. Through a window, they can see people across the hall working behind a big glass window. "Maybe this is the Department of Homeland Security. I don't know. They don't tell us."

After another fruitless try to reach Mary at her office, I hear again from Regina. Officers took the other two, she doesn't know where. She feels afraid. We pray together. At 10:00, she calls again. We pray together until both of us are quieted.

After hanging up, I suddenly realize this is not a dreaded Thursday, but—hey! It's Wednesday, June 1: the day Mike Anderson of Channel 12 is scheduled to interview Mary. I reach him on his cell phone.

"They took her? Oh, no! We're almost there, Sister. I'll tell Mary to call you immediately. Where is Regina? I've got a cameraman . . ."

As I finish talking to Mike, Regina calls. I quickly tell her what's happening.

At 10:25, Mary Sfasciotti finally calls. "Oh, Sister. This could be it. If they're flying her out immediately, they'll have her call David to bring a suitcase today or tomorrow. Then again, if they don't have a passport, they may be working out a travel plan with a third country—South Africa or some place—and will need her signature on a visa application, so we may still have time. I'll call the BIA immediately. This gives her case high priority. Dr. Val's report just came in, so I'll add that as an immediate amendment. If Regina calls again, tell her to insist on phoning her lawyer. Then I'll know what we're dealing with. And please tell her, no matter what happens, even if they put her on a plane, not to give up. I will do everything in my power to stop the plane—on the runway if need be. I will not abandon her."

Between calls, I contact David and committee members, our pastor, Father Art, and the school principal, Jeanne Siegenthaler. Tracy promptly notifies the media and sets up an afternoon press conference. Bob e-mails me that Congresswoman Gwen Moore's office phoned the

BIA and was assured that Regina's case now has priority status. This means that within a day or two, the BIA will study Sfasciotti's motion to decide if the case merits review. If they decide to reopen it, they will stay the removal.

At noon, almost two hours since her last call, Regina phones again. "They finally took me. The guy says they cannot wait anymore for the BIA to rule on my case, so they made travel plans. He wants me to sign for the visa because they send me through South Africa. Then I tell them I want to take my children. But, Sister, they complain about the *cost*!"

I hold my breath—she *still* wants to take her children.

"I insist they call Attorney Mary Sfasciotti. Mary says to them in a mean voice, 'These little ones have a father here! They are American citizens! You want to send two little American citizens to die over there in Congo?' Then she told me, 'Honey, don't worry about the children now. We'll talk more later. Just sign the paper.'"

Thank God for Mary Sfasciotti!

Processing the visa will take a week, so Regina says she'll be returned to Kenosha today. On Tuesday, June 7, they'll take her back to the ICE processing facility in Broadview, Illinois. (When I later phone ICE for the exact name, I'll be told only that it's a staging area they call "Broadview"—hmm, welcome to the secret world of ICE.) Regina says David is to bring her suitcase, and Wednesday, June 8, she will fly out. They gave her a paper listing suitcase dimensions and regulations.

"Thank God, Regina. A lot can happen in one week."

"God's gonna do something, Sister."

"By the way, I want to thank you for calling me so often. Sometimes I was close to panicking. I needed the reassurance of your calls."

"Me, too, Sister. I call you every time when I was start to panic. That's when I phone."

Only later will I learn that Custom Teleconnect, contracted by Chicago DHS/ICE, charges $11.99 to connect and 98¢ per minute. Eight calls, thirty-nine minutes: $134.14.

At four o'clock, St. Mary's Gathering Space is heavy with silence. Tracy accepts my purse and gestures for David and me to go directly to the bank of microphones. Behind the grim TV crews stand a line of somber teachers and staff and a handful of school parents, some weeping. I recount the day's events, answer a few questions, then step aside for David, but he hesitates.

He hunches toward me, his eyes frantic. "What?" he whispers. "What I gonna say?"

I huddle closer. "Just thank the people for their concern. Ask them to pray."

He steps up to the microphones, juts out his chin, glances quickly around, then hesitates again—the emaciated prisoner, still staring in silent dread. I move closer, putting my hand, fingers splayed, between his shoulder blades.

"It is a very hard time for my family. I thank you for your prayers for my wife and our family." He hesitates, shifts his stance, clears his throat. "Thank you. Thank you very much."

Tonight at 8:40, Regina calls from Kenosha. Tired as she is, she sounds elated. "I did not know that these women care so much about me!"

When the guard had unlocked the heavy door and Regina walked into the dorm, she says, everyone froze for a moment, then burst into cheers. They ran to hug her, several of them crying.

"I was so surprise! I did not know they love me like this! For weeks, they follow the TV stories, but"—her voice drops—"I did not know they really care. Then I explain that if nothing happens, ICE will deport me Wednesday. Leticia says, 'You're *not* gonna be deport. When they come Tuesday, you're gonna go to your house.' Then they ask to pray for me."

She describes how she stood with her eyes closed and her palms upraised as the women joined hands in a great circle around her.

I hang up the phone, tears running down my face.

━━━━━━━

Thursday midmorning I swirl into St. Mary's parking lot. Darryl's car is already here. The guy is always early, his tall-dark-and-handsome self impeccably dressed in a tailored dark suit and crisp white shirt with a conservative tie, every inch the gracious and successful businessman. I have never seen him out of uniform or out of sorts. As I walk into the main office, he gives me a hug. "How are you, Sister?"

"OK, I guess . . . exhausted."

While he goes to welcome David and US congressman Paul Ryan, I head down the hall to the conference room.

Ryan, personable and clean-cut with intense blue eyes, is even better looking than in his campaign ads. Nonetheless, he strikes me as little more than a fidgety, fast-talking politician. Trailed by two staffers, he swings into the room, shakes hands, and sits down. His female staffer pulls out a notebook. Nobody wants coffee.

"Here's your copy of Regina's current case, Mr. Ryan. On top is a signed affidavit from David authorizing you to examine her documents."

He pushes the unopened box back to me. "That won't be necessary, Sister. Gwen Moore is the hands-on person for her constituent." Then he folds his hands and asks what he can do for us. With every idea I suggest, either he quickly turns to the aide with the notebook and asks, "We've already done that, haven't we?" or he says that the separation of powers won't allow him to do it.

Our meeting is over and photos taken in less than ten minutes. After Ryan's entourage is gone and David has headed back to work, I comment, "Well, that was much ado about nothing."

Darryl maintains his smile but shakes his head. "Sister, even if he's limited in what he can do, Paul Ryan genuinely cares about Regina. He's a good man, Sister. A very good man."

"I'm not impressed."

Only much later will I learn that Paul Ryan himself crossed the aisle in the US House of Representatives to advise Milwaukee's junior congresswoman on how to help Regina.

I hand Darryl the box Ryan pushed away. "You'll need to understand her case before flying to Washington Sunday. I'm not going with you, Darryl. I can't be that far from her family during this crisis."

His face softens. "You belong here, Sister. I just hope I can do a good enough job on my own." He looks down, his eyes watery. "If there's anything else that might help me . . ."

I put my hand on his arm. "Darryl, you're perfect for this. You're intelligent, personable, savvy, and just humble enough to do a great job. In fact, this may be why God sent you to us."

He puffs out a stream of air.

I give him a hug. "We'll talk more before you go."

Mary Sfasciotti calls tonight. While I was trying to organize a "Save Regina" prayer vigil for Sunday night, she was in federal court filing for an emergency stay of removal to keep Regina in America. "Hopefully it will work. Keep prayin', girl!" she says.

Praying and working like a maniac, partly to stave off my own fear and partly to keep hope alive in everyone else. Meanwhile, Tracy is feeding the media, Bob and Leon are working the officials, and Darryl is tracking our BIA lobbying effort.

I open my e-mail. A parent writes: "As of 9:30 this morning the lady I spoke with at the Board of Immigration Appeals had already received twenty-six phone calls about Regina's case. They are overwhelmed by all the support. Her bosses' bosses—the higher-ups—are now reviewing her case." Bob also e-mails, noting that Representative Gwen Moore's office is "upbeat." He wonders if she knows something we don't.

A Saturday wedding of one of my RCIA candidates transports me into another world, but only for a while. Home by 8:30, I change clothes and dash to St. Mary's to meet Darryl so we can talk while I photocopy additional information for his trip to Washington.

"So who is this mysterious connection you have in Washington, D.C., Darryl?"

"Hector Flores, my father's best friend. They were migrant workers whose families grew up near each other in Texas. Hector went to college, became a police officer, did civil rights work for the federal government, and now works for the Dallas Independent School District. He's also the president of LULAC, League of United Latin American Citizens, the oldest Hispanic civil rights organization in the United States. LULAC also has the largest immigration lobby in Washington. Executive Director Brent Wilkes set up a Monday appointment for me with legal counselors to the Senate Judiciary Committee for our senators, Feingold and Kohl."

"That's terrific!"

"Brent will also get me phone access to immigration higher-ups, but a connection depends on who's in, when." He takes a deep breath. "Keep praying for me, OK? I've been up until all hours studying Regina's case. I keep thinking she could die if I blow it."

"Ohh, don't put yourself under that kind of pressure, Darryl. Just do your best."

"That's what I mean. I have to do my best."

After Sunday Mass, Darryl says he woke up rested and at peace. A small group of us lay hands on him, asking God's blessing.

On Sunday, the sky is purpling and the sun has faded to an orange smear above the treetops as the full bevy of media personnel and 200 to 250 somber people gradually gather in St. Mary's for tonight's prayer service, "Let My People Go!" In the church's amber glow, we listen to God's words to Moses from the Book of Exodus 6:5–6 : "I have heard the cries of the Israelites. . . . I am mindful of my covenant. I am the Lord. I will free you . . ." We weep, we pray, we sing.

In a closing reflection, our pastoral minister, Mary Matestic, says, "In reality, Regina could lose this battle, but I believe that she will not lose the war." She calls us to stand in solidarity with the Bakala family, absorbing the pain. "All prophetic insight begins in grief, but it does not stay there. It moves to righteous anger, which seeks to change systems. It moves toward setting *many* captives free. And it moves to an in-break of the Reign of God."

The Reign of God. I sit up straight. How often have I taught that the Reign of God is the loving care we freely give one another? It's happening . . . in *me.* This struggle has broken my heart, opened my eyes, set me free to act for justice. And in the process, I've found a huge family. I no longer "feel like a motherless child, a long way from home."

Channel 12's ten o'clock extended coverage begins with various clips of Regina, the school principal, and me. Then Mike Anderson interviews Gail Montenegro, Chicago spokesperson for Immigration and Customs Enforcement, a beautiful brunette, probably in her thirties, with an up-to-the-minute short hairstyle. She wears a pale blue suit and white collared shirt. Her earrings are small dangling discs. Behind her a bright blue flag bears a stylized white eagle in flight, ringed by the words "United States Department of Homeland Security."

"Ms. Bakala had every opportunity to present her case to the Immigration Courts, and it was denied. It was also denied on appeal," she says. "She has exhausted all legal avenues, and we are doing our job now in enforcing the deportation order against her."

"So, basically, you're saying it's her own fault?" asks Mike.

Her words are measured. "I'm saying she had her day in court and was unable to prove her claim, and now she has been ordered deported from the United States, and as ICE under the Department of Homeland Security, it is now our responsibility to enforce that judge's order." Ms. Montenegro leans forward, her face animated. "How can anyone be sympathetic to someone who was found to have *lied* to an immigration judge and presented *false* documents in the courtroom?"

"She did that?"

Her eyes widen. "Yes!"

The scene switches to a foot-high stack of legal papers as another woman says, "I read her transcript. I thought the judge just walked all over her. And her attorney just sat there passively."

The camera zeroes in on a frowning blond woman, sixty-something, with law books and papers lined up on one side of her gray desk. She wears a sharp black suit and collarless, cream-colored top with swirling black lines. As she continues talking, Mike's voiceover introduces Regina's "new tough-as-nails Chicago lawyer, Mary Sfasciotti."

So that's what she looks like, I muse. Large capiz shell hoop earrings and stylish short hair frame a pretty face, which at the moment is riveted on Mike.

He asks, "Is it true that her story had been fabricated?"

"No. The problem with her case is that the court didn't recognize rape as persecution." As she continues, Mike's voiceover summarizes the issue. Mary picks up again, cocking her head in mock horror, "Rape? Feminists note when a woman cried rape, they'd ask, 'How many men she had slept with?' She was treated in a really derogatory fashion. He [the judge] didn't think rape fit under the asylum statute as persecution and didn't know what was happening in Congo to begin with!" She clips her words. "Now we know that what she was saying was probable. Was credible. Was true."

The camera switches to David before tonight's service. He lifts his chin in a futile attempt to stave off tears. "I'm very . . . to all the people"—as he starts to cry, he swipes his hand from forehead to chin, but the mask barely holds—"who . . . help my family . . ." He looks down, swipes his face again, then jerks up, turning away as he struggles to finish: ". . . help Regina case."

As he breaks down, the camera returns to a head shot of Regina in jail: "I can't go back to my country." She, too, looks close to tears, but her voice manages to stay steady. "I can't. They gonna kill me." She pauses slightly, her eyes riveted on Mike. "I wanna save my life."

25

"Now, God, Now!"

Monday morning, I sit at my cluttered kitchen table thinking about Regina as I pore over my notes on trauma: "Early childhood abandonment exacerbates any adult trauma."

The death of her mother, the loss of her childhood, her arrest, the double rape in Idiofa, months in Idiofa's jail, the death knell of that final rape, the loss of husband and homeland, the struggles with lawyers, the judge's decision, nine years of uncertainty, then being snatched like a criminal from her terrified children, her psychological pain—"like somebody is burning me, but I cannot die"—being carted in shackles from Kenosha to Broadview to Chicago with no clarity about what was happening—layer upon festering layer. "Is too much, Sister. Too much," she said in this morning's call.

Last week, before sending Dr. Val's detailed psychological report to the BIA, Mary had assured me, "Not only did Dr. Val find that Regina is telling the truth, but in her report, she cites clear examples from Regina's various tests of the rapes' long-lasting and devastating effects."

Trauma alters a person's worldview, replacing a personal sense of well-being and safety with pervasive fear. I spent decades in hypervigilance, and my panic attacks lasted into my early forties. What must it be like for Regina and David?

I remember the terror I saw in both of them on September 11. Earlier that day, I had been too dazed to check on them, but on my way home from a tearful Mass that night, I drove to their apartment.

"It's OK. It's me—Sister Josephe," I called through the chained and dead-bolted door.

Regina fussed with the locks then carefully pulled open the door.

They stood like lost waifs, their eyes saucers.

"What we gonna do now, Sister?" she said, her voice small, her shoulders hunched.

"What do you mean?" I asked.

"We can't go out anymore!" said David with a sweeping gesture toward the street.

"You've been locked in this apartment all day?" I was stupefied. "Why?"

Regina leaned toward me, her upturned palms shaking. "We are immigrants!"

"The American people," said David, "we don't know what they will do to us."

For a moment I could not speak. "No, David. You're OK," I insisted. "Besides, the immigrants who hijacked the planes were from the Middle East."

Regina's eyes pleaded with me. She was insistent. "Our skin is black."

I wanted to weep.

When I got my bearings, I said in my best common-sense tone, "Look, there are plenty of black Americans in Milwaukee. You'll be OK. And you are personally loved by many white people—hundreds from St. Mary's alone!" I dropped my voice, hoping my firmness would help. "You are safe. You can leave the house." I looked from one skeptical face to the other. "*Really . . . I promise. You'll be OK.*"

The conversation had haunted me.

Today, their lives *do* hang in the balance. Shuddering, I stand up and step out onto my tiny kitchen porch. The bright air, cold against my skin, jars me into the present where firecracker tulips and spears of sturdy new grass are all shouting hope as loud as wedding bells. I take a deep breath. Regina seemed OK this morning, grateful that each day her dorm mates join hands, encircling her in prayer. But David . . . his weight loss—eighteen pounds these eleven weeks—his repeated need for a translator, his dismay in front of the microphone. I remember now how befuddled he seemed on Easter, while I was preoccupied with our late start. Regina herself chided him for Lydia not wearing her Easter dress. Gosh, he even forgot to give the kids their Easter baskets for six weeks. I walk back inside and plunk myself down at the table, tears flowing. I can see his furrowed face and sad eyes, his stooped shoulders, the lost look that barricades him from others. "Every trauma prolongs and deepens the effects of every subsequent trauma," I had once written.

O God, David is being undone.

My tears become sobs. I hammer my fist against the table top. *NOW, God! You've got to stop this NOW!* Grabbing my Bible and a wad of tissues, I walk into my bedroom where I kneel against my unmade bed, hugging my Bible and burying my wet face in the crumpled bedding.

"Hi, Sister. Who was it you wanted me to ask the judiciary lawyers to contact?" asks Darryl, calling mid-morning from D.C.

"Wesley Lee, the acting head of ICE's Office of Detention and Removal."

"Well, guess what." He laughs. "I myself just talked to him."

"That's incredible!"

"I was amazed at how quickly LULAC got him on the line, someone we had no other way to reach. After about ten minutes of conversation, Mr. Lee said he was already familiar with the case and agreed to personally look into it."

Days later Darryl would tell me that after lunch, he had caught a cab to the Hart Senate Office Building, where Attorney Lara Flint from Senator Russ Feingold's office welcomed him. Though *ABC News* was not allowed into the meeting, they filmed him saying, "We will not give up until we have saved Regina." As he entered the room, the camera zoomed in on the glass door: "Office of the Judiciary Committee to the US Constitution."

"See these petitions? Twenty-seven on a page," he began, fanning a four-inch stack. "I could fill this room with the names of people supporting Regina." Carl Hampton, also from Feingold's office, and Nate Jones from Senator Kohl's office told him not to rush. "Good," said Darryl as he slid inch-thick packs across the table to each of the three lawyers, "because we're going to review this entire case. Since it's is so complex, I also wrote an overview of all pertinent points." He handed each a presentation folder.

Two hours later, Ms. Flint said, "I can't believe you're not an attorney." Carl thanked him. Nate Jones added, "Coming into this meeting, I was prepared to ask some tough questions, but you have answered them all." The three left determined to take immediate action.

"I knew I had their support and they would talk to the senators, but was it enough? Did I miss anything?" While packing up, Darryl had still worried, "*Regina could die if I messed up.*"

It's 3:10 and I am restlessly awaiting news from him when the phone rings.

"Hi, Sister. It's Mary."

"Oh, Mary, wait till you hear what Darryl's been doing in Washington, D.C."

"Sister—"

"He's gotten wonderful access. This morning he—"

"Sister!"

"Let me tell you briefly—"

"*Sister!*"

I stop.

"I just got word. The BIA reopened her case."

I can't breathe. "O my God." Sobs belch up from somewhere too deep for words.

"Don't you cry now, girl!" says Mary. Her voice lowers. "I really can't believe it, Sister. You have no idea what a long shot this is!"

"Does Regina know? Did you call her?"

"Not yet. I don't want to label anything a victory until it's a sure thing. Indulge me, please. I need to phone them directly just to be really, really sure. I'll call you back as soon as I find out."

I have no doubts, only awe. *Oh, thank you, God. Thank you. Thank you.*

I quickly change clothes and am pinning a silk rose on my lapel when the phone rings again. "It's true," Mary says. "They based their decision on her husband's favorable ruling. I'll fax it as soon as it arrives. They're remanding her case back to the original judge in Atlanta. We'll try later to get the venue changed to Chicago."

"Thank you, Mary," I squeak out between tears. "When will they free her?"

"That's a separate action. Probably in a few days. The big news is that she is getting a new hearing." Her voice turns solemn. "Sister, I can't tell you what an outright miracle this is."

It is the attorney's role to notify her client. "Did you call Regina, Mary?"

"No, Sister," she says. "You call her."

I tear up again. The only way to reach Regina is to phone the Detention Center and ask to have her call me, but as I grab my day planner for the number, the phone rings again.

"This is Correctional Billing Services . . ."

Wow. Is she clairvoyant or what? "Regina! We just got the best news. The *best news.* The Board of Immigration Appeals has decided to reopen your case."

"Oh! Oh! Thanks to God. God did it," she cries. I hear cheering in the background. "I cannot talk now. I have to tell the others," she shouts, then hangs up, leaving me laughing.

David's response is equally exuberant. "Ooh, praise to God!" His voice swells. "We prayed last night in the church that God would do it, and God did it. Thanks to God."

"There's a 4:30 press conference at St. Mary's. Be there with the kids *before* 4:30, OK?"

After calls to St. Mary's, the team, and my family, I head out the door into a blast of sunshine. Television trucks with tall antennas are already parked near the church entrance. Father Art and the staff are all smiles and congratulations. Carolyn hands me the faxed decision.

While I head for the photocopier, I spot-read the four pages.

Since the respondent's husband was found to have established that he would face a clear probability of persecution if he returned to the DRC, the respondent believes that the security forces in the DRC would impute to her a political opinion based on her husband's activities in the CNRD [political party]. The respondent indicates in her motion that security forces would seek retribution against her, and in support of her claims she has submitted Country Reports and articles regarding the troubling country conditions in the DRC. The Board finds that, in this case, the respondent has met the general requirements for reopening . . .

They point out that their decision should not be misconstrued as overturning the judge's determination of adverse credibility. They are troubled that the dates in her court testimony do not match those in her affidavit. They also note that she offered no explanation as to why she failed to mention the August 30, 1994, customary marriage when she applied for asylum.

"We're ready for you, Sister!" says Tracy, swinging into the office. "The media are all here and a small crowd is gathering."

"Wow, I guess the word is out."

"Channel 12 interrupted *Oprah* with a crawling banner: 'Breaking news—Regina Bakala's asylum case is reopened!' Hey"—she laughs— "we knew we'd get on *Oprah* one way or another."

I quickly scan the closing paragraph.

. . . respondent's deportation proceedings will be reopened . . .
record will be remanded to the Immigration Judge. . . . The respondent and DHS will also have the opportunity to present evidence
at the hearing regarding conditions in the DRC and the respondent's persecution claim. The respondent may also request that the
Immigration Judge consider an application for deferral of removal
as provided by the Convention Against Torture.

As Tracy and I arrive in the gathering space, cameras swing in my
direction and a cheer goes up from staff, teachers, parents, and friends.
Giddy with delight, I leap into a quick two-step and pump my fist.
"Yes!" I shout. "We did it!"

Tracy had directed the media to set up the bank of microphones in
front of a bold four-panel tapestry depicting the rising sun with jubi-
lant, swirling rays. Next to the tapestry, tall maple doors open into the
church. She distributes copies of the decision as Bob runs back to photocopy more.

I take my place in front of the mikes. The room quiets. Though
David has not yet arrived, reporters signal me to start. I share how the
news came, explain briefly why her case now rests on David's, marvel
at what an amazing victory this is, then answer questions and thank
everybody.

David is expected any minute. Photographers train their cameras on
the big cedar doors.

We wait and wait. And wait a little more.

Finally folks near the windows spot his car. Cameras move in, a hush
comes over the group.

When the door swings open, David's arms are spread wide, holding
up the hands of his children on either side. His eyes are bright, his face
alive, his grin radiant. I see why he's late. He's wearing a white, short-
sleeved camp shirt over brown slacks and sandals, and his children are in
fresh, bright-colored shorts and T-shirts. Behind them traipse a number
of Congolese in African shirts and dresses, everyone clapping and cheer-

ing. Flanked by his children, David heads straight to the microphones. He needs no prompting, no hand on his back, no translator.

"Today we thank God," he proclaims. "Last night we pray *right here* . . . in *this* church!" He gestures toward the maple doors. "And today God answer our prayer." He does not fumble for words. "Next I want to thank everybody who support us. You are wonderful. I feel happy, not just for myself"—he opens his arms wide—"but for all the people working for this case."

A reporter bends down to Christopher, who stands close to his daddy's leg. "How do you feel now that your mommy will be coming home?"

The little guy does not smile. He leans toward the reporter, jabbing the air with his fist. "I'm gonna BREAK the MEER!"

"The meer?" A murmur ripples through the group.

Lydia translates, "He wants to break the mirror . . . the glass. The big glass in the jail between him and Mommy."

On Mother's Day, Christopher had not been allowed to give Mommy the dandelion he had picked for her. He had to leave the little flower on the ledge in front of the thick Plexiglas.

When I arrive at the crowded Bakala home tonight, Lydia swings open the screen door then runs to the kitchen, Christopher on her heels. "Daddy, Stir Zhsseff is here!"

Former Congolese senator Gauthier Sikisi Mukubi, whom we all call Sikisi, and his wife, Charlotte, are all smiles when they see me. They, along with their children, had won asylum years earlier. However, the United States decided his two brothers were not in danger and deported them. Neither was ever heard from again.

I hug them both. "You are such brave people. Thank you for all your support."

Papa Kadima and a few others are also preparing to leave. David tells the children it's bedtime, and one of the women shepherds them to their room. The rest of us crowd into the tiny living room late for the nine o'clock news. David and I are given prime seats on the high-backed living room couch, our knees pushing against the mahogany cocktail table. Pascal and two others take the settee and chair. The rest perch on chair arms. All eyes are fixed on the FOX 6 News anchor, whose face fills the thirty-six-inch screen less than six feet in front of us.

Last year after putting the down payment on their first home, David, drawing on his twelve years as purchaser for Kinshasa's Hotel Intercontinental, had picked out this handsome burgundy-and-forest green furniture with matching drapes, mahogany tables, and brass lamps. But what seemed perfect in the expansive showroom felt strangely crowded in their modest living room. The day it was delivered, Regina shook her head. "It's too big." But like most immigrants clinging to big American dreams, David had folded his arms. "No," he had said. "The house is too small."

As the station goes to commercial, Pascal remarks that we probably missed Regina's story, but someone else assures us that all newscasts should have it at ten.

"Well, tomorrow will be the *big* story," says David, "when we pick her up!"

My heart sinks. "Oh no, David," I moan. "I'm so sorry to tell you this, but we will not be able to bring her home until ICE gives the order to release her."

He laughs. "Yes! Tomorrow. We pick her up in the morning."

"No, David. We have to wait for—"

"Regina called me at suppertime. We pick her up in Broadview tomorrow morning."

I bolt upright. "Regina called? Wow! Tomorrow? This is huge." Everyone laughs as I fumble for my cell phone to call Tracy.

At 10:00 P.M., all Milwaukee channels lead with: "Breaking news! This just in."

A few more phone calls, and plans are set: Principal Jeanne Siegenthaler and the school kids will plan a two o'clock surprise celebration to welcome her home. The media will be there.

Home before midnight, I post details on the website, send a lengthy e-mail to the multitudes, then print out directions to Broadview. It's almost 4 A.M. when I hit the pillow.

The phone blasts me out of bed at 6 A.M.

"Good morning, Sister. This is Paul Kern of WLIP, Kenosha."

I have trouble masking my fury. "You woke me after two hours of sleep, Paul. I sent you an e-mail at 2:15 A.M. to be sure you had all the details in writing."

"Is she going to be released from Kenosha or Broadview, Illinois?"

The guy didn't read the e-mail. "Broadview."

"Thank you, Sister." He pauses. "Sorry."

I bite my tongue, blow away the fog, try to say something nice, then bumble my way back to bed. Another hour of sleep would be delicious, but I quickly give up and get dressed.

At 7:40, Regina calls from Broadview. ICE had picked her up at 4:00 to go to Illinois.

"Good Lord! You've been in Illinois since what? 5 A.M.? 6 A.M.?"

She laughs. "These people, Sister. *Tsk.* Why they can't release me in Kenosha? Why they have to come in the night, lock me in the handcuffs and chains, all that? Make my family come extra miles to Illinois to get me? It's crazy."

"Where are you now? In that little room?"

"No. They give me a choice. I can wait in that room in my jail clothes or I can change into my own clothes, but then I have to wait outside. So I tell them I will wait outside."

"In your pajamas?"

"Yes."

We both laugh.

"I'm going to tell the media—'The Department of Homeland Security has Regina Bakala waiting for her family outside, shivering in her pajamas!' Is there a place to sit down?"

"No, I just stand. When are you coming?"

"We won't be there for another three hours, ten thirty or so. Tell those people they must let you wait inside . . . on a chair."

"*Nooo*, Sister. They say once I sign out, I am out. I signed right away."

Later, I will find out that as Milwaukee's TV trucks began arriving, the officer in charge invited Regina to wait inside.

"He was nice. He says he wants to protect me from their questions until my family comes."

Right.

The village of Broadview is a mere 1.8-square-mile patch in the vast quilt of metropolitan Chicago. Thirteen miles west of downtown Chicago, we turn off the Eisenhower Expressway to wend our way quickly into a nondescript, mostly treeless industrial area.

"Wait, this can't be right," I say, looking again at the map.

"Look! The media is here," says driver Pascal.

Milwaukee's TV trucks are parked on the weedy gravel under the blaring sun. Seeing us, the cameramen swing into action, stepping out to train their cameras on David's Honda Odyssey.

To our left is the barren-looking Lehigh Press–Cadillac Printing plant and loading docks. To our right, a makeshift bank of microphones wait in front of a locked chain-link gate, and farther down, back from the road, a mostly windowless, brown brick building squats behind a clump of trees and bushes, offering no clues on the outside as to what it is. Only much later will I notice the tell-tale security cameras trained on the building and adjacent lot. We bumble down a short stretch of road, Pascal looking for a place to park, the rest of us straining to find Regina. Just beyond the mysterious brick structure, Pascal turns the minivan around to head back toward the TV trucks.

As we pass the brown building again, the kids suddenly come alive. "Mommy! Mommy!"

Regina has materialized from inside. She stands shadowed by the trees in her slippers and pajamas—black bottoms and grey top with two red stripes down the long sleeves. Her short hair is in tiny cornrows. She stays near the building while Pascal maneuvers the minivan toward a parking place, but with the kids clambering to get out, he stops in the road.

Lydia flies into Mommy's open arms with Christopher right behind her. Regina bends down, holding them both, tears flowing. Congolese friends in bright African dress run squealing and cheering to hug her. One of them, Claudine Tezzo, had come with us. Charlotte and Sikisi drove in their own car. Regina reaches out her arms for me, both of us crying. As she finishes hugging all of us, she walks toward David, who has been watching patiently from the gravel roadside about fifteen feet away.

We stand back in silence as he gathers her in, pressing her head against his chest. In a few moments, he loosens his hold enough to look into her face, then kisses her, and again closes his eyes and holds her close. The media keeps a respectful distance, though I presume cameras are rolling. As they finish, David steps back.

"When you're ready," says one of the reporters, gesturing toward the microphones twenty yards down the road.

David takes her hand as the children bounce ahead. The rest of us follow.

Facing a bank of microphones for the first time, Regina momentarily closes her eyes, then looks into the face of a nearby reporter. "First of all, I thank God for everything he do for me!" She then thanks all who supported her and her family. She's glad to be out of jail and eager to go home.

As the interview draws to a close, Lydia clambers for her attention. "Mommy! Mommy! Now can we go to the zoo?"

The laughter feels wonderful. (Later, after the quote hits the news, two families will offer the Bakalas tickets for the Milwaukee County Zoo.)

We climb into the minivan, David and Regina in back, Claudine and the kids in the middle seat, Pascal and myself up front. My cell phone rings. The *Charlie Sykes Show* stands by as I hand the phone back to Regina for her second interview. Somehow we manage to keep the kids quiet as we drive to a local McDonald's and wait in the parking lot for the interview to end.

When we get inside, Regina heads for the restroom, carrying the small bag of clothes David brought and, a few minutes later, emerges in black slacks and a soft, gray top patterned with small white flowers. Her feet are in black slides. "At last I'm in my own clothes!"

The phone calls do not stop. Congolese friends call her on Claudine's cell phone; the Associated Press finds her on mine.

On the way home, I suggest we stop first at St. Mary's to thank God together. "I think some people there will also want to welcome you home."

The air conditioning keeps a steady hum while in the seats behind Pascal and me the voices of the children on either side of Charlotte gradually soften into intermittent chatter. I hear David and Regina in the backseat, talking in sibilant Lingala and periodically breaking into laughter. I look at Pascal. He, too, is grinning.

The parking lot is full of parents' cars at this time of day, but media trucks are also here. As we pull up to the main church doors, a few cheering adults are outside to greet her—parishioners, her boss, some of the Save Regina Committee and at least five cameramen. Claudine keeps the kids buckled in until Regina and David climb out from the back. As soon as folks see her, they rush to hug her. She moves to the next and the next, cameramen backpedaling in front of her to catch every angle. As we go through the cedar doors into the large gathering space, more are waiting in a hodge-podge line leading toward the church doors.

In the church itself, four-hundred-some children plus parents, teachers, staff members, Regina's co-workers, parishioners, and friends are waiting in whisper quiet for her to appear in the doorway. As she nears the church doors, principal Jeanne Siegenthaler holds her in a prolonged hug, tears flowing freely, then leads her through the doorway.

With deafening cheers, the church explodes in joy—kids everywhere, arms thrust in the air waving American flags, homemade signs, big posters, cards. The din is overwhelming.

Regina throws her arms up, then clutches her hands to her heart and bursts into tears. As her knees buckle, Jeanne and Claudine grab her to keep her from falling. The *Journal Sentinel* photographer squats in front of her to get the perfect shot while TV cameramen bob and weave with her every move. The jubilation continues as she makes her way up the aisle, cameramen in front, family and friends behind. Shell-shocked, she pauses at random pews to hold some people's hands, to hug others. "Thank you! Thank you!" she says. At times she just bows her head and crosses her hands over her heart, too overwhelmed to speak.

The podium is ringed with microphones. When she gets to the front, David, Lydia, and Christopher walk with her up the three sanctuary stairs to the podium. Lydia's kindergarten friend presents a multicolored spray of flowers as big as she is. Cheers continue as two older girls, one of them Lydia's big sister, Cara, carry up a huge, signature-filled banner that shouts in bright red, "Welcome home, Mrs. Bakala!"

Regina pauses, then speaks slowly, deliberately. "First, I have to thank God. If I'm here, it's because of him!" She points upward. "My faith in God kept me strong in the jail." She thanks everybody for the prayers and support. Looking around, tears roll down her face. "I have never seen this love in all my life. Thank you for your love." She can hardly speak. "Thank you! Thank you!"

On the evening news, Andrew Cesarz, a bright, lanky seventh grader, offers his comment along with a caution. "I was surprised. I really didn't think her case would be reopened. I'm very glad she's free, but it isn't over yet, you know. She still has to go through another hearing."

PART IV
WHERE IS HOME?

26

BLESS THE CHILDREN

Three days after her release, I pick up Regina for her first office appointment with Mary.

"It's good to be home. To sleep in my own bed is a big relief." Regina buckles her seatbelt, then shakes her head. "But I worry about my children. Last night when I tell them I must go to Chicago today, they was *very* upset, afraid I won't come back."

I wince. Mental health professionals warn that the abrupt removal of a parent leads to separation anxiety, depression, post-traumatic stress, and even suicidal thoughts in children.

"Finally, I tell them, 'But *Sister Josephe* is going with me.' Then they was OK, because they think the police will not take me if I am with Sister Josephe." She catches my crooked smile. "Yeah, I'm glad I thought to say that, but, Sister, they want to be with me *all* the time, even just to go to the grocery store. And they are *very* scare of the police. Yesterday I was driving, they see a policeman, they quick get down"—she swirls her hands near the floorboards—"tell me to get away quick. I say, 'No, these police are not the ones took Mommy away. These are the *good* police who help us.' But they are still afraid . . . all the time they are afraid."

"I'll help you find a good child counselor," I say, but inside, I feel a thrumming anger.

The Convention on the Rights of the Child, the most widely and rapidly ratified human rights treaty in history, states:

> In all actions concerning children, whether undertaken by public or private social welfare institutions, courts of law, administrative authorities or legislative bodies, the best interests of the child shall be a primary consideration. . . . [Article 3 (1)]
>
> The child shall in particular be provided the opportunity to be heard in any judicial and administrative proceedings affecting the child, either directly, or through a representative or an appropriate body. [Article 12 (2)]

Only two countries in the world have not yet ratified the Convention on the Rights of the Child: the failed state of Somalia and the United States of America.

Nowadays, our country, which once worked so hard for international human rights legislation—including the family's right to protection by the state—is tearing apart thousands of families, many of them families of *legal* permanent residents like Leticia and Emma. In other immigrant families, an estimated 3.1 million children who are American citizens by birth have at least one parent living here illegally. Though illegal presence is not a criminal offense, ICE daily rips away their parents, leaving our most vulnerable little citizens at profound psychological risk. For every two adults ICE detains, one American child is left behind. Most have one parent left, but some lose their only parent or both parents. The majority of these little American citizens are under age ten.[1]

Mary Sfasciotti enters her tiny reception room, all smiles and flashing brown eyes, "It's so good to see you, Regina! And to finally meet you, Sister." Her modest office is on the twelfth floor of a matronly old building in Chicago's Loop. After warm hugs and accolades, I comment on the fresh floral arrangement on a side table. "What a gracious way to welcome your clients."

"A surprise from your committee." She grins. "It made my day. Truthfully, without God's help, I could never have done this. I remember exactly where I was standing the night you asked me to take her case, Sister. I told you I was exhausted, but what you didn't know is that my ninety-year-old mother was close to death. She still is. I don't know how much longer I'll have her."

Regina's response is immediate: "Oh, Mary!"

"She's a wonderful mother, Regina. At age twenty-three, she and my dad immigrated from Italy, so my becoming an immigration lawyer was a big deal. 'Remember one thing,' she would say. 'Always do things in the image of God. When you get one dollar, you give two dollars of service.' Her heart was for the little guy, the one with no one to help him. When she saw me on TV talking about your case, she told everybody, 'I'm so proud of her!'"

"You share her heart, Mary." I smile.

Her face looks worn. "I fought so hard for Regina, all the while fearing that whatever I did would not be enough. Last weekend was terrible for me. I'm so sorry, Regina. I just couldn't get myself to visit you in jail. I was exhausted and depressed every morning." She looks at me, remnants of worry around her eyes. "These last minute petitions are almost *never* successful!"

She puts an arm around Regina. "I'm so glad you're still in America!" Then she walks us into her office. Motioning us toward the two guest chairs, she takes the swivel chair behind her desk. "We don't yet have a date for your master calendar hearing in Atlanta, Regina, but when we do, I'm hoping to get Judge Cassidy to transfer your case to Chicago. Meanwhile, until your case is resolved, you are officially on parole. This means you must report monthly to the Chicago Office of the Department of Homeland Security."

"Wait a minute," I say. "Why not have her report to the DHS Office in Milwaukee?"

Mary leans forward, mischief in her eyes. "Sister, you forget we are dealing with the Great Immigration Bureaucracy. Logic is not part of the equation."

"Right!" I laugh. "That's why ICE could not release Regina in Kenosha or in Milwaukee. They had to transport her sixty miles farther to Broadview, Illinois . . . in shackles! . . . before daylight! . . . so she could stand outside at 6 A.M. in her pajamas . . . for hours until—oops!—the media showed up."

Before Sunday's 9:30 Mass, Father Art invites Regina into the sanctuary. TV cameras are rolling as nine hundred parishioners stand applauding. She looks lovely—straight black skirt and patterned white top, her hair professionally cut and smoothed back from her radiant face. There's something humble about Regina—humble but elegant. Maybe it's her courage, maybe her faith. I remember sitting with her in my living room when she would open her worries to me. Afterward, we would close our eyes in prayer. Each time, I was invited into a luminous sanctuary all her own, so rich with the assurance of God's love that her clamor for solutions was quickly hushed. That would be all she needed. "Thank you, Sister. It's gonna be OK now."

Today she stands at the podium looking too nervous to smile as she waits for the applause to die down. She blinks rapidly, then regains her composure as the congregation sits down.

"The first thing I want to say is to thank God. It is because of God that I am here today."

The congregation applauds again.

"And I thank each of you for your prayers and your letters, for how you help my family, for everything you do for me." She weighs each word. "I tell you the truth. *You* are my family that God give to me. I never experience love like this, not in my *whole* life. Thank you for your love!"

More applause.

"I am a mother, so you know it was very hard for me in the jail. All the time I was worry about my little children, how they can grow up without their mother. If I am deport, I want to take them with me. But

I also know in my heart, it is too dangerous for them to go with me to Congo. This was the hardest thing. All the time I struggle.

"Last weekend you was praying for me. That's the time I know God wants me to be like Abraham in the Bible who give up his son Isaac. God was testing Abraham to see if he can trust that God's not gonna hurt Isaac. So finally I said yes to God's decision. 'You are my Father. I trust you. If you want me to stay here in America, I will thank you; if you want me to leave my husband and children and go back to my country, I will thank you.' Then I give my children to God."

As we head for the parking lot after stopping at a bake sale for the Regina Bakala Fund, I ask Regina, "What happened to the other mothers, Leticia and Norma, who were jailed with you?"

"Leticia's family told me this week she was deport. We were good friends—Leticia, Norma, and me. We pray together. Leticia told me at the very beginning, 'You not gonna be deport. God told me you gonna stay here with your family.' I think she knew she was gonna be sent back to Mexico." She shakes her head. "Norma, too, is gone. Leticia and me, we tell her to get a lawyer, but she was too depress, no hope. Finally, when she sees my case on TV, she says maybe she get a lawyer, but it was too late. In a day or two, they sent her back to El Salvador." She turns to me, pain in her eyes. "I worry for their children, especially for Norma's little boy."

Three weeks after Regina's release, Congolese music sets a festive tone and scents of fried plantain entice patrons into Club Timbuktu's fundraiser. Patrick Ntula slides into a chair next to me, his voice insistent. "We *saved* Regina, Sister! We *did*!"

"I know, Patrick. Local Congolese said their relatives in Kinshasa are arming themselves with machetes in fear of a government crackdown next week on June 30."

"I'm not talking about the delayed elections, Sister. Read what the BBC posted today." He thrusts a web printout in front of me: "June 24, 2005: Netherlands halts Congo returns."

The Netherlands suspended the return of failed asylum seekers to the Democratic Republic of Congo. . . . Congolese officials are reported to have obtained confidential documents on several deportees and then abused them. . . . Human rights organizations had warned that deportees faced the serious risk of imprisonment, extortion and assault if unmasked as asylum-seekers.[2]

"Regina's Uncle Jérôme Akiewa warned about this in his letter," I say. "Thank God she's safe!"

Across the dining room, I see Regina laughing with a friend. Her mom has surely been praying with us. From this angle, they look so much alike—same mouth, same beautiful eyes.

Today, July 15, is Regina's birthday. I put the restored photo of her mother in its rustic, fourteen-by-sixteen wooden frame. The outer gilded edge has a wide inner frame stained deep red with gold filigree. Around the five-by-seven photo is a narrow, raised edge, also in gold. Josephine looks regal. Sister Caroline had prayed through the many hours it took her to restore the damaged image. I set the finished gift on my coffee table and stand back. Beautiful. Just beautiful.

Early this evening, I ring their doorbell.

"Mommy! Mommy!" shouts Lydia. "Stir Zhsseff is here with a present for you."

"Happy birthday," I call as she comes smiling from the kitchen. After hugs, she sits down on the settee, unties the blue satin ribbon, then pulls back the paper. The kids jump around urging her to hurry. I lift away the wrapping paper and ribbon as she opens the tissue.

"Oh! Oh! My mom!" she gasps, then hugs the photograph. Her eyes brim. "Thank you, thank you!"

As the kids scamper off, I return the original to Regina, then hand her a brown envelope with duplicates for Uncle Basil and Aunt Julienne, her brothers and sisters, and her own children.

"My mom was wonderful, Sister. Everybody love her, *everybody*. She married too young—only fourteen years old. Her parents were divorce, so she took in her two younger brothers and sister and her mom. Besides caring for them, she raised nine other kids—eight from our family and the son of Aunt Véronique, who was not so good with children."

Regina looks again at the photo. "I remember the day she help one homeless lady, let her take a shower at our house, and treat her sore foot. She gave her some of her own clothes and something to eat at our table. Later, my brother refuse to use the plate or the fork, but my mother said, 'No, Lucién. She is a person just like you.' They became friends, my mom and this lady. That's why David and me, we welcome poor people in our house. For myself, my mom taught me how to cook the cassava leaves and chicken. That's why I am a good cook." She studies the photo. "I remember sitting under the lemon tree while she put polish on her fingernails. I ask her to put on my nails, too. She said, 'Yes, honey'—she always call me 'honey'—then she do for me."

She clears off a mahogany side table. "My mother belongs right here in the living room with me and my whole family."

———

During break time at an SSND gathering, I run into Sister Miriam Cecile Ross, the wise spiritual director who had helped me through my roughest years dealing with mother issues.

"Josephe!" she laughs, bright blue eyes wide, arms open. "Congratulations on all you've been doing for Regina! I'm so proud of you."

"Miriam, helping Regina is changing something in me. I can't explain the peace I feel. Can you believe—I'm no longer yearning for my mother?"

Her eyes soften. "I'm not surprised, Josephe. You've been like a mother to Regina. Every woman mothers the lost parts of herself as she mothers her children through the various stages of their lives. While helping Regina, you've been mothering your adult self."

Something catches in my throat. "Miriam, I've finally come home."

27

"Don't Stop Now, Girl"

"Hi, Sister. This is Robin from Attorney Block's office. The BIA's decision on David Bakala's case arrived this morning. Mr. Block asked me to fax it to you and to Mary Sfasciotti. I presume he expects you to share it with David. I'll fax it to your attention at St. Mary's."

I thank her, grab my keys, and head out into the stifling August air. At St. Mary's, Carolyn hands me the three pages. "How's retirement?"

"I highly recommend it." I laugh. With Regina's case reopened, I had canceled my sabbatical. In my car, I flip past the two cover pages to reach the one-page decision.

The respondent, a native and citizen of the Democratic Republic of Congo ("DRC"), has timely appealed from the Immigration Judge's decision denying his asylum application pursuant to section 208 of the Immigration and Nationality Act ("Act"), 8 U.S.C. § 1158, because it was untimely filed. . . . The sole issue on appeal is whether the Immigration Judge correctly denied the respondent asylum. The respondent's appeal will be dismissed.

What? I feel an iron fist slam into my gut.

I scan the rest. One paragraph summarizes Judge Brahos's findings, the other Block's arguments. No reasons, no nothing. Exactly what lawyers detest—a summary affirmance without opinion. I flip back to the cover page: "Panel Members: Juan Osuna."

So Judge Osuna was too busy whipping through a pile of cases to explain, was he? Well, I for one would like to know, on the scales of justice, how an arbitrary one-year rule could ever outweigh the fact of a man's brutal torture, which, after all, was undisputed in David's case. And if it all hinged on David's PTSD diagnosis, how dare he dismiss Dr. Collins's own refutation?

I lean back, too stunned to cry. This is a disaster. Two months ago this board linked Regina's case with his, now they deny him asylum? Who are these faceless judges anyway?

Mary Sfasciotti once worked at the BIA. She had told me that previous administrations tried to balance judicial appointments between private lawyers (immigrants' advocates) and government lawyers (the equivalent of prosecutors). George W. Bush's administration, however, appointed political loyalists, some with little or no immigration experience. Those with immigration background had worked either as "prosecutors" or in enforcement jobs. In 2002, when Attorney General John Ashcroft slashed the number of BIA judges to eleven, he kept only government types then streamlined the process, requiring the more liberal use of summary affirmances. The year before his changes, 43 percent of cases represented by lawyers received favorable decisions. By 2005, the number had dropped to 13 percent.[1]

All week I've struggled to bring myself to tell David. He hates the perpetual limbo of withholding of removal. Without the full embrace of asylum in America, how can he—torture survivor for democracy—ever feel safe? Now he, his family, their future—all are as friable as the papers Osuna once whisked through.

I wave to the Bakala kids as I follow Regina into the house, then sit down in her kitchen. "I've got news, Regina, but it's not very good."

Her eyes register alarm.

I wait until she pulls up a chair. "The BIA denied David's appeal."

She jerks back. "No!"

I reach across the table to take hold of her hand. "Don't worry. You're still OK—both of you. This decision does not stop your case; it just makes it harder."

She turns quiet, stares unseeing at the tabletop. When she looks up, her voice is firm. "No, Sister. Trust me. It's gonna be OK. God's gonna do it." Then suddenly, her eyes widen. "But *David*. He will be *very* upset to hear this. Sister, you are the one who must tell him. Wait till Friday when I'm in Chicago and he is home with the kids. He won't be so tired."

I rub my temples. "I can't tell him, Regina. It will break his heart."

"You can do it, Sister. I know you can."

———

Midafternoon Friday my phone rings. "Guess what? I finally got my work permit."

After two anxious months of needless, bureaucratic rigamarole, Regina had turned to Mary for help. I can see the harrumphing Attorney Sfasciotti marching her client through Chicago's Loop into the DHS Office to insist that, at the very least, they grant her an emergency, temporary work permit—*now*. With no appointment, they had to wait three hours.

"I'm so happy. But I missed my train, so I have to wait. You tell David about his appeal?"

I moan. "I've been avoiding it all day."

"*Tsk*. Sister, you *must*. Call now. This is the best time."

Shortly before five, she phones again, this time from the train station. "I can't reach David, Sister. Please tell him my train is late, not to worry. You talk to him about the appeal?"

I groan, make another promise, hang up.

The worst part of PTSD is powerlessness to stop the trauma, to feel in control. But America has David trapped on a hamster wheel of perpetual powerlessness. I lean back on the settee, remembering how, when the BIA reopened Regina's case, I had quickly credited David for his heroic hours of testimony years earlier. "In the end, David, *you* are the one who will save Regina." For that one moment, his face had lit up.

I lean forward now, my head down, elbows on my knees. I, too, hate being powerless.

Suddenly, it hits me: this immigration system is like my disturbed mother—mercurial and arbitrary. I straighten up. God, I want no part in this cruelty. You want me to be like Abraham? OK, I entrust David to you, but I refuse to be the one putting him on some altar to scare him to death, got that? I refuse to undermine his hopes.

I lean back and close my eyes, taking deep, slow breaths to still my anxiety.

Gradually, I enter the stunning immensity of God's love . . . for me . . . and for David. I feel myself settling into the calm that inevitably accompanies deeper truth: God loves this man beyond anything I can imagine. Gradually, I realize that what I *can* do—*all* I can do—is stand with him, trusting God . . . even if I must deliver this terrible news. Maybe my faith can strengthen his. After another deep breath, I open my eyes. OK, God, help me do what I must.

As I stand up, the phone rings.

"Hi, Sister. Hal Block here. What do you think about that BIA ruling on David's case?"

"Oh, it's terrible, just terrible. I haven't been able to tell him."

"Oh, for heaven's sake," he sputters, "don't tell David and Regina anything. They've been through enough hell." Hal reverts to his usual matter-of-fact tone. "Tell you what: I'm going to appeal that decision. David has already met the higher proof for withholding, so why would the BIA let Brahos deny him asylum on a procedural matter based on two words that Dr. Collins himself insisted do not equivocate his diagnosis? More important, why did Brahos not telephone Dr. Collins himself, as a judge is required to do if he has lingering doubts about written testimony? No judge has the authority to overrule an expert witness. Collins has the PhD in psychology, not Brahos. The government should produce their own expert witness if they don't trust Collins."

I hang up, my spirit dancing in thanksgiving for Hal Block, the timing of his call, the wondrous ways of God.

———————

Thursday, October 27. Thanks to road construction on Atlanta's narrow streets, plus a chatty Mary Sfasciotti in the passenger seat, the taxi driver misses his turn, so we arrive at the massive Martin Luther King Jr. Federal Building with little time to spare. My brain, stuck in morning mode, loses track of what Mary is saying. All I can focus on is Regina next to me staring out the window, the courtroom trauma of years earlier still with her.

We step out of the cab to face a wide bank of stairs leading to a sprawling plaza—all stone, no greenery, no life. Like other federal buildings of the early 1930s, the majestic structure that once served as a central post office looks down on us like a stodgy judge, dowdy and dull.

Room 112, one of three immigration courtrooms, is a low-ceilinged, windowless room on the basement level. We enter the gallery where several twosomes and small groups with solemn faces wait in the few rows of worn benches or on the cheap side chairs crowding the back and side walls.

Beyond the waist-high wooden bar are two large tables facing the judge—one on the left for the immigrant's lawyer, the other on the right for the government attorney, and between them a podium at which a sandy-haired lawyer stands addressing the judge. The court clerk sits at her small table near the front. From his raised bench, the large, graying Judge William A. Cassidy glances at us with a trace of a smile. Behind him stands the American flag and, on the wall, the great seal of the Department of Justice, Executive Office for Immigration Review—a large bald eagle with a single olive branch in one claw and in the other, a slew of arrows. Far too many arrows, I'd say.

Judge Cassidy calls Andes Imwa next. As Mary grabs her stuffed briefcase and opens the gate to the podium, he smiles briefly toward Regina. "I am very familiar with this case," he says, patting the foot-high stack of documents next to him, most of them Mary's motions.

Mary brings greetings from Chicago, tosses in a compliment from a mutual acquaintance, then banters a bit about the pile of documents he had patted.

He seems congenial enough, though I know not to trust him. Cassidy was appointed an immigration judge in 1993 after six years as a government lawyer ("prosecutor"), years in which he also directed training in Washington, D.C., for other government lawyers. Since immigration courts are part of the executive branch of government, federal judicial rules of evidence do not apply. The mind-set of the judge is critical. Like other judges whose law careers began in an adversarial role, Cassidy rarely grants asylum. When he heard Regina's case in 1997, he ranked fourth in asylum denials among the nation's 203 immigration judges, denying 95.8 percent of his cases.[2]

Mary gets down to business. "Based on the fact that Ms. Imwa's case now hinges on that of her husband, we respectfully request a change of venue, Your Honor. Since Judge O. John Brahos in Chicago is already familiar with her husband's case, this would save Your Honor the extra work of studying both cases. It would also eliminate expensive travel and lodging as well as much inconvenience for the family and all involved."

"Chambers for pretrial," he says, and all three—Judge Cassidy, Mary, and the government lawyer—grab their papers and briefcases and disappear behind a closed door.

Regina looks at me, a hint of worry in her eyes.

I shrug my shoulders, glance at my watch, then reach for her hand. She closes her eyes. I know she is praying. So am I.

An eternal ten minutes later, the three emerge. The judge repeats their conclusions for the record: Mary will submit a formal written motion for change of venue. In the event that he denies her motion, another master calendar hearing will be held by telephone on January 4, 2006. Regina will need to be with Mary for the telephonic hearing.

When the government lawyer asks if the petitioner is present in court, Regina stands up.

"That's all right, ma'am. You may sit down," smiles the judge. "I recognize you sitting there . . . with a Catholic nun beside you, right?"

Hmm. Must be my stereotypical white hair and skin. (Vitiligo, beginning in childhood, stole my freckles and eventually all pigmentation.) I return the judge's smile.

Mary reenters the gallery, causing a small commotion when she can't find her purse. Judge Cassidy goes back into chambers and returns quickly, purse in hand. "I wasn't sure it was yours, it doesn't match your outfit," he teases. She laughs and thanks him as he hands her purse over the bar. He smiles directly at Regina. "God bless you," he says.

Out in the hall, Regina says, "Wow. Last time he was *mean*! He never smiled, not once."

Mary seems edgy, eager to leave the building. "Start praying. We've got to get this case moved. I didn't like the way he brushed aside my motions in chambers. He didn't want to hear anything about the rapes, her trauma in court, nothing. He was dismissive and abrasive. 'We're not going to rehash any of that' was all he said. I know we're not retrying the original case, but he was not even open to the *possibility* that his ruling was wrong."

"Regina and I were praying for you, Mary. I prayed for wisdom," I add, "and that God would keep you calm."

"*Calm?*" She swings toward me, eyes ablaze. "Don't you *ever* pray for me to be calm. I have to be absolutely alert. I must hear not only what's being said, but what's not being said, what's in the air, what's likely to happen next. Don't ever pray for me to be calm."

I pull back, hands up in surrender. "OK!" I say, quelling a joke about throwing God into a quandary. "I'll just stick to wisdom." Mary is obviously scared. No wonder her earlier jabbering with the cabdriver, the string of niceties to butter up the judge, the embarrassment of forgetting her purse. I turn to Regina. "What did you pray for?"

"I just thank God," she says calmly, as if her deliverance were a done deal. "If God wants me to go back to Congo, I say OK; if I stay here, OK. God knows what is best."

At Hartsfield-Jackson Atlanta International, I turn to Mary while we await our flight. "We brag about being a nation of immigrants, but our system seems intent on keeping them out. Is this because of 9/11?"

"Not entirely. In 1995, remember how we immediately jumped into blaming foreigners for the Oklahoma City bombing of the Alfred P. Murrah Federal Building, *even* after two native-born Americans were convicted of the crime? Fear of immigrants escalated, giving right-wing, anti-immigrant groups the chance to push for the most punitive laws. Congress came down hard. In 1996, AEDPA and IIRAIRA reinstated McCarthy-era 'guilt by association' for anyone donating to a group now labeled 'terrorist,' gave border inspectors unprecedented power to remove people without judicial review, ordered mandatory detention of asylum seekers, redefined aggravated felonies while removing all waivers. I could go on and on." She gives her head a quick shake. "Honestly, Sister, in their application, these laws violate human rights."

She describes a pattern. Congress takes its cues from the mood of the country, often passing ill-conceived laws with unforeseen consequences. Then, as happened with the Real ID Act, the bill is misrepresented to the public. In the end, innocent people suffer.

"After 9/11, it got even worse. The USA Patriot Act authorized unparalleled surveillance of American citizens and gave the attorney general power to detain any foreign-born person as a possible terrorist—no proof, no hearing needed. In what amounted to racial profiling, he required all male noncitizens, age sixteen and up, from twenty-five mostly Muslim countries, to register with immigration authorities, then secretly detained and deported thousands. Your Wisconsin senator Russ Feingold was the only one voting against it."

The Midwest Airlines attendant announces our flight.

"As the daughter of Italian immigrants, I feel privileged to be an immigration attorney in a country that was so hospitable to my parents. But in recent years, I've been terribly discouraged, struggling to represent deserving families in the face of such inhumane laws."

As we get in line, Mary talks about the months after 9/11, when President Bush redistributed the functions of the old INS, putting immigration under the new Department of Homeland Security, then giving DHS a single mission—to secure the homeland against terrorists. Her eyes pierce mine. "You see what that did? Immigrants are now linked with terrorism."

"Yes. So, the war on terrorism became a war on immigrants."

The plane is full. After settling in our last-row seats, Mary continues, "In the beginning, people just came. Our founders encouraged it, and from President George Washington until the mid-1800s, almost everyone presumed immigration was good for the nation. However, there were always those who claimed that only white people had enough intelligence to live in a democracy."

"What?"

"And by that, they meant Anglo-Saxon whites from the British Isles and people from the Nordic countries. The darker your skin, the less intelligence they assumed you had, so the closer you got to the Mediterranean, the dumber they claimed you were." She juts up her Italian chin. "Never mind that democracy originated in Greece."

I can't help but laugh.

"Hey, you should read what Benjamin Franklin wrote about the Germans."

I will later find the quote in *Observations Concerning the Increase of Mankind*, 1791. Though Franklin eventually softened his stance, his diatribe sounds like today's talk radio.

Why should the Palatine boors be suffered to swarm into our Settlements, and by herding together establish their Language and Manners to the Exclusion of ours? Why should Pennsylvania, founded by the English, become a Colony of *Aliens*, who will shortly be so numerous as to Germanize us instead of us Anglifying them, and will never adopt our Language or Customs, any more than they can acquire our Complexion.

Mary went on about the 1800s—Jews fleeing the Russian pogroms; German Catholics seeking farmland; Irish Catholics fleeing the potato famine. This influx of Jews and Catholics plus the rising slavery crisis ignited America's first anti-immigrant mass movement. The violent group known as the Know-Nothings (their answer to anyone questioning their activities) went from forty-three members to more than one million in less than two years.

"California later started a ruckus to get rid of the Chinese who had come during the gold rush and worked on the continental railroad but were now 'taking our jobs.' A congressional committee decided Chinese brains were too small for democracy. The Chinese Exclusion Act 1882 led to a long string of exclusionary laws, reaching their nadir in the quota system of 1924."

I later discover that in the 1900s, intellectual elites latched on to social Darwinism, connecting culture with biological evolution. The logical outgrowth was eugenics, selective breeding for the perfect race—the rationale behind Adolf Hitler's massacres.

Many anti-immigrant groups today, fueled by fear of population growth—especially brown and black-skinned population growth—are fixated on preserving the purity of the white race. I learned that eugenics is the underlying philosophy of John Tanton, mastermind and financier behind America's largest network of immigration restrictionist groups. Tanton's own racist memos convinced the Southern Poverty Law Center to list his flagship, the Federation for American Immigration Reform (FAIR), as a hate group.[3]

Throughout our history as a nation of immigrants, two issues have dominated our dialogue: (1) Identity. Who are we as a people? At this point in our history, where on the spectrum of homogeneity and dissimilarity is our best future? (2) Economics. What immigration policies will best help our nation thrive in the global economy? On the spectrum of business interests and labor concerns, where are "We the People" best served?

While these are appropriate political questions, they don't raise the justice issues that deeply trouble me: Since when can we search a private home without a warrant? How dare we traumatize little children by snatching away one or even both parents? Who are we to deprive someone of due process? Or to permanently break up a family? Who gave us the right to flout international law, letting border guards either deny entrance to asylum seekers or lock up these psychologically vulnerable people with criminals, often for months on end? Why sign treaties we refuse to follow? Why pour billions into private prisons when alternatives have proven effective? Must everything involving immigrants be layered in secrecy? Is this the legacy we want our mother country to hand on?

An attendant announces that we will be landing shortly in Milwaukee. Mary turns to me. "You see why the demand for more fencing and detention centers is short-sighted at best?"

"It doesn't begin to address the injustices in the system."

She grips my arm. "Sister, until due process rights and human rights are recognized as basic to all immigration law, we will not have real immigration reform."

At Milwaukee's Mitchell International, Mary hugs Regina, then still holding her, says, "Girlfriend, you have my heart. And my mind. And, heck, my lungs and a whole lot more."

She hugs me, too, but her demeanor changes. She straightens up, her eyes pleading with me, then takes me by the shoulders. Her words, somber and firm, grip me tighter than her hands. "Don't you stop now, girl. There are thousands of Reginas and Davids out there."

28

2006

My thrumming expectation of some word from Judge Cassidy has slid from fear to dread and, today, just a flat, stark sense of the inevitable. Tomorrow, January 4, is Regina's telephonic hearing. As I mindlessly watch the dishwater swirl down the drain, the phone startles me.

"Good news at last," says Mary. "Our motion for change of venue was granted."

"Hallelujah!"

"Tell Regina, no hearing tomorrow. I don't know which judge will hear her case. Brahos's clerk told me that even for change of venue cases, they assign judges on a rotational basis."

My call catches Regina during her lunch break. "Praise to God!" she shouts. "I knew this would happen . . . but why they always wait till the last minute? *Why?*"

Busy at my computer January 30, I read on the *Business Wire* that former Haliburton subsidiary KBR—which overcharged the Pentagon millions during the Iraq War—announced a $385 million contract to construct more detention centers over the next five years for "an emergency influx of immigrants into the US, or to support the rapid development of new programs." (ICE declined to explain "rapid development of new programs.")

We already have the largest prison system on the planet. What in the world are we doing?

Googling, I find the forty-nine page answer: "ENDGAME: Office of Detention and Removal Strategic Plan, 2003–2012," published by the Department of Homeland Security. The goal of the multiyear enforcement expansion is "to remove all removable aliens" by 2012.[1]

My heart sinks. "Removable aliens" includes people like Regina and Norma and José, whom this rigid system, rife with cruelty, continues to betray. While Congress dithers, ICE turns en masse against them all, raiding private homes and workplaces, terrorizing families and communities—costing us taxpayers multi-billions. What sense does any of this make?

By 2008, the detention population will have grown by more than 60 percent in four years. Congress will also have approved "secure communities," irrevocably linking local biometric databases with ICE to ensure the deportation of every undocumented person arrested by local police for whatever reason. Regardless of its effects on local policing and public safety, secure communities will be mandated nationwide by 2013.[2]

I flick off the computer. Someday America will wake up from this nightmare to face not only what we did to untold thousands and their children but what we did to ourselves.

It's after five when Hal Block phones. "We have some news, Sister, basically good news. The BIA has decided to reopen David's case."

"This *is* good news."

"Yeah, but I'm disappointed. Why didn't they just give him asylum? Why make this poor guy go through another hearing? I don't know. It seems like an odd decision, a convoluted way to avoid doing the obvious." He reads, "On August 24, 2005, the respondent filed a document entitled a 'Motion to Reconsider,' which the Department of Homeland Security opposes. To the extent that the respondent moves to reconsider, the motion will be denied. We also construe the motion as one to reopen, which will be granted, and the record will be remanded for further proceedings."

Even Hal is puzzled, but later I will learn that under the 2002 BIA streamlining rules, an individual BIA judge cannot reverse an immigration judge's ruling but may remand the case to the original judge.[3]

"Well, the board is under fire right now, Sister. Did you see the *New York Times* article the day after Christmas about judges from US Circuit Courts of Appeal nationwide criticizing immigration judges for mishandling asylum cases? Failed asylum seekers keep appealing to their courts because they can't get justice in the immigration system. Federal judges have also had to rebuke them for using sarcasm and humiliating remarks against asylum seekers. Even conservative Judge Posner of our Seventh Circuit said the work of immigration judges has fallen below the minimum standards of legal justice."

"Do you think the article will make a difference?"

"Well, this, plus last year's *Report on Asylum Seekers in Expedited Removal* by the US Commission on International Religious Freedom has gotten the attention of Attorney General Alberto Gonzales. On January 9, he announced a review of the immigration court system. So we can hope. . . .[4] In any case, David's got another chance. I'll send you this decision along with our motion to reconsider. We'll probably combine his wife's case with David's and try to get Brahos to grant asylum to both at the same time."

"Congratulations, Hal. This is huge. David and Regina will be thrilled."

And so it happens. March 8, 2006, at Regina's master calendar hearing, Mary Sfasciotti is grateful to have Judge Robert Vinikoor combine the cases and transfer them to Judge Brahos. Raw with grief over the recent death of her ninety-one-year-old mother, Mary will insist in the weeks ahead that Attorney Hal Block take the lead on our case.

Holy Thursday, April 13. While I'm driving home from Pick 'n Save, Regina and David are in Chicago with both lawyers for their combined master calendar hearing. They took the kids, not only to see the judge who, Regina told them, "can give Mommy and Daddy the papers to stay in America," but to give Brahos a good hard look at the family whose future he will soon decide.

O. John Brahos was appointed to the bench in late 1982 after working eleven years as a prosecutor. For three years, he has also served as an alternate on the BIA. His asylum denial rate over the past five years has been 72.6 percent, twelve points higher than the national average.[5]

The year-long wait has been hard on both parents and children.

Last month when Regina apologized for forgetting something Lydia needed for school, Lydia said, "That's OK, Mommy. Sometimes your brain gets mixed up when you have to go to Chicago. When you get the papers, you won't have to go to Chicago." Counseling has helped, but Regina says they won't sleep unless their bedroom door is open so they know she is there. When she goes to evening class, "they do what they did when I was in jail—wrap up in my quilt and take turns sitting in my place on the couch—to be sure I come home."

My cell phone rings.

"The master calendar hearing went better than we expected."

As I pull into the parking lane to talk, Mary continues, "Judge Brahos made it clear that first he will decide whether to grant David asylum. Then, because, quote, 'America does not want to break up a family,' end quote—even though our immigration system does it all the time—he will decide on whether to grant Regina asylum on a derivative basis. This is perfect, Sister." I hear joy in her voice. "The hearing will focus on David's PTSD diagnosis. He may have to answer a few questions, but that's it. Regina will probably not have to testify at all."

"It will be that simple?"

"That's what it sounds like. Of course, I will continue preparing Regina to testify, just in case. But, Sister, I know Judge Brahos. He does what he says he's going to do."

"Mary, this is wonderful!"

"At the end of the hearing, the government attorney raised an objection for the record, but she's new to the case, and the stack of documents from both cases is two feet high, so her objection may just be pro forma. The key person is Brahos, and he's already set the agenda. The hearing is Friday, January 26, 2007, at 9 A.M."

Eight more months. "Besides the date, how much can we tell people?"

"Tell them what the judge said he plans to do, but remember, it ain't over till it's over, so tell them we are cautiously optimistic."

In his early afternoon call, Hal Block, in his own staid way, echoes Mary's positive report but raises his own caution, calling the government attorney's objection "a bit troubling."

Good Friday. I sit in my living room cloaked in a quiet sadness, aware of the suffering Christ in people today. It was Holy Week last year when Regina was taken, Good Friday when Shelley's husband, José, was "dumped" in Mexico. My heart is quickly drawn to the frightened new asylum seekers stuck in US prisons within criminal populations and then to other detainees, tens of thousands slated for deportation. I try to picture them—the only group of noncriminals imprisoned in America—whole families as well as individuals, pregnant women, babies, children, the elderly, mentally ill, sick, and disabled, penned up out of public scrutiny in a vast patchwork of about 350 facilities, a number of them run by private prison firms.[6]

Private prisons with no enforceable national standards, eager to maximize income and minimize costs, are particularly ill suited for detainees with language problems and few resources. Yet, regardless of lawsuits alleging sexual abuse, physical violence, medical neglect, and mismanagement, Corrections Corporation of America and their top competitor, GEO Group, Inc. (formerly Wackenhut), continue to win lucrative government contracts.[7]

With no status, detainees have no voice. Medical neglect is widespread. An alarming number have died in prison. Others, terrified of returning to dangerous homelands, have been drugged by ICE for deportation. Such horrors stay hidden until nosy journalists get involved.[8]

Until Regina was taken, I knew none of this. Now it haunts me.

This evening, I phone her.

"Today was painful, Sister. I went by myself to St. Mary's Good Friday Service, but I could not stop crying the whole time. I kept thinking about being in the jail last year. It was too hard. I was like dying with the nightmares . . . and in the days, the terrible memories, crying until I could not breathe. I could not escape from them. It was—I don't know how to tell you—like I was buried alive . . . like I was already dead, but I had to keep living."

For a moment I cannot speak. Regina usually glosses over her jail struggles with talk of God. Only now and then do I glimpse the fuller reality.

"Sometimes, Sister, I just want to kill myself . . ."

Kill herself? She has never said *this* before. "Regina . . ." I stumble for words.

"But then . . . I don't want my children to be *orphans*. To have no mother is the *worse* thing for my children. I cannot let them grow up like me, with no mother."

I close my eyes. How deeply scarred she is, still seeing the world through orphan eyes.

"How are you now, Regina?"

"I'm OK," she says, her voice quiet but sure. "I just cry a lot today, Sister."

After hanging up, I lean back in my chair. Miriam Cecile's words come to mind: "Every woman mothers the lost parts of herself as she mothers her children." I hope that Regina's deep love for Lydia and Christopher has also alleviated some of her own sense of loss.

What did it take for an orphaned nine-year-old to stand so tall that no one would suspect how fragile and lonely and, yes, how traumatized she really was? I wonder what happened inside as she stood with her brothers and sisters around her mother's coffin waiting for someone to want them, then stuffing all those feelings to take on the role of surrogate mother to her brothers and sisters, housekeeper for them, girl-servant fetching a chauffeur for her rich cousins. I imagine the cunning and bravado it took to insist that Uncle Basil send her to Lycée Matondo Boarding School. Was that the turning point—the day she shoved it all and took the reins?

Yet when her cousins enrolled in that same school, getting gifts and attention from home, she felt "like a charity case," weeping in private, missing her mother, always missing her mother. Years later, after the family had all fled Congo and Regina was a new teacher living with her beloved Grand-mére Gabrielle, grief struck again. Stunned by the death of Grand-mére, the woman who had been "like another mother," Regina dropped the reins and retreated to Belgium.

So what drove her back, not only to teach in Idiofa but to plunge into white-hot political activism? And if David made her feel protected, why did she leave him in Kinshasa for a solo mission back into the dangers of Idiofa, her father's home, and Elom, her mother's village? And months later, after being double-raped, imprisoned, and solemnly warned by her Idiofa jailer to stop all political work, what made her con David into letting her go back again? Why the devil-may-care decisions?

"I am a strong, independent woman," she has said in the past. Smiling. Her chin up.

But what I also see is the lifelong orphan, overcompensating just as I did for the nurturing she so keenly missed. Regina's life is more painful and complex than I can begin to fathom, but from what she's told me over the years, missing her mother seems to be at the heart of everything.

Somehow she made it—this traumatized rape survivor sitting in the bow of a stranger's pirogue, hanging on with both hands, grieving her husband and home, her mother's village, her father's house, her beautiful, beautiful mother country.

She steeled herself through every leg of that journey, even the humiliation of a police body search in JFK Airport.

But with minimal English, how did she negotiate the confusion of our asylum system with heedless lawyers? Or hold it together in the

Atlanta courtroom as one of the most intimidating judges in the nation shredded her case, accused her of lying, ordered her deported, and warned that any appeal would fail? Trauma piled upon trauma until US Immigration dealt the final blow—tearing her from her family.

This time, unable to escape the horrors of PTSD, she hung onto the only thought strong enough to stop her from suicide: "I can't let [my children] grow up like me, with no mother." What a powerful force—maternal love fortified by her own lifelong craving!

In the wonderfully intricate world of human relationships, yes, Lydia *did* save her mommy's life. And if Miriam Cecile is right, by attending to her children's need, Regina was also heeding the cry of her orphaned self. May the healing continue.

29

THE ELEVENTH HOUR

After most parishioners have left Sunday Mass on September 3, several knots of folks linger with their friends in the aisles to catch up on news. I ask the Bakalas, "What do you think of the Congo election results?"

A week earlier Congolese election authorities announced that since no presidential candidate won a clear majority, the top two contenders—current president Joseph Kabila and rebel militia leader Jean-Pierre Bemba, one of the four vice presidents—would face a run-off in October.

David smirks then shakes his head. "Kabila is cruel like his father, but Bemba will bring more war." He shrugs. "So what choice is that?"

"PALU's Antoine Gizenga was third," Regina says, "a good leader, but with thirty-three candidates, people voted for the one they knew."

More than 70 percent of Congo's 25.7 million registered voters had voted on July 30, in Congo's first free elections in forty-six years. They voted not only for a president but also for members of the federal assembly and provincial assemblies. Thanks in large part to $442 million from the international community and the presence of seventeen thousand international observers, all had gone smoothly. However, the announcement of the two finalists brought three days of violence—in

Kinshasa, twenty-three killed, forty-three injured, and in Équateur Province, eighty-four hauled to Camp Tshatshi by Kabila's Republican Guard to be beaten, threatened with death, and forced to confess their support for Bemba before being released.[1]

Two months later, on December 3, as we leave Sunday Mass, David pulls me aside. "Did you hear the run-off results? Joseph Kabila won by 58 percent. If he keeps working with the UN, he will be best for the country."

"And his past brutality may help your case," I say.

Or maybe not. Though US State Department reports on country conditions are a staple in asylum cases, they have also been known to present a rosier picture when the administration is cozying up to a country's rulers.

"Happy 2007, everybody!" Bob walks into St. Mary's upstairs meeting room two days after New Year's for our last official Save Regina Committee meeting, his winter jacket stuffed with soft drink cans. He slides them down the table. "My treat. Happy New Year—especially for Regina and David!"

"It's so good to see all of you. It's been forever." I grin.

Tracy turns to David. "How is Regina?"

"Regina is good. Me, too. We are nervous, but"—he smiles, hikes his shoulders, and gestures with upturned palms—"what can we do?" He laughs. "Nothing! So we just trust God." His voice takes on a serious tone. "God's gonna do it."

Heads nod. I feel the same, despite a tiny niggling about what effect, if any, Congo's elections might have on their case.

Teresa Lee has a happy announcement. "I'm pleased to report the Regina Fund is up to date on all payments, and we will easily cover upcoming expenses."

After all expenses are paid, the fund will be dissolved and, despite David's protests, remaining monies will go to the Bakala family.

With the asylum hearing just three weeks away, January 26, we turn to publicity.

"Lead attorney Hal Block strongly cautioned against notifying the media," I say. "He's afraid it might be perceived negatively by Judge Brahos. How should we handle this?"

"Let's say nothing to anybody," says Tracy. "It's in the morning, right? As soon as it's over, I can e-mail a press release and notify the media of a 3:30 press conference at St. Mary's."

Everyone agrees.

"And if they get asylum?" I ask. "What about a public celebration a week or so later?"

Major roles are assigned. We list dignitaries to invite. To thank the school for all their efforts I suggest we present the principal with some library books on Africa.

"Awesome," says kindergarten mom Teresa.

"Speaking of awesome gifts," I say, glancing around the table, "there simply are no words big enough to thank God, or to thank each other, for the gift of working together for such an important cause. Each of you offering to help . . . it just blew me away."

"For Amy and me, it's always been about the kids," says Bob. "I looked at our little Karly and Abby, and I had to get involved. To me religion is what you do and how you live. Regina's strong faith when she faced the ultimate test of losing her children, that's what inspired me."

Pascal nods. "Like Bob, I did not want Lydia and Christopher growing up without their mother. That's what I worried about."

"You know what struck me?" says Tracy. "The school kids. They really *got* it—working together for a cause, a lesson they'll never forget."

"My first grader was so proud to wear her button and make her poster," adds Teresa. "It's been a privilege for me, being new to the parish. St. Mary's has such a great sense of family!"

Tracy again. "Even the media got super involved!"

"One reporter said, 'I commend your efforts, Bob, but she's outta here.' I knew he was wrong. I never doubted Regina would be freed. When she was released, he actually apologized."

Darryl is somber. "Angela and I have never seen God work like this. It changed our lives."

Heads nod.

"When the League of United Latin American Citizens in Washington helped," he adds, "I sensed a new call. I've started a LULAC chapter in our area. Sister agreed to be our chaplain."

"Sure'n begorra, Irish me—with all the Latinos!" I laugh. "By the way, some of you know that I helped organize our archdiocesan Justice for Immigrants Committee, part of the national Catholic effort. We'll soon be setting up educational forums in parishes."

I look at my watch. "Let's keep each other posted by e-mail." I pause. My eyes look slowly from one end of the table to the other. "Each of you has a permanent home in my heart. I would do anything for you."

I turn off the vacuum and grab the phone just as it switches to voice mail.

"I'm here—don't hang up!"

"Hi, Sister. This is Mary Sfasciotti. I need to get a message to Regina about changing the time of our appointment."

"I'll have her phone you from work, Mary. I'm glad you called. We had our final Save Regina Committee meeting last night to discuss publicity around the hearing. Since Hal is very uneasy about media coverage, we decided to—"

"Why is he uneasy? The immigration court could use some good coverage. They've been brutalized by the press this past year for judges mishandling asylum cases. This case could help the court as a whole and boost Brahos's spirits as well. I say go for it."

"I didn't expect you, of all people—"

"The court may have regulations regarding media in the courtroom, but specifics might be up to the judge. Why not call his law clerk? Explain how this case has had a lot of press in Wisconsin and have her ask if he would be open to having the media in his courtroom."

"Great idea." I jot down the phone number. "Oh, and Mary, please reserve Sunday afternoon, February 11. If they get asylum, we want you at our celebration."

I leave a message for Hal Block that we're putting the media decision in Brahos's hands, then phone Tracy. "Tell the clerk we will abide by whatever Judge Brahos decides."

In less than twenty-four hours, she has the answer. "Each news organization must get individual permission from the national office in Virginia, but—good news—Judge Brahos is fine with it." She pauses. "Sister, Brahos would not agree to this unless he expects a good outcome."

After phoning the building manager to turn up the heat in her two-room office, Dr. Rhea Steinpreis swings her swivel chair back toward David and me. "I apologize," she says. "It can get pretty chilly in here. Can I offer you some hot coffee? Sister, a shawl for your knees?"

We both decline the coffee, but I'm grateful for the shawl.

"So, David," she continues, "you were a CNRD spy. Was CNRD separate from AFDL?"

"Yes . . . well, not after . . . but yes I was a spy after that."

"After what?"

He glances toward me. To bolster David's case with a current assessment, Hal Block had referred him to Dr. Steinpreis, a licensed clinical psychologist/neuropsychologist with expertise in post-traumatic stress disorder. I came along to help as needed.

"In September 1996," I explain, "CNRD joined with three other parties to form AFDL. David continued then as a spy for the AFDL alliance."

Throughout the two-hour interview, I marvel at how David maintains his composure, even when describing his torture. But I also notice one detail that differs from what he had originally told me. On the way home, I ask about it.

"David, back in 2000 when you first told me about the soldier striking your teeth, you said he used the butt of his gun; today you said he used his elbow."

"No, it was his elbow. Today I remember exactly. I don't know how to explain what happens in my brain. Sometimes . . . it's like blanks. I am talking and then part goes blank, so I say what I think must be right. But today, I know for sure it was his elbow."

A week later, after telling more painful details at his second appointment, I ask, "David, it's been nine years since you were tortured. Do you still have nightmares?"

"All the time."

I've finished straightening my bedroom and cleaning up from breakfast. Outside, heavy snow is silently wrapping all the trees in a cottony lace—a perfect setting for some quiet time, but I cannot sit still. Tomorrow, January 25, we'll stay overnight in Chicago to be in court by 8:30 A.M. Friday. My shoulders are tight, my stomach in turmoil. I don't know if it's fearing the outcome or just wanting this thing to be over. My clothes are ready, hotel confirmation and extra cash in my purse, and I've e-mailed the known world for prayers. While getting my carry-on out of storage, the phone rings.

"Sister, this is Mary Sfasciotti's office. Regina and David's asylum hearing has been postponed. Judge Brahos has been sick for days and his clerk is canceling everything."

"No!"

"We won't know the new date until he gets back."

As I watch the snow quietly transform the neighborhood, flake by flake, everything within me slides into slow motion. I don't know if it's sheer relief or the beginning of a slow burn.

30

"WHO WILL TAKE CARE OF US?"

Winter is supposed to be gone, but this year, it trails in its wake a string of drizzly, gray days. This morning as I walk into church, the usher hands me a fresh palm frond. Even after five weeks of Lent, Passion Sunday catches me emotionally off guard. Bright hosannas and fresh palm branches march us inexorably into the long, stark gospel account of Jesus' passion and death. Tomorrow, Regina, David, and I will leave for Chicago. Judge Brahos scheduled their hearing for 9 A.M. this Tuesday, April 2, 2007. By the end of the liturgy, my heart is heavy, the music has slid into a minor key, and palm fronds, stripped of all naivete, now carry the weight of Holy Week. I leave mine in the pew. I just want Easter.

It's almost four o'clock Monday as Regina, David, and I enter the narrow, unheated Amtrak Station. Regina, in a dark green quilted coat and black slacks, takes a seat along the wall. "Sister, you remember? Everything happens in Holy Week."

I join her on the bench while David stands next to her against the wall.

"In 2005, they took me to jail on Tuesday of Holy Week, last year the master calendar hearing was on Holy Thursday, and tomorrow our asylum hearing—again, Holy Week." She smiles up at her husband. "God is with us."

David returns her smile. In khaki pants and a plaid green and black sweater, he seems to be taking tomorrow in stride.

I can't imagine how Regina has lived here twelve years and David ten, always teetering between fear and hope. I pull the zipper closed on my light blue jacket. I want this settled.

"How are the children?" I ask. "Are they OK with both of you gone overnight?"

"They went home from school today with some friends." Regina glances at her watch. "They are there over an hour now. That part's OK." She sighs, her face turning somber. "But they know tomorrow is the big day that the judge can give us the papers so we can stay in America. Was they scare? Yes, but this morning we sit down with them, David and me. We try to help them so they're not so scare, you know?" She frowns. "Lydia, she ask, 'The judge gonna say you go to Africa?' I say, 'I don't think so.' She say, 'If the judge say you go back to Congo, who will take care of us?'" Her shoulders sink. "Oh, Sister, this break my heart."

David leans in closer.

"We tell them, David and me, 'We *never* gonna leave you. No matter what, Mommy and Daddy gonna be *with* you.'"

"Even if we cannot stay in America," he adds, "we gonna *always* be together as a family."

Her eyes expand. "But then Christopher, he got *very* scare! He jump up and pull away." She jerks back, palms up. "He say, 'No! No! I don't want to go to Congo! I don't want to die!'"

David shakes his head. "We don't know what to say. Regina just keeps saying not to worry, the judge gonna give us the papers, we sure we gonna be OK."

With the beep-beep-beep of my travel alarm, the big day begins. I peek down the hall to see David and Regina's empty breakfast tray outside their room. While my tea brews, I enjoy the two oranges brought from home, pack up everything, then sit quietly and open *Psalms for Praying* to Psalm 72: "Bring justice to the peoples, O Beloved, and your mercy to all generations! . . . May You heed the cry of the poor—the young and the old, setting free all those in need, melting the hearts of oppressors! . . . From injustice and oppression, You redeem their life . . ." The next phrase lingers, ". . . and precious are they in your Heart."[1]

Regina answers my knock, her eyes as bright as her earrings and the small gold cross glittering against her brown sweater. She wears black pants and black heels.

"You look great, Regina. How are you? Were you able to sleep?"

"I'm fine. I woke up early so I pray. Everything gonna be OK, Sister. God already touch the judge's heart. I just know it."

"I'm not afraid, Sister," says David as he flicks off the TV. He is wearing the same khaki pants with a long-sleeved black polo shirt and black dress shoes. "God is with us. We trust God."

"I just wish you didn't have to go through the ordeal of another hearing." I hug each of them. "Did you notice?" I say, tugging at my left earlobe. "No earrings today. Your lawyers want me to look like a nun because Judge Brahos is a devout Episcopalian."

They laugh.

I'm in a navy pantsuit with a white mock turtleneck, my Notre Dame pin on my lapel, and, around my neck, a silver cross. White hair. White skin. No makeup. Nun.

We check out, leave our carry-ons in the hotel luggage area, then head for court. On yet another drizzly day, Chicago's Loop is a cacophony of taxis, delivery trucks, cars, and pedestrians weaving their way through dark canyons of skyscrapers.

Known simply as 55 East Monroe, the building that houses the Midwest Immigration Court soars forty-nine stories high. A sign outside says the top floors are being renovated into the Park Monroe residences. Arriving at least a half hour early, we walk through the glassy entrance into a cavernous granite lobby.

The elevator lets us out on the nineteenth floor. Suite 1900 is carpeted in a burgundy pattern with peach highlights. The cream wall covering is herringbone textured—a sophistication probably lost on frightened immigrants who arrive silent and wide-eyed. The security guard, a meticulous older fellow, instructs us to put wallets and pocket contents in a basket. Purses are sent through the X-ray machine, and all cell phones and cameras are sealed in labeled envelopes not to be opened until we leave. After walking through the metal detector, we enter the short part of a long L-shaped corridor. Judge Brahos's now-familiar courtroom is just beyond the bend. Closed courtroom doors on the left side of the hallway each bear the name of one of seven judges. Burgundy upholstered side chairs line the opposite wall.

Tracy and Bob, who arrived by Amtrak, greet us with hugs. They, plus Pascal, who is coming later in the Bakala minivan, are the only committee members able to adjust their schedules. Clustered nearby are reporters from two Milwaukee TV stations as well as from the *Milwaukee Journal Sentinel* and the *Catholic Herald*.

"Good morning, David. Sister. Regina." Hal Block is wearing a natty, pin-striped black suit, white shirt, and conservatively patterned garnet tie. I notice he's gained weight, his thinning comb-over is whiter than I remember, and though he has not been well for several years, his cheeks are rosy and he looks rested. Gone is the battle-worn, over-stuffed briefcase of years past. Today he rolls behind him a spiffy, ten-inch-thick catalog case. Clearly, the low-key, dogged advocate went out of his way to look the consummate professional.

He turns to me. "Is Mary Sfasciotti here?"

"Not yet."

While he sits down with David, we mill about, talking quietly, checking our watches, speculating on Mary's whereabouts. Nine o'clock comes and goes. Another lawyer and her client walk past. Still no Mary. When the clerk notifies Hal that Judge Brahos is ready for a short pretrial, Hal asks if I can locate her. I hurry out of the secured area toward the elevator where cell phones are allowed. No one answers her three numbers. I'm listening to her office voice mail when the elevator opens and out she swirls in a crocheted, multicolored shawl, spouting, "What a time for them to change the damn 'L' schedule!"

After a short time, we spectators file into the courtroom gallery. On the dark blue wall behind the raised bench hangs the great seal of the United States Department of Justice, Executive Office for Immigration Review—the eagle with all the arrows. The American flag stands beside it. David and Regina sit in adjacent chairs along the left wall while their attorneys confer quietly at a nearby table. At the table on the right, the DHS lawyer, a middle-aged brunette, shuffles through her stack of papers. Tracy, Bob, and I step up into the first row of the small, raised gallery while the reporters take the back row. We watch the clerk set a cassette recorder on the judge's bench then return to her table.

A door in front opens, admitting the Honorable O. John Brahos, his open robe swinging over a white shirt, navy tie, and dress pants. Brahos is a sprightly man with thinning white hair and a deceptively kind face. He quickly mounts the dais, turns on the recorder, then establishes for the record the presence and identity of each respondent, their lawyers, and the attorney for the government—not the one we expected but a woman named Alexandra Kostich. All the while, a small smile plays about his face. I don't trust the guy. I remember him smiling at David's hearing just before filleting him with demeaning remarks.

After a slew of preliminaries, Brahos asks Attorney Block if Dr. Rhea Steinpreis is available for telephonic testimony. Assuring the judge that she has kept her entire morning open, Block hands him her number.

We sit in silence as the court sound system picks up the dial tone, the dialing, then the persistent ringing. No one answers.

He tries again.

Nothing.

No one in the courtroom moves.

Again.

Zilch.

My shoulders zing into knots.

On the fourth try, the judge waits for voice mail, then leaves the court phone number.

We wait again.

Forever.

Finally the judge asks, "Mr. Block, if the witness were to testify, do you know what her testimony would be?"

"Yes, Your Honor, ah . . ." Block stands, leaning down to rifle through his papers. "If Dr. Rhea Steinpreis were testifying on a full, ah . . . testimony basis, she would in fact, testify, ah . . . in conformance with her report that we had submitted in our January submission and more particularly, ah . . . what she would say is that after interviewing Mr. Bakala in the presence of Sister Josephe Marie ah . . ."—still rifling—"in the event that there were any additional information she could provide, that Mr. Bakala testified in great length to his own personal experiences and in the manner in which . . ."

I feel my anxiety mounting.

Bob leans closer, muttering from the side of his mouth, "Jeez, what's with this guy? C'mon already."

I see David lean forward a bit, his hands in his lap, his face calm. Regina sits straight. Both focus on Hal Block.

". . . a number of classic tests that are done by professional clinical psychologists, in coming up with an evaluation regarding the mental status of the person and to arrive at some type of a current diagnosis and conclusion on current psycho-social functioning and more particularly, in conformance then and consistent with her written report, she would discuss . . ."

Bob straightens up, folds his arms. Tracy mutters something. My shoulders are now tying knots within the knots.

". . . the Minnesota Multiphashic Personality Inventory II test, which is one of the classic profile tests. . . . She also would go on to report that in addition . . ."

David, still slightly hunched, is now studying Judge Brahos, whose smile has not waned.

Block plods on. ". . . In going over the MMPI-II results . . ."

The phone rings.

"Thank God," whispers Bob.

When I phone Dr. Steinpreis later today, she will tell me, "I had a terrible crisis. I charged my phone last night, but when I got up this morning, it was dead. I left for work super early to use the charger in my office, but it didn't hold the charge. By the time I realized the phone itself was the problem, I had no time to run and get another one, so I tried frantically to call Hal on my fax line to tell him he should call the fax number. When that didn't work, I ran out to my car and drove around the block using my car charger. This charged the phone just enough so I could listen to the judge's message. I ran back to my office and tried to call the judge on my fax line, but he had left the wrong courtroom extension, so the courtroom I dialed into kept saying I was disturbing their proceedings! They kept hanging up on me!

"By the time I figured out how to get the switchboard to have them patch me into the correct courtroom, I was practically in tears, fearing I was too late and all would be lost. When I finally reached Judge Brahos's courtroom, I was out of breath and literally shaking."

"Dr. Steinpreis, good morning to you. This is Hal Block."

In response to Block's calm, careful questions, Steinpreis confirms the PTSD diagnosis as well as David's inability to function well enough during his first year in the United States to have testified in his own defense. Gradually, she finds her stride. The testimony gets interesting.

MR. BLOCK: A person with PTSD with a marked severity such as Mr. Bakala's, that condition—how long would that be expected to last?

DR. STEINPREIS: Quite frankly, it varies based on the severity of the trauma that the person was exposed to. It can last until death. . . . The problem with PTSD is that the symptoms can come and go, come and go, without a whole lot of predictive information. They can rear up at any time. They generally last for years afterwards, even more in severe torture cases—which I consider his case to be.

MR. BLOCK: Now ultimately, through the passage of some time, Mr. Bakala . . . did in fact move ahead and propound a claim for asylum although, as we are all well aware, it was considerably after the one-year period from his entry. Is that something that is surprising?

DR. STEINPREIS: Actually, that's relatively par for the course. People with PTSD . . . just can't seem to do anything. They won't act. They don't move. They know what's at stake sometimes. Sometimes they're not even capable of gathering information to figure out what they're missing in the outside world and they just are completely frozen.

MR. BLOCK: . . . [T]he fact that at a point in time, he was actually able to move forward on his propounding a claim for asylum, is this something you think is not so surprising?

DR. STEINPREIS: It's not surprising at all. Sometimes they function better than others and, unlike lay people who haven't been through the same sort of trauma as torture victims, their valleys are ten thousand times lower than we would [have] . . . .

Judge Brahos introduces Dr. Steinpreis to the government attorney. Her first question startles me. "Ma'am, are you being paid to testify today?"

"Yes, I am."

The smiling Brahos interrupts, "Ma'am, the fact that you are receiving an honorarium does not at all impinge on your veracity."

After a string of questions on PTSD, Ms. Kostich asks what caused David to be able to file for political asylum when he did. Dr. Steinpreis explains that the social support system developing around him is what gradually freed David to act.

"So the fact that his wife had already filed for asylum and he did not, you can explain that away through this whole post-traumatic stress syndrome diagnosis?

"I'm not sure that I understand what you mean by 'explain it away.' To be honest, I'm not sure that it would have mattered if President Clinton would have shown up at their house. . . . Whether you are a human or an animal, if you are exposed to uncontrollable torture or uncontrollable shock or uncontrolled sensory deprivation, you stop acting on your own behalf and you simply freeze."

Kostich twice rewords the question, but Steinpreis is unflappable. "It wouldn't have mattered if the courts would have shown up at his door . . . the man was not functioning. . . ."

David betrays no emotion. His eyes are fastened on Brahos-of-the-perpetual-smile.

"Did you ask him, 'Why didn't you file?'"

"In several different ways."

As Ms. Kostich finishes, Mary whispers to Hal, who then asks the judge to please allow Ms. Sfasciotti to question the witness.

Bob grips Tracy's knee and mine, whispering through his teeth, "Here she goes!"

He's right. Mary rattles off a series of statements, each ending with, "Is that correct?" Steinpreis rhythmically answers, "Yes." Mary probes deeper. "Would you describe what he told you happened to him in the Congo as horrific?"

"Oh, yes. As horrific as it gets. He was electrocuted, he was lying in his own feces, he was hit repeatedly in the front teeth with an elbow chipping his teeth, he was beaten, he was starved to death, he contracted diseases and was untreated, he was given very little food, he was given very, very little fresh water. It was awful. It was nothing that I would ever want any human being on the face of this planet to go through." She later testifies that manifestations of PTSD can also be "extremely destructive."

When Mary asks what circumstances would cause a person suffering from chronic PTSD to contemplate suicide, Dr. Steinpreis describes being reexposed to any reminder of the trauma, "or they are just having a particularly bad day, or they are getting really, really super malnourished and they're thinking, 'We get any more afraid, we're going to have a flare-up,' . . . any odors, any sights, any sounds, just, you know, having a nightmare—all these things can cause a flare-up in their symptoms to the point of suicidal ideation."

In answer to whether David would have experienced a severe flare-up had he tried to apply for asylum, Steinpreis says, "Yes. But he [would have] had the recurrence whether or not he filed for asylum. Would it have made it worse? . . . Yes, because . . ."

David, still staring at the judge, betrays no emotion.

When Mary finishes, Mr. Block, ever the alert prognosticator, staves off a last possible argument by asking if David, for all his intelligence and education, could have faked his symptoms to trick both psychologists into this diagnosis.

Dr. Steinpreis explains how the MMPI questions are designed to prevent cheating. "You have to literally memorize where 552 questions go and on which scale and whether to mark the answer true or false. Who has time for that? Who does that? . . . It's just not possible."

After Ms. Kostich declines cross examination, Judge Brahos thanks Dr. Steinpreis, calling her testimony "most helpful," then hangs up. He laces his fingers together and, continuing to smile, says in gentle tones, "I'm inclined to grant the asylum for the male respondent . . ."

Loud clapping breaks out from Tracy.

Mary spins around, shushing her in a loud whisper.

As Brahos continues, David takes Regina's hand. They sit ramrod still, eyes fixed on him.

"I find that the failure to file the application timely has been excused," says Brahos. "In view of that, Mr. Block and Ms. Sfasciotti, granting the asylum for the male respondent, the female respondent becomes the derivative. Do I hear anything further on her application?"

Bob grips Tracy's hand and mine. Lifting them waist high, he leans forward.

Mary says, "Judge, if you're inclined to grant it, it should be by order of the court."

"All right. But before I do enter that order, what is the government's position?"

I hold my breath.

"Well, Your Honor, the wife gets something she was unable to get on her own, which was the fact that her political asylum was denied and that denial and her appeal [were] dismissed by the Board of Immigration Appeals. However, I think her name does appear on his application. Derivative asylum is contemplated by the law, and so that's her legal right."

Brahos continues, "Both cases are now before the court as a joint hearing with the husband's case, and therefore, I'm going to grant the asylum application for the male respondent. And before I go on to a brief decision, are you both rested?"

Bob tightens his grip and bites his lip, but his tears are already coming.

Judge Brahos turns to David and Regina. "I'm pleased to grant your joint application for asylum and hope you will have a long and happy life in the US."

We burst into tears—all of us—tears and cheers and applause.

My shoulders suddenly release. I feel every muscle in my body relax. The pent-up tears of two years are finally free. Through the wavy flood, I see David take Regina into his arms. Shaking with sobs, they bury their faces in each other's shoulders. Even the reporters are crying, clapping, cheering. Bob and Tracy hug me, then pull me down the row to be first through the gate. The rest is a happy blur of hugs and congratulations and thanks. The guard opens the door for Pascal who, having arrived when court was already in session, had to wait in the corridor.

When I thank Judge Brahos, he says, "You're welcome, Sister."

Ah, he recognizes me as a nun. And, at least for now, I can finally trust his smile.

He adds, "And may you have a happy Easter!"

"Your Honor, this is it." I gesture toward Regina and David. "*This is Easter!*"

As we leave the courtroom, Tracy is already phoning the school principal to tell Lydia and Christopher that the judge said Mommy and Daddy can stay in America. And as we step off the elevator and head down the granite hallway, she is notifying news organizations.

Outside, just beyond the waist-high barrier—a black band stretched between silver posts—cameras are rolling, their zoom lenses trained on Regina and David coming through the revolving glass door. Once on the sidewalk, the new asylees, their faces wreathed in laughter and palms lifted high, lean back then quickly bow forward, thrusting their hands toward the ground and shouting in unison, "We're home!" and again "We're *home!*" and again, "*We're home!*" On each bow, the word *home* seems to root them deeper in the land beneath their feet.

St. Mary's parking lot is full when we arrive. This time the media are set up and waiting inside the church proper. Regina, David, and the four of us cluster in an alcove watching as the school children, carrying American flags—Lydia had the honor of distributing them—file through the large gathering space on their way into church.

In the long line of first graders, their eyes focused straight ahead, is little Lydia. She turns her head in our direction. Spotting her mommy and daddy, she springs to life. "Mommy!" Bob had been moving to take her out of line, but she bolts past him, her arms open. Leaping up, she throws herself into her mother's embrace, wrapping around her mommy with both arms and both legs. Daddy also gets a generous hug. I brush away tears as she scampers off to church.

Minutes later, Christopher's reaction is entirely different. Walking single-file with the kindergartners, he stares blankly in our direction, and even though we gesture for him to come, he keeps following his classmates. Bob scoots over, tugging him out of line to come hug Mommy and Daddy. He seems dazed and walks slowly. There is no smile. Though Regina and David embrace him warmly, his part in the hugs is lackluster at best.

It won't be until early the next morning that Christopher will "get" it.

Regina later tells me that when he was all dressed and ready for school, he looked her in the eye and asked, "Mommy, *now* is it *over*?"

"I say, 'Yes, Christopher. *It's over.*'" Her voice was strong and sure. "'We gonna stay in the United States.' He look at me. His eyes get really big. And then! Oh! Then he was *soo* happy he start to sing! Sing and dance! Dance all over the living room!"

EPILOGUE

———   ——   ———

Today, Regina and David are grateful to call the United States home. They live in the same house, belong to the same parish, work the same jobs, and take classes as they can. In February 2010, they applied for their green cards as legal permanent residents of the United States. Though eligible in 2008, the fee for the four-page application had soared out of reach the year before from $325 to $930 plus $80 for biometrics, a whopping $2,020 for the two, not including medical exams and vaccinations. (On November 23, 2010, the fee would again increase to $985, plus $85 for biometrics.)

In September, seven months after they sent in their applications, USCIS questioned a discrepancy in the spelling of Regina's surname, an error caused fourteen years earlier by her first lawyer, who had misspelled it "Imua." When Mary Sfasciotti heard about the delay, she sent Regina right to the Milwaukee County Courthouse to officially change her name to "Imwa," matching her birth certificate—another $263.00— but by early November, Regina had her green card.

David, however, was still waiting and worrying. In a late February 2011 phone call to USCIS, he learned that spouses often receive their green cards months apart. As we go the press, he is still waiting.

After five years of permanent residency, each will be allowed to apply for citizenship. Current fee with biometrics, $680 apiece.

The Bakala children attend St. Mary's School. Lydia (twelve) dreams of becoming a fashion designer. Chris (eleven) has his eyes on a football career and maybe, just maybe, becoming an immigration judge.

Author's Note and Acknowledgments

What a privilege to be welcomed into Regina and David's lives! I thank both of them for their trust and their friendship, and for the honor of sharing their stories. While our interviews appear at various places in the book's timeline, most were recorded after Regina was released from detention. I also rephrased some quotes for clarity. Regina and David each worked closely with me throughout the process, then carefully reviewed the final manuscript.

I was able to reconstruct the events in this story from my daily notes, correspondence, legal documents, news articles, and online accounts. While I changed the names of a few people for privacy, nothing else about them or their roles was altered. It goes without saying that any errors are mine. If some parts offend, so be it. I wrote this book not to soothe our consciences but to inflame them.

Writers are advised to write what we know, but it's what I did not know that kept me fighting and prodded me to write. Struggling for the safety of two torture survivors from a country foreign to my own had swept me into the equally foreign culture of ICE and then into the dark recesses of our asylum system, where—contrary to all that I cherish about America—a lawyer's mere slipup had become Regina's death sentence. I had to write.

Learning the history of the Democratic Republic of Congo took extensive research on my part. I also thank Colonel Christophe Opanga for sharing his firsthand experience of the 1997 Congo war, and Tshimankinda Kadima-Kalombo, who double-checked my account.

To help me navigate the intricacies of America's convoluted immigration system, I turned to consultant and author Godfrey Y. Muwonge, JD (*Immigration Reform: We Can Do It, If We Apply Our Founders' True Ideals*, 2009). Growing up in Africa, Godfrey first learned to cherish the US Constitution from his Ugandan father. I cannot thank him enough for patiently teaching me as I wrote, then reviewing each part of the manuscript for legal accuracy.

Special thanks to the Save Regina team and all who helped: Theresa Ambord, Tracy Borgardt, Lyonel Delva, Papa Tshimankinda Kadima-Kalombo, Teresa Lee, Angela and Darryl Morin, Bob Mutranowski, Patrick Ntula, Leon Todd, Jeanne Siegenthaler, Father Art Heinze, staff and parishioners of St. Mary's in Hales Corners, and countless others near and far.

Thanks, too, to US representative Gwen Moore and her capable staff, who advised us to "shine a bright light" on injustice, and to the full bevy of Milwaukee media that helped us do it.

Immigration attorneys Mary L. Sfasciotti and Harold D. Block, you are our heroes.

To my sisters and their families—Ruth and Ken Vonderberg, Eileen and Geno Mosconi—I treasure your love and support.

Abundant thanks to my religious community, the School Sisters of Notre Dame, who believed in me, supported me, and prayed for me as I wrote. I am grateful to all my praying friends, especially Dennis Boudreau, Deacon Mike LeBeau, and Sarah Opanga.

To writing coach Judy Bridges, whose help and enthusiasm spurred this book; Kris Babe, who got me started; and local editor Carolyn Kott Washburne, whose encouragement and skill gave me wings: abundant thanks! Thanks too to all who slogged through the trenches with me—my readers, writers, Dutch translator Jan Van Den Kieboom, and especially Carol Thomas, whose wonderfully picky comments over many versions proved invaluable. To my agent, Sheree Bykofsky, you've been perfect! Thanks, also, to salesperson Janet Rosen.

To my superb editor Susan Bradanini Betz, in-house designer Jon Hahn, and all at Lawrence Hill Books/Chicago Review Press, thank you for honoring me as an author and for treating this important story with such meticulous care.

Notes

1. "They Took Regina!"

1. See Nadira Lalji, "The Resource Curse Revised: Conflict and Coltan in the Congo," *Harvard International Review,* December 31, 2007, http://hir .harvard.edu/economics-of-national-security/the-resource-curse-revised.
2. See "GDP (Per Capita) Statistics," NationMaster.com, www.nationmaster .com/graph/eco_gdp_percap-economy-gdp-per-capita.
3. By 2008, the monthly death toll averaged 45,000. See International Rescue Committee, "IRC Study Shows Congo's Neglected Crisis Leaves 5.4 Million Dead," news release, January 22, 2008, www.theirc.org/news /irc-study-shows-congos0122.html.

2. "Never in America"

1. Withholding of removal, a.k.a. withholding of deportation, arises from the nonrefoulement doctrine of the 1967 UN Protocol Relating to the Status of Refugees, part of the United Nations Charter. Article 33 bars member nations from returning refugees or asylum seekers to countries where their lives and freedom would be in danger. Thirteen years later, the US Congress enacted and President Jimmy Carter signed into law the Refugee Act of 1980. See title 8 of the *United States Code*, section 1521.

   Since both withholding of removal and asylum are assumed to be sought by an asylum seeker, the application is titled "Request for Asylum and Withholding of Removal." However, each grants different relief, and each requires the applicant to meet a separate and distinctly different burden of proof. The standard for asylum in INA § 101(a)(42)(A) and

(B) requires the applicant to prove a *well-founded fear* of persecution based on race, nationality, religion, membership in a particular social group, or political opinion. Withholding, on the other hand, which has its standard under INA § 241(b)(3)(A), requires a higher burden of proof, *clear probability* that the applicant's life and freedom will be in danger.

A third form of relief is withholding of removal under the United Nations Convention Against Torture and Other Cruel, Inhuman or Degrading Treatment or Punishment (UNCAT), which was ratified by 142 nations, including the United States, and signed by another nine that have not yet ratified it. Taking effect in June 1987, it requires an applicant to prove that *it is more likely than not* that he or she would be tortured by the government of his or her country or that the government would acquiesce to the torture. This third relief under UNCAT does not require a motivating factor for the torture in terms of race, nationality, religion, membership in a particular social group, or political opinion. Since David had already met the higher proof required under the INA, the judge wrote that it was unnecessary to grant him withholding under UNCAT.

4. A Rag in the Weeds

1. See Kevin R. Johnson, "Court Challenge to 'Stipulated Removal,'" *ImmigrationProf Blog*, November 12, 2008, http://lawprofessors. typepad.com/immigration/2008/11/court-challenge.html; also, Jayashri Srikantiah and Karen Tumlin, "Stipulated Removal," (background paper, n.d.), http://lawprofessors.typepad.com/immigration/files /backgrounder20final1.pdf.

2. See Paula Donovan, "The War That Never Ends: Sexual Violence in DRC," Aids-Free World, February 22, 2008, www.aidsfreeworld.org /Our-Issues/Sexual-Violence/The-War-that-Never-Ends.aspx; also see Michael Gavshon and Drew Magratten, producers, "War Against Women," *60 Minutes,* August 17, 2008, transcript available at www.cbsnews.com/stories/2008/01/11/60minutes/main3701249.shtml.

5. In the Eyes of the Law

1. See "Immigration Enforcement: The Rhetoric, the Reality," Transactional Records Access Clearinghouse, Syracuse University, May 28, 2007, http://trac.syr.edu/immigration/reports/178.

2. See Megan Davy, Deborah W. Meyers, and Jeanne Batalova, "Who Does What in US Immigration," *Migration Policy Institute*, December 2005, www.migrationinformation.org/USfocus/display.cfm?ID=362.
3. In the mid-1990s, Bessel van der Kolk, M.D., observed and documented the dissociation in live brain scans. See Mary Sykes Wiley, PhD, "The Limits of Talk: Bessel van der Kolk Wants to Transform the Treatment of Trauma," *Psychotherapy Networker* 28, no. 1 (2004), 30–41, available at www.traumacenter.org/products/pdf_files/Networker.pdf.
4. See Attorney General John Ashcroft, "Administrative Change to Board of Immigration Appeals," (news conference, February 6, 2002), transcript available at www.usdoj.gov/archive/ag/speeches/2002 /020602transcriptadministrativechangetobia.htm.

6. WHY AMERICA?

1. "Transportation (Land Transportation)," *2000 Detention Operations Manual*, US Department of Homeland Security, www.ice.gov/doclib/dro /detention-standards/pdf/transp.pdf, 14. The full manual and updated "2008 Performance Based Detention Standards" are available at www.ice.gov/detention-standards/2008/.
2. The constitutional rights of immigrants in deportation proceedings were clarified in the court cases Delgadillo v. Carmichael, 332 U.S. 338 (1947); and Wallace v. Reno, 24 F. Supp. 2d 104 (D. Mass. 1998), quoting Ng Fung Ho v. White, 259 U.S. 276 (1922).
3. See Wong Yang Sung v. McGrath, 339 U.S. 33 (1950). Regarding ICE administrative procedures, see above, ch. 4, n. 1; also see "New Data on the Processing of Aggravated Felons," Transactional Records Access Clearinghouse, Syracuse University, January 5, 2007, http://trac.syr.edu /immigration/reports/175/.
4. The rights of immigrants in deportation proceedings were clarified in three cases: Wong Yang Sung v. McGrath (1950); Woodby v. INS, 385 U.S. 276 (1966); and Addington v. Texas, 441 U.S. 418 (1979).
5. See "Inspirational Gifts," Caroline Design official website, www .carolinedesignonline.com/cart/index.php?act=viewCat&catId=18.
6. The human right to save one's life trumps the civil matter of illegal entry into another country. The emphasis in Genesis 12:10–20 is on God's unwavering fidelity to the divine promise, not on Abraham's decision to save his life by putting Sarah at risk of being raped.

7. This definition of *refugee* is used in § 101(a)(42)(A) of the Immigration and Nationality Act (INA) as amended by the Refugee Act of 1980, and it generally conforms to the international definition in the 1951 United Nations Convention relating to the Status of Refugees.

8. See "US Refugee Program," Cultural Orientation Resource Center official website, www.cal.org/co/refugee/; and "The Asylum Process," Transactional Records Access Clearinghouse, August 7, 2006, http://trac.syr.edu/immigration/reports/159/.

8. Searching for a Lawyer

1. See "Elizabeth's Story: The Women of Bulawayo," *Medical Foundation Annual Review*, 2000–2001, available at www.torturecare.org.uk /survivors_stories/338.

2. See Donald Kerwin, "Revisiting the Need for Appointed Counsel," *MPI Insight* 4 (April 2005), www.migrationpolicy.org/insight/Insight_Kerwin.pdf.

3. See "Immigration Judges," Transactional Records Access Clearinghouse, Syracuse University, July 31, 2006, http://trac.syr.edu/immigration /reports/160/.

4. The record of proceedings includes the transcript of the hearing and the exhibits (application, affidavit, and supportive documents).

9. David's Tragic Past

1. Jeffrey Tayler, *Facing the Congo: A Modern-Day Journey into the Heart of Darkness*, (New York: Three Rivers Press, 2000); and Michela Wrong, *In the Footsteps of Mr. Kurtz: Living on the Brink of Disaster in Mobutu's Congo* (New York: HarperCollins, 2001).

2. For my portrait of Mobutu and his times, I rely on Wrong (n. 1, above), and Robert B. Edgerton, *The Troubled Heart of Africa: A History of Congo* (New York: St. Martin's Press, 2002).

3. Alliance des Forces Démocratiques pour la Libération du Congo-Zaire (AFDL) included: (1) Conseil National de Résistance pour la Démocratie (CNRD), a military party with an army of thousands; (2) Partie de la Révolution Populaire (PRP), whose current members were Laurent Kabila and son Joseph; (3) Mouvement Révolutionnaire pour la Libération du Zaïre (MRLZ), with members from the Congolese Bashi tribe; and

(4) Alliance Démocratique des Peuples (ADP), the Banyamulenge, exiled Tutsis living in Congo.

4. See Osei Boateng, "The Second Scramble for Congo," *New African*, December 2005, http://findarticles.com/p/articles/mi_qa5391/is_/ai_n21384287.

5. See Amnesty International, *"Our Brothers Who Help Kill Us"*: *Economic Exploitation and Human Rights Abuses in the East* (Amnesty International, April 1, 2003), www.amnesty.org/en/library/asset/AFR62/010/2003/en/8bf8b529-d70a-11dd-b0cc-1f0860013475/afr620102003en.html.

11. Befriend the Fears and Angers

1. Nan C. Merrill, *Psalms for Praying: An Invitation to Wholeness* (New York: Continuum International Publishing Group, 2002), 154–156.

2. John Boardus Watson, *Psychological Care of Infant and Child* (New York: W. W. Norton, 1928).

3. See the memoir of Watson's granddaughter: Mariette Hartley and Anne Commire, *Breaking the Silence* (New York: G. P. Putnam Sons, 1990); also see Mariette Hartley, quoted in "Lecture Notes on John B. Watson," website of Victor Daniels, Sonoma State University, www.sonoma.edu/users/d/daniels/Watson.html.

12. Good Friday

1. For information on naturalization, see US Citizenship and Immigration Services, *A Guide to Naturalization* (US Department of Homeland Security, revised August 2010), www.uscis.gov/files/article/M-476.pdf.

Citizenship can be revoked for a person who lied on the naturalization application. The Intelligence Reform and Terrorism Prevention Act of 2004 (IRTPA) also allows deportation of a naturalized citizen for acts of torture or killing. See Anwar Iqbal, "New Law Allows Deportation of Naturalized US Citizens," *Dawn*, January 6, 2005, http://archives.dawn.com/2005/01/06/top11.htm.

2. Throughout this section, I rely on the analysis of Melissa Cook, "Banished for Minor Crimes: The Aggravated Felony Provision of the Immigration and Nationality Act as a Human Rights Violation," *Boston College Third World Law Journal* 23, no. 2 (2003), www.bc.edu/dam/files/schools

/law/lawreviews/journals/bctwj/23_2/03_TXT.htm. Also see "Aggravated Felonies and Deportation," Transactional Records Access Clearinghouse, Syracuse University, June 9, 2006, http://trac.syr.edu/immigration /reports/155/.

3. For Xuan Wilson, see Celia W. Dugger, "After Crime, She Made a New Life, but Now Faces Deportation," *New York Times*, August 11, 1997, www.nytimes.com/1997/08/11/world/after-crime-she-made-a-new-life-but-now-faces-deportation.html. For Olufolake Olaleye, see Ronald Weich, Esq., *Upsetting Checks and Balances: Congressional Hostility Toward Courts in Times of Crisis* (Washington, DC: ACLU, October 2001), www.aclu.org/files/FilesPDFs/ACF1B82.pdf, 30. For Sal DeWitt, see Betsy DeWitt, "How My Family Became the White 'Poster Child' in the Debate," New American Media, March 15, 2007, http://news .newamericamedia.org/news/view_article.html?article_id= c990f7a9de1f35b7a1c906269a12fe99.

13. In Good Times and in Bad

1. See "Elizabeth's Story: The Women of Bulawayo," *Medical Foundation Annual Review*, 2000–2001, available at www.torturecare.org.uk /survivors_stories/338.

15. "It's Hard to Be Here"

1. See National Immigration Forum, "The Math of Immigration Detention," *Backgrounder*, July 7, 2009, www.immigrationforum.org /images/uploads/MathofImmigrationDetention.pdf.

2. See Bob Libal, "Intelligence Bill Signals Boon for Immigrant Incarceration Industry," *ZNet*, February 20, 2005, www.zcommunications.org /intelligence-bill-signals-boon-for-immigrant-incarceration-industry-by-bob-libal. Also see Renee Feltz and Stokely Baksh's award-winning online publication *The Business of Detention*, www.businessofdetention.com.

16. "My Children Need Me"

1. The Midwest Immigrant and Human Rights Center (MIHRC) is now the National Immigrant Justice Center (NIJC). NIJC's official website is www.immigrantjustice.org.

17. "THEY ASK ME WHY I CRY SO MUCH"

1. To better understand PTSD, see Mark I. Levy, M.D., "Stressing the Point: When Is a Post Traumatic Stress Disorder Claim Legitimate . . . and When Is It Not," *For the Defense*, November 1995, expanded version available at http://expertpages.com/news/ptsd.htm.

2. See Physicians for Human Rights and the Bellevue/NYU Program for Survivors of Torture, *From Persecution to Prison: The Health Consequences of Detention for Asylum Seekers* (Boston: Physicians for Human Rights and the Bellevue/NYU Program for Survivors of Torture, 2003), www.physiciansforhumanrights.org/library/report-persprison.html; also see Allen S. Keller, M.D., et al, "Mental Health of Detained Asylum Seekers," *The Lancet* 362, no. 9397 (November 22, 2003), 1721–1723, www.thelancet.com/journals/lancet/article/PIIS0140673603148465/abstract.

3. Immigration and Nationality Act, § 235(b)(1)(A)(i). Also see Alison Siskin and Ruth Ellen Wasem, *Immigration Policy on Expedited Removal of Aliens* (Congressional Research Service, September 30, 2005), available at http://trac.syr.edu/immigration/library/P13.pdf.

4. The four questions on Form I-867B are: 1) Why did you leave your home country or country of last residence? 2) Do you have any fear or concern about being returned to your home country or being removed from the United States? 3) Would you be harmed if you are returned to your home country or country of last residence? 4) Do you have any questions or is there anything else you would like to add?

5. A year-long study mandated by Congress recommended no expansion of expedited removal until grave problems were remedied. See US Commission on International Religious Freedom, *Report on Asylum Seekers in Expedited Removal* (USCIRF, February 2005), www.uscirf.gov/index .php?option=com_content&task=view&id=1892&Itemid=1. Two years later, DHS had not only failed to respond but also expanded expedited removal to include the entire land and sea border. See US Commission on International Religious Freedom, *Expedited Removal Study Report Card: 2 Years Later* (USCIRF, February 2007), www.uscirf.gov/images /stories/pdf/scorecard_final.pdf. For excellent analysis, see Michele Pistone and John Hoeffner, "Rules Are Made to Be Broken: How the Process of Expedited Removal Fails Asylum Seekers," Villanova University School of Law Working Paper 49, June 2006, http://law.bepress.com/villanovawps /papers/art49.

6. Serious errors do occur. Rosebell N. Munyua successfully sued the US government for wrongful deportation back into danger. See Dean E. Murphy, "In Rare Accord, Spurned Asylum Seeker to Get $87,500," *New York Times*, April 28, 2005, www.nytimes.com/2005/04/28 /national/28asylum.html.

7. See UN High Commissioner for Refugees, *Revised Guidelines on Applicable Criteria and Standards Relating to the Detention of Asylum Seekers* (UNHCR, February 1999), www.unhcr.org.au/pdfs/detentionguidelines.pdf.

19. SAVE REGINA

1. See American Immigration Lawyers Association, *The Real ID Act of 2005: Summary and Selected Analysis of Provisions Included in the Emergency Supplemental Appropriations Package (H.R. 1268)*, (AILA, 2005), available at www.shusterman.com/pdf/realid-aila.pdf.

2. US Constitution, article 1, section 9: "The privilege of the writ of habeas corpus shall not be suspended, unless when in cases of rebellion or invasion, the public safety may require it."

3. See Mary Sykes Wiley, PhD, "The Limits of Talk: Bessel van der Kolk Wants to Transform the Treatment of Trauma," *Psychotherapy Networker* 28, no. 1 (2004), 30–41, available at www.traumacenter.org/products /pdf_files/Networker.pdf.

20. IT WAS A DARK AND STORMY NIGHT . . .

1. See Jonathan Pikoff and Charles J. Crimmons, "Lost in Translation: Texas Notary Public vs. Mexico *Notario Publico*," Texas Secretary of State official website, www.sos.state.tx.us/statdoc/notariopublicoarticle.shtml.

21. THROWING GARBAGE CANS

1. See Human Rights Watch, amicus brief in the case of Wayne Smith and Hugo Armendáriz v. the United States of America, Inter-American Commission on Human Rights, June 6, 2007, www.hrw.org/pub /amicusbriefs/armendarizvUS071007.pdf.

2. For an analysis of DHS data, interviews of affected families, and a comparison of US deportation practices and international standards, see the combined report of the International Human Rights Law Clinic and the

Chief Justice Earl Warren Institute on Race, Ethnicity and Diversity at the UC Berkeley School of Law, and the Immigration Law Clinic at UC Davis School of Law, *In the Child's Best Interest? The Consequences of Losing a Lawful Immigrant Parent to Deportation* (IHRLC, Warren Institute, and ILC, March 31, 2010), www.law.ucdavis.edu/news/images/childsbestinterest.pdf.

3. See Human Rights Watch, "Sexual Violence in the Congo War: A Continuing Crime," in *Seeking Justice: The Prosecution of Sexual Violence in the Congo War* (Human Rights Watch, March 2005), www.hrw.org/reports/2005 /drc0305/4.htm. To understand the persistence of rape as an act of war, see Stefan Kirchner's well-documented article "Hell on Earth: Systematic Rape in Eastern Congo," *Journal of Humanitarian Assistance*, August 6, 2007, http:// jha.ac/2007/08/06/hell-on-earth-systematic-rape-in-eastern-congo/.

22. TEAMWORK

1. Millions of time-limited *nonimmigrant visas* are issued annually for students, business travelers, visitors, temporary workers, and others, but only an *immigrant visa* makes one a United States legal permanent resident (LPR, or green card holder). After five years as a legal permanent resident (three if married to an American citizen), a person can apply for naturalization (citizenship).

    Only 675,000 immigrant visas are issued annually in three categories. (The fourth has different limits.) Each requires sponsorship.

    1. Family-based visas: 480,000 (71 percent) are for the immediate family of LPRs and for the immediate family and close relatives of US citizens. The citizen or LPR who applies for the visa must demonstrate financial resources to support the immigrant(s) as well as those in his or her own household at 125 percent above the poverty line. To prevent an immigrant from needing public assistance, INA § 213A also requires the sponsor to sign an affidavit of support, a binding contract that the federal government will enforce if need be. The contract lasts "forty qualifying quarters" (ten years).

    2. Employment-based visas: 140,000 (21 percent) are requested by employers who show evidence of having advertised the position to US applicants and guarantee the prevailing wage for the position as determined by the US Department of Labor. The five prioritized work categories include 135,000 high-skill jobs and only 5,000 low-skill jobs.

3. Diversity (DV) Lottery visas: 55,000 (8 percent) are set aside by the State Department for people from approximately 170 countries with low immigration rates. Applicants must have a high school education or two years of work experience in a field requiring two years of study. Of the 55,000, 5,000 are reserved for use under the Nicaraguan and Central American Relief Act of 1997 (NACARA).

4. Humanitarian visas: The number of political refugees is set annually by the president in consultation with Congress. The US government contracts with nonprofit groups, mostly churches, to use federal, state, and local aid as well as private assistance to provide them with food, housing, jobs, health care, etc. Asylum seekers come as they can but do not qualify for any government support until after they receive asylum.

In addition, a per-county limit is set at 7 percent of the total family-sponsored and employment-based preference limits. For current visa data and the visa bulletin with wait times, see the website of the US State Department's Bureau of Consular Affairs, http://travel.state.gov /visa/visa_1750.html.

2. See Erin Patrick, "The US Refugee Resettlement Program," Migration Policy Institute, June 2004, www.migrationinformation.org/USFocus /display.cfm?ID=229. For statistics, see Audrey Singer and Jill H. Wilson, "Refugee Resettlement in Metropolitan America," Migration Policy Institute, March 2007, www.migrationinformation.org/USfocus/display .cfm?ID=585.

3. Regarding refugees being denied human rights protection, see Amnesty International, "World Refugee Day 2007," news release, June 21, 2007, www.amnestyusa.org/document.php?lang=e&id=ENGPOL300142007; also see the Flash presentation "World Refugee Day 2007," US Committee for Refugees and Immigrants official website, www.refugees .org/wrd2007/.

4. For an analysis commissioned by the US State Department's Bureau of Population, Refugees and Migration, see David A. Martin with Suzette Brooks Masters, *The United States Refugee Admission Program: Reforms for a New Era of Refugee Resettlement* (Washington, DC: Migration Policy Institute, 2005), executive summary available at www.migrationpolicy.org /MPI_Mar_ExecSum3.pdf.

5. See National Immigration Forum, "Real Faces Behind the REAL ID Act," *Backgrounder*, March 17, 2005, www.policyarchive.org/handle/10207 /bitstreams/11692.pdf.

6. See *Conference Report on H.R. 1268*, H.R. Rep. 109-72, at 174–175 (2005), available at www.gpo.gov/fdsys/pkg/CRPT-109hrpt72/pdf /CRPT-109hrpt72.pdf. The American Immigration Lawyers Association (AILA) had resisted this move (see ch. 19, n. 1, above), but court challenges later upheld its constitutionality.

26. BLESS THE CHILDREN

1. A 2008 UN study concluded that the US detention and deportation system violates international law. See Jorge Bustamante, "Promotion and Protection of All Human Rights, Civil, Political, Economic, Social and Cultural Rights, Including the Right to Development" (report to the UN Human Rights Council, March 5, 2008), available at www.texascivilrightsreview.org/tcrr/docs/bustamante08a.pdf.

On the importance of family unity in immigration policies and legislation, see James D. Kremer, Kathleen A. Moccio, and Joseph W. Hammell, *Severing the Lifeline: The Neglect of Citizen Children in America's Immigration Enforcement Policy; A Report by Dorsey & Whitney LLP to the Urban Institute* (Minneapolis: Dorsey & Whitney, 2009), www .dorsey.com/files/upload/DorseyProBono_SeveringLifeline_web.pdf; and International Human Rights Law Clinic and the Chief Justice Earl Warren Institute on Race, Ethnicity and Diversity at the UC Berkeley School of Law, and the Immigration Law Clinic at UC Davis School of Law, *In the Child's Best Interest? The Consequences of Losing a Lawful Immigrant Parent to Deportation* (IHRLC, Warren Institute, and ILC, March 31, 2010), www.law.ucdavis.edu/news/images/childsbestinterest.pdf.

2. "Netherlands Halts Congo Returns," BBC News, June 24, 2005, http:// news.bbc.co.uk/1/hi/world/europe/4618807.stm.

27. "DON'T STOP NOW, GIRL"

1. See Amy Goldstein and Dan Eggen, "Immigration Judges Often Picked Based on GOP Ties," *Washington Post*, June 11, 2007, www.washingtonpost.com/wp-dyn/content/article/2007/06/10 /AR2007061001229.html. For BIA approval rates before and after Ashcroft's reforms, see "Asylum Requests Dwindle, As Do Approvals," *Dallas Morning News*, May 31, 2007, www.dallasnews.com/sharedcontent /dws/news/world/stories/060107dnintasylumprimer.2dbcaae.html.

2. "Asylum Denial Rates by Immigration Judge, FY 1994–1999," Transactional Records Access Clearinghouse, Syracuse University, 2006, is no longer online. Judge Cassidy's later records are available at Transactional Records Access Clearinghouse, http://trac.syr.edu /immigration/reports/judge2008/00004ATL/index.html.

3. See Heidi Beirich, "The Teflon Nativists: FAIR Marked by Ties to White Supremacy," *Intelligence Report*, Winter 2007, www.splcenter.org/intel /intelreport/article.jsp?aid=846. More Southern Poverty Law Center reports on Tanton are available at www.splcenter.org/search/apachesolr_search /Tanton. Also see Deepa Fernandes, "U.S. Immigration Policy and Racism: How White Supremacists Are Writing Immigration Policy and Democrats Are Asleep at the Wheel," in *Targeted: Homeland Security and the Business of Immigration* (New York: Seven Stories Press, 2007), 201–238.

28. 2006

1. Bureau of Immigration and Customs Enforcement, *ENDGAME: Office of Detention and Removal Strategic Plan, 2003–2012* (US Department of Homeland Security, June 27, 2003), available at www.cryptogon.com /docs/endgame.pdf.

2. For the detainee statistics, see Donald Kerwin and Serena Yi-Ying Lin, *Immigrant Detention: Can ICE Meet Its Legal Imperatives and Case Management Responsibilities?* (Washington, DC: Migration Policy Institute, September 2009), www.migrationpolicy.org/pubs/detentionreportSept1009 .pdf, 7. Regarding secure communities, see Michele Waslin, PhD, *The Secure Communities Program: Unanswered Questions and Community Concerns* (special report, Immigration Policy Center, November 2010), www.immigrationpolicy.org/special-reports/secure-communities-program-unanswered-questions-and-continuing-concerns.

3. See Human Rights First, *Summary of Recommendations Relating to the Comprehensive Review of the Immigration Courts and Board of Immigration Appeals* (Human Rights First, May 15, 2006), available at www.rcusa.org /uploads/pdfs/recs-doj.pdf.

4. See ch. 17, n. 5, above, for more on the USCIRF's *Report on Asylum Seekers in Expedited Removal*. On August 9, 2006, Gonzales announced twenty-two measures to improve the system, but his successors dropped the ball. See "Bush Administration Plan to Improve Immigration Courts Lags," Transactional Records Access Clearinghouse, Syracuse University,

September 8, 2008, http://trac.syr.edu/immigration/reports/194/. Also see Julie Preston, "Lawyers Back Creating New Immigration Courts," *New York Times*, February 8, 2010, www.nytimes.com/2010/02/09 /us/09immig.html.

5. See "Judge O. John Brahos," Transactional Records Access Clearinghouse, 2007, http://trac.syr.edu/immigration/reports/judgereports/026/index.html.

6. In October 2009, DHS secretary Janet Napolitano and ICE assistant secretary John Morton announced new immigration detention initiatives to eventually move civil detainees out of the penal system. See "Fact Sheet: 2009 Immigration Detention Reforms," ICE official website, www.ice.gov/news/library/factsheets /reform-2009reform.htm. For current facilities, see "Immigration Detention Facilities," ICE official website, www.ice.gov/detention-facilities/. An interactive map of current US detention facilities is available at Detention Watch Network, www.detentionwatchnetwork.org/dwnmap.

7. See Mark Dow, *American Gulag: Inside U.S. Immigration Prisons* (Los Angeles: University of California Press, 2004), 9–10; also see Deepa Fernandes, "This Alien Life: Privatized Prisons for Immigrants," *CorpWatch*, February 5, 2007, www.corpwatch.org/article.php?id=14333.

8. See the four-part series by Dana Priest and Amy Goldstein questioning US secrecy around immigrant deaths, "Careless Detention," *Washington Post*, May 11–14, 2008, www.washingtonpost.com/wp-srv/nation/specials /immigration/cwc_d1p1.html, and Goldstein's follow-up, "Immigration Agency to Reveal Some Death Data," *Washington Post*, June 5, 2008, www.washingtonpost.com/wp-dyn/content/article/2008/06/04 /AR2008060403757.html.

For detainee names and causes of death, see the website Homeland Guantanamos, www.homelandgitmo.com/memorial.php.

29. THE ELEVENTH HOUR

1. "DP Congo to Hold Historic Presidential Election," *People's Daily Online*, July 30, 2006, http://english.peopledaily.com.cn/200607/30 /eng20060730_288146.html.

30. "WHO WILL TAKE CARE OF US?"

1. Nan C. Merrill, *Psalms for Praying: An Invitation to Wholeness* (New York: Continuum International Publishing Group, 2002), 142–144.

INDEX